The Fracture of Good Order

The Fracture of Good Order

Christian Antiliberalism and the Challenge to American Politics

Jason C. Bivins

The University of North Carolina Press • Chapel Hill and London

The introduction has been reprinted with permission in
revised form from "'Watch!': Postwar American Politics
and Christian Anti-Liberalism," *Polygraph* 12 (2000).

Designed by Chris Crochetière
Set in Cycles and Officina Sans
by B. Williams & Associates

The paper in this book meets the guidelines for permanence
and durability of the Committee on Production Guidelines
for Book Longevity of the Council on Library Resources.

Library of Congress Cataloging-in-Publication Data

Bivins, Jason.
    The fracture of good order : Christian antiliberalism
and the challenge to American politics / Jason C. Bivins.
        p. cm.
Includes bibliographical references (p.   ) and index.
ISBN 0-8078-2793-2 (cloth)—ISBN 0-8078-5468-9 (paper)
1. Christianity and politics—United States.
2. Liberalism—Religious aspects—Christianity.
3. Political activists—Religious life—United States.
4. Liberalism—United States.
I. Title.
BR526 .B58 2003
261.7'0973—dc21

                                        2002153735

cloth 07 06 05 04 03   5 4 3 2 1
paper 07 06 05 04 03   5 4 3 2 1

For my parents,
Royal Gardner Bivins Jr.
and
Kathleen T. Noerr

Contents

Acknowledgments

I have always enjoyed reading the acknowledgments in other people's books, not in the morbid way in which some people enjoy obituaries—as if a book and its concerns are being laid to rest—but because they are often more revealing about authors than are their arguments, regardless of how compelling and provocative the latter may be. So it is that I happily acknowledge the many people who have helped me, encouraged me, and pushed me while I wrote this book.

This work began during my graduate school years at Indiana University, an ideal place for me to write the first of many versions of this book. I benefited not only from that institution's generous financial support but also from the intellectual rigor and collegiality of its Department of Religious Studies. Since arriving at North Carolina State University I have also been the happy beneficiary of such support.

It is my pleasure to acknowledge my colleagues at North Carolina State, particularly Bill Adler, Mary Kath Cunningham, Natalie Dohrmann, and Tony Stewart. Their intellectual dedication and warm friendship are much appreciated. I must also thank Randy Carter, Ron Endicott, Tim Hinton, and Doug Jesseph for their collegiality and refreshing skepticism. Hal Levin and John Carroll have been able and understanding administrators, and Ann Rives and Vicki Corpening have been sources of good cheer and much-needed practical wisdom.

I am grateful to Elaine Maisner at the University of North Carolina Press, not only for her faith in this project but for her keen intellect and expert criticism. I am also thankful to Paula Wald, Adrienne Allison, and Grace Buonocore for their help with this project. Thanks, too, to the anonymous readers of this text, who gave such helpful comments.

My colleagues in the field are sources of constant strength and inspiration to me. I am fortunate to live in an area that is unusually rich for the study of religion. In addition to my departmental colleagues, I have met so many kind and brilliant people—fellow faculty and graduate students alike—in seminars, reading groups, and other arenas. I would like to acknowledge Richard Jaffe's friendship and support. And I would like particularly to express my gratitude to Tom Tweed, whose friendship and collegiality—not to mention his incisive engagement with this book—have enriched my time in North Carolina so far. Thanks also to Jessica Baldanzi, Christie Fox, Shane Graham, Maurice Meilleur, Kristy Nabhan-Warren, Doug Padgett, Eric Saidel, and Lisa Sideris.

I wish to thank my teachers, too. David Haberman, Michael Jackson, Mike Michalson, Sam Preus, David Smith, and Grover Zinn all enriched this work in various ways. Special thanks go to my dissertation committee, Jeff Isaac, Richard B. Miller, and Mary Jo Weaver. Jeff Isaac continues to be a cherished colleague and friend. And I do not know exactly how to begin acknowledging Bob Orsi. As my dissertation adviser, he continually challenged and encouraged me in the crafts of research, writing, and teaching. He has also—throughout, and especially now—been a friend. For the countless hours of gracious listening, hospitality, good humor, and friendship, I express my deep and sincere gratitude.

It goes without saying that the religious practitioners I have written about and communicated with deserve acknowledgment. Thanks to those in Sojourners who were helpful in correspondence and conversation, particularly Kari Jo Verhulst. Thanks to all at Jonah House for their generosity and hospitality, especially Liz McAlister. And to the members of the New Christian Right I have met with over the years, I appreciate your willingness to listen and your patience with my questions.

I would be remiss without acknowledging all the friends whose company I am fortunate enough to enjoy and whose love and support have seen me through some tough times. Hans Spencer Indigo, Heather Keith, Ted Leventhal, Dodie Morris, and Matt Smith have been friends for so long that I cannot remember my life without them. Thanks to my partners in the sublime sport of ultimate Frisbee. And huge thanks to my partners in music making, particularly Ian Davis, the Family Vineyard road dogs, the Micro-East Collective, and my brothers in the Unstable Ensemble.

It is a special joy to acknowledge my family. To my stepfather, Peter Noerr; my dear sister, Kristina Hammond, and my brother-in-law, Jeffrey Hammond; Sarah Burns and Dennis Gannon; Luther and Lorraine Bivins; my late father, Royal G. Bivins Jr.; and especially my mother, Kathleen Noerr, my deepest thanks. Thanks finally to Sonja C. Rice, my attorney and co-conspirator, who understands how meaningful it is if I say that, for once in my life, words fail me.

The Fracture of Good Order

"Watch!"

The Meanings of Christian Antiliberalism

At dawn on Ash Wednesday, 1997, Philip Berrigan, a former Josephite priest, and five young activist colleagues climbed aboard the naval destroyer USS *The Sullivans*, docked in Portland, Maine. The members of the group, part of the so-called Plowshares Movement, commandeered the ship and began to perform the sorts of actions that Berrigan had developed throughout his decades-long career as a Catholic social activist. Some of the members produced hammers and, pounding on the destroyer's missile hatches and guidance system, enacted the biblical injunction to "beat swords into plowshares." Others ceremoniously poured their own blood from containers filled earlier onto walls, decks, and control panels. For the participants, the blood symbolized the suffering of Christ crucified and also the potential suffering caused by the weapons carried aboard *The Sullivans*. But the blood also heralded for them the possibility of transformation and redemption. Within minutes, the six protesters were seized by the ship's authorities. They went peacefully, seemingly almost with joy, into detention.[1]

Months later, the Plowshares activists were tried and convicted of conspiracy and destruction of government property. Philip Berrigan, a veteran of such trials and subsequent jail terms, seemed unperturbed until the sentences were pronounced in November 1997. Berrigan, then seventy-three years old, was given two years in prison and two years under federal supervision. At the sentencing, with his brother and frequent collaborator, Daniel, present, Berrigan availed himself of the public space of the courtroom to issue a scathing condemnation of U.S. nuclear weapons policy. Drawing on many of the same prophetic images and themes he had used since first protesting U.S. involvement in Vietnam, Berrigan intoned before the judge, "God did not provide one reality for governments and another for human beings like you and I. If it is criminal for me to kill, it is criminal for my government to kill."[2]

Although it was unusual for Berrigan to speak of the U.S. government as "his," since he had made quite public his disdain for the state, the argument made in this Portland courtroom perfectly exemplified Berrigan's brand of religiously motivated challenge to the state. Drawing on the oft-cited distinction between God's law and human law, Berrigan subordinated human law to the divine in order to expose what he perceived as the state's immorality. Both the judge and the U.S. attorney had grown weary of Berrigan's speeches; on the basis of his apparent lack of remorse, they had forgone a lighter sentence and given Berrigan two years in prison. In defiance of a gag rule on religious language that had been imposed by the judge presiding, Berrigan continued to excoriate the court and the government for which it stood. He read from the Gospel of Mark (13:35–36): "'Watch ye, for ye know not when the master of the house cometh . . . lest coming he suddenly find you sleeping.' That's what I say to you all: Watch!"

Although the issues raised in this incident might seem to be obvious, concerning the legality of Plowshares actions independent of their religious and political significance, it also highlights important and less obvious concerns. In order fully to grasp its religious and political implications, such protest should be considered as "political religion," action conducted in political spaces or contexts for explicitly religious reasons.[3] As political religion, the protest aboard *The Sullivans* raises new questions. Was Berrigan's act one of trespass, of the destruction of federal property? Or was this demonstration an act of conscience or moral outrage? Are his continued protests simply a part of one marginal group's tenacious cry against militarism? Or are they part of a wider pattern of religious protests that challenges the legitimacy of the liberal state and the political order in post-1960s America?

What are we to make of the presence of this disruptive, antagonistic political religion? Such self-consciously Christian protests against what practitioners perceive as the state's excessive power or lack of moral authority have been proliferating since the 1960s. In convention halls and outside abortion clinics, in America's ghettos and at weapons manufacturing facilities, on school boards and in prisons, such protests are staged again and again. Across the United States, Christian voices of all political inflections have been raised against "big government," "politics as usual," "the military-industrial complex," or "the big brother state." These folksy terms and clichés resonate deeply in American religious and political history. Indeed, one might argue that there is no political impulse more American than the denunciation of political power, an impulse doubtless shaped in part by the Puritan flight from England during the seventeenth century and by the Revolutionary War's goals of shaking off foreign influence to create a society of free enterprise and self-government.[4] Since the Founding era, religious outsiders and dissidents—including the abolitionists, the populists, and the early waves of Christian fundamentalists, to name only some of the most widely recognized examples—have frequently challenged the moral legitimacy of the state or of particular policies. One might say of these religious criticisms that, like broader suspicions of state power, there are few critical impulses in American religion that are more American than the insistence that this country falls short of the exacting standards of various deities.

Yet although such religious challenges to government and political order have occurred frequently in our national history, American culture in recent decades has become saturated with new forms of collective action, protest, and public disturbance that call into question conventional understandings of politics. Among the most vocal practitioners are Christians who, like Philip Berrigan's Plowshares activists, assail the contemporary political order of American liberalism by engaging in specifically Christian forms of protest. I call this mode of critical action Christian antiliberalism because it self-consciously uses religious protest—rituals, symbols, narratives, and communities grounded in Christian traditions— to denounce features of American liberalism as it is understood by the practitioners. By liberalism I refer not to the opposite of conservatism but to the broad political tradition commonly associated with John Locke, Adam Smith, John Stuart Mill, and others. At the most general level, liberalism is associated with representative democracy, has tended to privilege individual over collective rights, favors negative liberty (freedom from coercion) over positive liberty (freedom to participate in politics in active, constructive ways), and seeks to protect moral and religious pluralism by separating public from private realms of society, keeping the public free from contentious moral or religious beliefs that are regarded as threats to political stability. Christian antiliberals reject many of these features of liberalism—particularly its conception of citizens, its emphasis on negative liberty, and its strict division between public and private—as well as many of the institutional forms that have developed in the United States to pursue these political ends. Christian antiliberals believe specifically that post–World War II liberalism has made it increasingly difficult to practice religions faithfully in the United States. They believe that by increasing the power of a centralized state and by divesting public life of moral and religious participation, liberal political order in the United States lacks a moral orientation.

I find that, today, the new forms of such challenges to political order move beneath our "interpretive radar" or, even when recognized, are understood inadequately. Such challenges are not necessarily ignored, but too often they are seen simply as a popular political reflex, a self-evident feature of the American political ecology. What is unique or compelling about such protest, particularly its religious manifestations, is often lost in the attempt to render it hospitable to extant analytic categories.

Many, perhaps most, accounts of the political development of the modern West have either left religion out of the picture or striven to write religion out of history as irrelevant. Transformations in American political culture, however, have always been intertwined with religious developments. One recent transformation has been a growing legitimation crisis facing American democracy, visible not only in the proliferation of protest phenomena such as Christian antiliberalism but also in the widespread dissatisfaction with conventional forms of political identity and affiliation. These developments are growing beyond the descriptive and analytic capacity of older vocabularies and categories. Cultural presences such as Christian antiliberalism are, among other things, signs of the inability of reigning political discourses either to document these changes or to capture the needs and the self-understandings of many (religious) citizens.

As an example of this shift in interpretive frameworks, consider the manifold changes emergent during the post–Cold War era of American politics, which has seen a marked increase in antigovernment rhetoric. From the congressional elections of 1994, when Newt Gingrich and his followers successfully appropriated Ronald Reagan's strategy of commandeering the government by denouncing its bigness, to the antigovernment violence committed at Waco, Ruby Ridge, and Oklahoma City, criticisms of the state's legitimacy or of the federal government's efficiency have once again assumed prominence in American public discourse. The very commonality of this critical impulse inures us to it, lulls us into taking it for granted. When critiques of political order are enacted in religious terms, it is tempting simply to interpret them as one part of a larger political drift toward decentralization, rather than to essay a deeper understanding of the specifically religious motivations that lie behind such critiques. The religious critique may be shrugged off as "an ongoing morality play at the margins of American society,"[5] lacking the substance to merit hard-nosed political scrutiny.[6] Contrarily, when theorists or others seek to take seriously a religious presence in politics, it is often in one of two standard forms: religion is either acknowledged only as a "private" phenomenon that has no place in public politics, or it is somewhat uncritically welcomed as a beneficial source of "values." Neither view, however, necessarily captures the rise in American religious activism in recent decades, particularly actions that, like Berrigan's, directly challenge the political authority of the liberal state.[7]

A new framework and a new vocabulary are needed to understand these religious creations. This shift in frameworks helps reveal the complexity and the challenges of religious protest. Such efforts aid not only in understanding the particularities of Christian antiliberalism but also in reconfiguring conversations about American political religion. I document the complexities of Christian antiliberal thought and practice by focusing on the concerns and strategies that are central to its practitioners. This process reveals, at the same time, both Christian antiliberalism's continuities with older forms of protest and its contemporary power.

When seeking to understand actions such as the protest on *The Sullivans*, a conventional analysis might begin with questions about ideology ("Is this an action of the Right or of the Left?") or about institutional affiliation ("To what denomination or movement does this action belong?"). These questions focus on externals; they are ex post facto applications of analytic terms and categories that are often not central to the motivations or the practice of political religionists such as Christian antiliberals. Clearly, the "internals" and the "externals" exist in a relationship of dynamic interaction; there is no considering the one without the other. Still, when focusing explicitly on the concerns practitioners have about liberal political order and the ways these are dramatized in activism, it is evident that questions about ideology or institutional affiliation only scratch the surface of what is most compelling about political religion.

I shift the focus away from exterior categories and toward what animates and energizes political religion: the elements, the sources, and the motivations of these practices as described by the activists themselves. If the religious protest that has increased in both visibility and fractiousness in the past few decades is to be addressed, it must be more fully understood. To focus this understanding on Christian antiliberalism, I chart the history and practice of three Christian groups with vigorous, although different, antiliberal impulses: Catholic peace activists Daniel and Philip Berrigan, the New Christian Right (NCR) movement for homeschooling led by Michael Farris's Home School Legal Defense Association (HSLDA), and the evangelical Sojourners Community of Washington, D.C. Christian antiliberalism is a broad religio-political impulse, a persistent register of religious discontent with political order. It is also enacted in specific ways by practitioners such as those above. Thus, Christian antiliberalism can be seen as a decentralized form of religious social criticism, which can be studied using the comparative categories I outline below, or as a more specific form of religiously grounded dissent that rejects not simply a particular institutional form but the very ways in which politics is conceived and practiced in a liberal regime. Concentrating on the way such dissent is organized around shared antipathies that stem from religious commitments, as opposed to being organized around institutional affiliation or political ideology, helps one to appreciate the distinct qualities of this activism as well as to push toward new ways of interpreting political religion more broadly.

Christian antiliberalism is one sign among many of important shifts under way in American religious and political culture. Where once American government and politics enjoyed fairly widespread legitimacy and popular consensus, the past three decades have seen this faith eroded by economic instability, voter apathy and cynicism, dwindling support for public institutions, and the growing desire among citizens for new identities and modes of political participation.[8] Christian antiliberalism is a part of these trends and a reaction to them. To grasp its complexity and significance, I use a method that fuses the interpretive worlds of religious studies and political theory. This analytic combination gives some empirical grounding to the wider cultural and political issues raised by this form of religious social criticism, and it expands the interpretive frame within which political religion is generally understood.

Earlier I defined political religion broadly as acts conducted in political spaces for explicitly religious reasons. Although the breadth of this definition serves usefully to suggest the multiple ways in which religions and politics might intersect, or by which religions define themselves through engaging political matters, the term requires more specificity with regard to Christian antiliberalism in particular. Clearly there are many religious groups, associations, or movements that either have themselves served as political spaces or have occupied these spaces for religious purposes. So there is more to say about Christian antiliberalism than that it engages political spaces. I focus specifically on the context of American liberal political culture to track an impulse embodied by religionists who erupt into and disrupt political order, bringing with them as they do so a set of experiences and assumptions—about power, authority, and meaning—that they perceive to be contrary to those generally tolerated in such spaces. These groups shatter political, and perhaps religious, convention. It is precisely this intrusive, confrontational dimension of Christian antiliberals—their tendency, even hunger, to blur or break boundaries—that distinguishes them from other political religionists.

As Christian antiliberalism is enacted, the sacred narratives, moral imperatives, and embodied practices of specific communities are used to define grievances that practitioners experience with regard to specific issues in specific times and places. These activists are concerned less with political strategy and organization, as these are customarily understood, than with issues of meaning and the experience of identity. Liberal political order rests on the notion that common legal and political principles or practices can constitute something like a shared political faith that can unite a citizenry in spite of its differences. The critics and protesters I describe worry, along with many others, that such a project asks us to ignore some things that are crucial to us as humans.

The stakes in this potential discrepancy among identities are high owing to the meanings and functions of both religions and politics in citizens' lives. Both religion and politics are ways of imaginatively configuring and ordering the world. They are grand narratives or systems of meanings by which people make sense of and make livable their worlds. Each system claims to possess "truths," as with a Marxist claim that the wheels of history are oiled with the blood of the workers or the Buddhist claim that conventional reality is a form of suffering brought about by desire or attachment. If it is true that both religious and political systems of meaning are, among other things, ways of organizing and experiencing reality, then it is not difficult to appreciate why there is such a powerful reaction when they mix. Sometimes the reaction is harmonious, and religious ends overlap with political ones. But just as often, as with Christian antiliberals, the reaction is hostile, and religions find themselves at odds with politics.

Religious practitioners such as Christian antiliberals position themselves against political order because they believe that an injustice has been committed or truth obscured. They sense that the world is out of order and must be set right. Opposition to political order often develops around these perceived infractions of religious norms, and allegiance to a particular form of religion is felt to require protest. The various forms of Christian antiliberalism are linked, as are other variants of religious protest, by the presumption that there is a fundamental distinction between human laws and sacred laws. In order to preserve the integrity of the sacred, religious protesters risk violating human laws and challenging political order in various ways.

Christian antiliberalism is concerned primarily with liberalism's political and institutional order rather than with liberal political philosophy. The two are related, especially insofar as the state has been ordered by liberal principles, but the distinction makes clear exactly what antiliberals most oppose. Two other methodological decisions bear mentioning. First, it is apparent that the religious challenge to political order is exclusive neither to Christianity nor to the United States. Even the casual observer of politics cannot have failed to notice that, since 1979 and Khomeini's violent deposition of the shah in Iran, political religion has dramatically reared its many public heads. Since then, religious struggles in the public arena have proliferated across the globe, in Algeria, Chiapas, India, Ireland, Sri Lanka, and places too many to mention.[9] I am concerned with precisely this sort of interaction between religion and political order, but I seek to excavate the meanings it has for the American political context in particular.[10] For this reason, I purposefully use the term "Christian" antiliberalism rather than "religious" antiliberalism. Although the phenomena I describe undoubtedly extend beyond the boundaries of tradition, the cultural and political influence of Christianity far outstrips, at least for the present, that of other religious traditions in the United States. It is the specificity of this tradition's antiliberalism I interpret.

Second, let me say a bit about my criteria for the selection of case studies. Readers may balk at my choices and wonder why I have not focused on the so-called Christian patriot movements, the Sanctuary movement in the American Southwest, the Catholic Worker movement, Barrios Unidos of Santa Cruz, Texas Valley Interfaith, the East Brooklyn Congregations, the now defunct Operation Rescue, or the 10-Point Coalition of Boston, to name but a few of the many activist groups that might be considered antiliberal. My omission of the Christian patriots is deliberate, for though they are certainly the most violent critics of liberal political order, they also are not part of the political spectrum that truly engages the liberal state and American political culture. I have chosen to focus on the Berrigans, the NCR, and Sojourners because they have publicly engaged the political legitimacy of liberalism in a more direct fashion than many of the groups just mentioned; they now remain directly involved in these sorts of protest; and each is a significant presence in post-1960s American religious history. However, my claim is not that these three groups exhaust the conversation about Christian antiliberalism but rather that they exemplify many of its characteristics in a highly suggestive and informative way. Thus, these three groups help to shed light on the broader impulse of Christian antiliberalism. That there are more exponents of antiliberalism seems only to underscore its significance.

In a time of declining church attendance in mainline denominations,[11] increased communication between religious communities, and religious diversity, it is no surprise that religious creations such as Christian antiliberalism have not yet been consciously categorized by scholars. The phenomenon has links with movements and activists in the past, though its presence also exemplifies trends from the current moment in American religious and political culture. Christian antiliberalism is most distinctively a response to the religious and political watershed of the 1960s. It has been in the wake of the sixties that the critique of liberalism, and the role of Christian activists therein, have reached their apex. Whereas activists in earlier movements, such as the abolitionists or the Catholic Workers, focused on specific issues and sought largely to correct or render more effective the system, Christian antiliberals have used their idiosyncratic and agonistic protest practice to deny the very legitimacy of contemporary liberal political order (even if they are occasionally willing to work with that political system in order to restore its legitimacy).[12] To do so, they have combined new political tactics and an explicitly dramaturgical public style with older modes of activism such as confrontational direct action.

Because of these and other innovations, Christian antiliberal protest cannot simply be captured by extant ideological discourses or denominational concerns; rather, it is constructed around concerns and antipathies manifested in groups that might not otherwise be seen as kindred. This protest does not generally seek redress from the state, as other religious activists have done in the form of rights or legislation; instead, Christian antiliberalism is an explicitly critical idiom, which calls into question the very legitimacy of the system (at times even retreating into "intentional communities" in order to escape the reach of political order or to establish a space wherein their members can participate more directly in the decisions affecting their lives).

I am not suggesting that there is an "official" subculture or movement of activists who recognize and declare themselves to be Christian antiliberals. I use the term, rather, to denote what Linda Kintz calls "a coalition of resentments."[13] Instead of focusing solely on organizations or ideology, which I believe provide only a partial picture of what is happening with American political religion, I concentrate on the salient features and defining characteristics of Christian protest against and criticism of political order.

In my observations of American political religion, I have been particularly compelled by activists whose challenge to political convention is particularly agonistic, directly confrontational, and willfully out of step with expectations about what it means to be religious. As I began this study, my questions were—I thought—quite simple ones: Why do people do this? What makes Christians so angry about American politics? How do these people, when they engage in specific forms of protest, perceive themselves and their intentions vis-à-vis those of liberal political order? These are the questions that still compel me and that I strive to answer in this book. To understand the sources of this protest, the shapes it takes, and the self-understandings of these religionists, I have put aside some of the conventional guidelines for interpreting political religions and have worked with a new series of categories. These qualities are not generated by conventional markers such as ethnicity, denomination, or social class; instead, these features span traditions, institutions, and ideologies to get at the sources of outrage and strategies for criticism that are common to Christian critics of political order. I do not propose that they serve as structural parallels to terms such as "liberal" and "conservative"; rather, they give us some new angles of vision on the shapes of American political religion.

The first of these qualities I refer to as *political illegibility*. This concept, indebted to James Scott's broader notion of "illegibility," is suggestive of the ways in which the specificity and robustness of religious beliefs (particularly Christian antiliberal concerns about political order) cannot be "read" or understood using the political logic of "left" and "right" or perhaps by any political ideology.[14] The second of these qualities is *the sacred register of politics*. This is the tendency among Christian antiliberals (and other religious activists) to politicize what is most intimate to them: their very identity and self-understanding as religious practitioners. The use of the term "register" indicates the *felt* quality of this perceived conflict between religion and politics, that it is at this intimate level of religious devotion that Christian antiliberals claim to feel or to register the negative impact of liberalism. This quality is linked to the broader rise of "identity politics" since the 1960s, the turn to particular features of the self or community such as race or gender, instead of "traditional" political affiliations such as party or union, as a central component of political action. The sacred registers are, however, of a somewhat different order, since they are less clearly linked to a social movement and not nearly as concerned with recognition or legislative redress as are many forms of identity politics.

Whereas identity as a category denotes a group defined as a number of people sharing a characteristic or quality of experience that demands recognition, the sacred registers call attention additionally to a mode of self-understanding whereby the existence of Christian antiliberals—as thinking, feeling, morally committed agents—draws on the shared history, experience, culture, and connections of their group or community as this is shaped by antiliberal sentiments. So the sacred registers call greater attention to the felt and experiential quality of political existence for religionists in particular; more specifically, it is in the sacred registers that the *difference* between religious and political worlds of meaning is experienced.

The third category evident across the range of Christian antiliberalism is *ritual protest*. Antiliberals use a variety of methods to dramatize their concerns, call attention to the state's perceived shortcomings, or disrupt the stability of political space, decorum, or discourse. The most common, and most effective, of these methods involves the performance or reenactment of religious rituals, narratives, or moral codes in the very public spaces that Christian antiliberals feel are hostile to these religious meanings. By contrasting their understanding of the sacred with what they denounce as merely profane, Christian antiliberals are establishing these acts as protests, denunciations, and critiques. They are ritualized in the sense that, for the participants, they possess the symbolic and transfigurative power of ritual and something of ritual's demonstrative impact.

Finally, Christian antiliberals display a propensity for local or grassroots activism, which I refer to as *koinonia*. This is the biblical Greek term for "community," a term of common usage found most explicitly in the Book of Acts. I use this language to call attention to Christian antiliberals' efforts, in the face of their perceived persecution from political order (through the courts, the police, or the political process itself), to control the decisions that shape the way they live and to carve out an existence that reflects their worldview. In attempting to maintain a degree of political and religious self-determination in this context, to decide what shape their home will assume, the activists often feel that they are seeking or creating a communal refuge from a social and political context both alien and threatening.

Each of these four features is manifested in the varied groups I document herein, and this breadth demonstrates something of Christian antiliberalism's significance. By focusing on these qualities and these modes of enacting political religion, a far clearer understanding of both Christian antiliberalism's breadth and specificity is achieved. The Sojourners Community has, since its inception in 1971, sought to challenge the state's lack of responsiveness to citizens' concerns. Liberalism, Sojourners claim, codifies a brand of politics that is too bureaucratic or administrative to capture the nuances of the religious concerns that animate their practice. They charge that the liberal state privileges only a narrow type of political understanding, one that emphasizes themes of individual liberty over group identity and parliamentary representation over vigorous citizen participation. Hence, according to Sojourners, the liberal state's salient features often sit awkwardly with the very democratic virtues it claims to uphold. Further, it has sullied itself with morally dubious endeavors such as the nuclear arms race, and it has failed to act on issues such as widespread poverty and racism. As part of their religious social criticism, Sojourners practice political illegibility.

The NCR is also averse to what it sees as the theological rigidity of the liberal state, but for very different reasons. Unlike Sojourners, NCR activists seek not to steer the state toward broader concerns of social justice but to prevent it from imposing its authority or stamping its identity on them. Among their primary concerns, in other words, are the sacred registers of politics. To shore up the boundaries around its communities, the NCR has become increasingly insistent on making its concerns known in public, whether in local elections or in national lobbying organizations. Michael Farris's and the HSLDA's efforts are particularly exemplary of these concerns.

Finally, the Berrigans contend that the liberal state is now all but unworthy of reform. Once staunch "connected critics" of both the Catholic Church and American democracy, the Berrigans have devoted their recent practice not to reform but to the cultivation of the resistance community at Baltimore's Jonah House and to the performance of ritual protests associated with the Plowshares Movement.[15] Participation and self-government are necessary but cannot salvage the wreck of the liberal state; in serving as moral witnesses, the Berrigans hope to provide a genuine communal alternative to the spaces acknowledged and sanctioned by the state.

Each group shares concerns about the authority and the direction of the political order; to a lesser degree, each shares certain religious goals. Some choose to enact an immanent critique of liberalism, hoping to transform the regime from within, whereas others dramatize their distance from conventional political operations. Just as methods and tactics differ, doctrinal, liturgical, and ideological differences also exist among the groups. But their common antipathies toward and critiques of liberal political order demand to be analyzed and understood. It is for this reason that I have chosen to focus on antiliberalism as a window into the broader culture of

American political religion. This protest idiom captures many of the concerns, motivations, and tactics of religious social critics active on the American scene today, as well as some from previous eras of American history; and the interpretive categories I have generated shed light on new domains of politicization being enacted by Christian antiliberals. Certainly there are religious and political differences among different groups of Christian antiliberals. This multiplicity, along with the presence of antiliberalism in different communities, helps capture the breadth of this religious challenge to political order. My analysis is not intended to be a comprehensive study of any of these groups; rather, it is a thematic exploration of a presence, perhaps even a style, in American religion and politics. My aim is not solely to narrate the story of each group but to focus on and make clearer Christian antiliberalism's thematic characteristics.

The study of this impulse and of these groups has independent merit. But I also hope that the interpretive categories I proposed earlier can serve a comparative purpose broader than this particular study: that they can begin to be suggestive of the kinds of questions that might more fruitfully orient the study of American political religion. Examining these areas of practice and politicization can serve as a useful supplement to standard accounts of religion and politics, which can often be detached from the concerns, practices, and history of actual practitioners or from the historical and political circumstances that inform their work.[16]

As a way of bridging these gaps, I place the four features of Christian antiliberal politics in conversation with the three groups I have chosen as exemplars of this protest. Although each group manifests all four characteristics of Christian antiliberalism, each also exemplifies one of the qualities in particular. Thus I use the history and practice of a particular group to explore a quality that each group shares. Even though it is possible to discuss each group in the context of each quality, I have chosen to highlight a feature at the fore of each group's practice: Sojourners exemplify Christian antiliberalism's political illegibility; the NCR and Michael Farris's HSLDA activism illustrate the concern for the sacred registers of politics; Daniel and Philip Berrigan are masters of ritual protest, and they dramatize this dimension of Christian antiliberalism; and koinonia is discussed in a summary chapter on the broader implications of Christian antiliberalism for American religion and democracy.

Actions such as the Berrigan protest described at the outset form the horizon of this study. This work aims to provide a sociologically and historically grounded account of the origins, components, and practitioners of Christian antiliberalism, but it is also a work of political interpretation that seeks to situate this protest phenomenon in its proper sociopolitical context and to explain its many meanings. Without an understanding of this context, it is impossible to grasp either the religious or the political motivations of Christian antiliberalism. The work of the following chapter, therefore, is to tease out these understandings through historical interpretation.

In chapter 2 I begin exploring Christian antiliberalism by way of the new categories I propose for comparative work in this area. This journey begins with the Sojourners Community's use of political illegibility. Sojourners insist that theirs is not a politics of "left" or "right" but simply a life of obedience to the Gospels. They believe this life is "illegible" according to conventional political analysis, which ultimately only trivializes religious devotion and activism. Sojourners present their activism as a politics beyond politics; their concerns are frequently neither legislative nor programmatic but exemplary of what they call the "prophetic" nature of Christian activism, which the rigidity of political logic cannot capture.

Chapter 3 explores the sacred registers of Christian antiliberal politics, documenting how antiliberals attempt to preserve those features of their shared history that they feel are most at risk in a liberal regime. The NCR waves the banner of its religious identity as an overt challenge to liberalism. Yet unlike identity politics, the NCR does not always seek redress or recognition; rather, it seeks to defend, educate, and cultivate the sacred registers of those in its confessing community. The NCR is nowhere near as discrete a phenomenon as Sojourners or the Berrigans. For this reason it is tempting to focus on impulses, such as homeschooling or antiabortion, that are common throughout its organizational breadth. But to do so would court a methodological disparity. Since my goal is comparative, I have chosen to focus on the activism of Michael Farris and the HSLDA. Like Sojourners and the Berrigans, this movement has a national representative, writings, and resources. Although it is clear that the NCR is broader than this movement, focusing on the ways in which Christian identity is geared toward a specific issue will enable me to draw a sharper comparative picture as well as to discuss the concerns that are more widely shared by the NCR as its practitioners variously attempt to renegotiate the boundaries of the political sphere.

The challenges of Christian antiliberalism are often most acutely felt in the presence of its ritual protest. The fourth chapter unpacks this idiom by interpreting the practice of the Berrigans and Plowshares actions. Together with a small coterie of like-minded activists, the Berrigans have carved out a unique style of ritual protest designed to undermine the workings of a political system they link to ongoing violence. They have conducted masses around burning draft files, smeared their foreheads with ash in Lenten significance, and hammered on nuclear warheads; they hope such actions, violations of state laws in order to bear witness to the higher laws they feel are being disobeyed, will disrupt daily work and the political process, challenging both the rhetoric and the decorum that support these activities. Ritual protest uses religious ritual and narrative as symbolic resources for critique. I document the tactics used, the varieties of ritual protest, symbolism, and religious activities to show that the Berrigans employ these tools to challenge not only particular policies or laws but also our very understandings of what it means to be religious and political. This they do through, among other things, incorporating satire and theater into their actions and by manipulating the plasticity of symbols or ritual in order to create alternate worlds of meaning to the liberal state.

My concluding chapter knits together the themes of the previous three in a discussion of the shared characteristics of the broader political culture of Christian antiliberalism. Here I think through some of the questions Christian antiliberalism raises about the new American religious landscape and American democracy. The shared antipathies found among Christian antiliberals gesture toward the promise of community democracy but also court the dangers of religious particularity.

If it is not obvious already, it will soon become apparent that I share some of these activists' concerns about liberal political order. This does not mean that I identify with them or that I endorse their tactics or concrete responses to what I believe is a moment of importance and risk in American life. I have long had an interest in religious social criticism, both in its second-order discursive forms and in its first-order embodied forms, and this interest has served as my entry into the study of American religions more generally. Yet I am—by training and by choice—something of a hybrid student of religion, pulled in roughly equal measure by theory and history or sociology. This study, then, is also hybrid. I attempt to think through some of liberalism's limits along with these critics, even as I simultaneously document Christian antiliberalism and its place in American religion. Throughout I attempt to withhold judgment—both political and religious—as best I can, though doubtless my own position and voice saturate this book. These limitations, however, are those that every scholar in the field faces, and I happily embrace them, for they are what make our work so vexing, challenging, rewarding, and hopefully enlightening. By working through these limits—both disciplinary and political, both historical and theoretical—I strive to contend with the complexity of this confrontational form of protest.

The Irony of the Liberal State

Law is order, and good law is good order.
—ARISTOTLE

The things that Americans were taught and still wish to believe about self-government—the articles of civic faith we loosely call democracy—no longer seem to fit the present reality.
—WILLIAM GREIDER

Sociological or political interpretations of religion often tend, in the words of anthropologist Clifford Geertz, to look everywhere for explanations of religious phenomena but to religions themselves.[1] New religious creations, particularly those that might be regarded as political, are often described as epiphenomena of larger geopolitical shifts such as the decline of the nation-state and the turn to local forms of identity; as a reaction to the travails of modernization; or as a response to disillusionment with the "master narratives" of the West, such as socialism or liberalism. Although such pronouncements can indeed border on a kind of intellectual reductionism, filtering the richness and complexity of religious expression down to a single causal factor, they also possess some explanatory merit.

In this chapter, I synthesize such "macrolevel" explanations of Christian antiliberalism with my focus on practitioners' religious concerns and activities. My goal in so doing is to distinguish three levels on which Christian antiliberalism may be understood: as a religious phenomenon, with rich theological and doctrinal motivations at the heart of its critique; as the outgrowth of a specific constellation of historical circumstances in the United States since the 1960s; and as an impulse with independent political significance. Religiously, it is notable for its denominational and political diversity, and its shared qualities and its political aims transect the denominational and traditional boundaries that were once more reliable guides to the religious topography of American culture. An impulse whose political concerns and religious tactics are present in Baptist, Roman Catholic, Pentecostal, Evangelical, and other Christian communities, Christian antiliberalism is evidence that the shape of new religious movements is not easily captured by denominational or institutional affiliation.[2]

Historically, Christian antiliberalism is linked to older forms and traditions of religious social criticism and protest. Yet it is also part of a more recent shift in American political culture, one linked to the legitimation crisis of political liberalism and the rise of new social movements. Traces of American anarchism are evident in the antiliberal disdain for organized political logic; the fierce use of Christian moral rhetoric in the public sphere has accompanied protest movements as long as there has been political order in the United States; and ritual protest, too, has been acutely felt in American religious history, an early and notable example of which was William Lloyd Garrison's burning of the American Constitution.[3] Yet in the era since the civil rights movement, ritual protest has reentered public politics dramatically, in ways that are often unique to our historical moment.

Politically, Christian antiliberal action is frequently not only tied to specific issues but linked in addition to systemic critique of political order. Further, antiliberalism's propensity for local politics represents a historical shift from earlier protest movements that, like the Populist campaigns of the 1890s or the fundamentalist "campaigns" of the 1920s, were aimed at influencing politics or culture on a national level. Contemporary critiques of liberalism often share normative concerns about the way society is organized and the way the state regards religious belief. Specifically, each group contends that liberal political order lacks legitimacy for two reasons: because it is bereft of the moral authority that it requires to align itself with the norms and ideals of a democratic society and because it provides insufficient resources for citizens to participate in the democratic process. Christian antiliberals give shape to these normative critiques through quite different communal or theological elaborations, varied issues around which antiliberal sentiments cohere, and different programmatic responses to their critiques.

Without appreciation for all these constitutive elements—particularly the religious worldviews that shape its motivations and practice—Christian antiliberalism cannot be understood. This complex religious creation is both heir to older traditions of American religious dissent and a product of its contemporary sociopolitical context. A phenomenon with deep historical roots but one that is also new and challenging, it must be seen in light of the changing nature of American politics.

Traditions of Dissent

Christian antiliberalism is both continuous and discontinuous with earlier movements and activists, both religious and nonreligious. The challenge to the legitimacy or the reach of the state has been prevalent in American politics, in both its religious and nonreligious forms, at least since the Federalist debates during the Constitutional era. Throughout the recorded history of the United States—stretching from long before the War of Independence into the twenty-first century—religious people from multiple traditions have debated the legitimacy, scope, character, and direction of political power. Indeed, there seems to be something uniquely American about the obsessive regularity with which such debates are held; and religious groups in particular have long found sport in denouncing the government that, at least on some level, guarantees them the freedom to utter such denunciations. In the twentieth century, debates about the state animated groups ranging across the political spectrum, from the Students for a Democratic Society to *National Review* conservatives.

Drawing power from its ability to name historical and critical forebears, Christian antiliberalism captures themes deeply embedded in the American political and religious imagination. A comprehensive list of its antecedents would extend back quite far in American history. Indeed, the historical range of Christian dissent itself is vast, stretching from the resistance of early Christian communities to Roman assimilation through the antinomian communities of the radical Reformation to peasant uprisings such as that led by German Thomas Müntzer, among many examples. Even within the United States, there are countless examples of Christian protest, such as Roger Williams's rejection of theocratic government in Massachusetts in 1636, the religious presence in popular uprisings such Bacon's or Shays' Rebellion, the abolitionists of the 1830s–50s, Christians working for woman suffrage in the decades following the Civil War, trade union activism that churches spearheaded in the 1880s and 1890s, and dozens more. I purposefully do not touch on this broader history; nor even do I attempt to treat Christian dissent in the United States exhaustively. The purpose of my historical discussions here is simply to suggest, first, that Christian antiliberalism is continuous with some specific forms of earlier American dissent (most obviously the populism of the 1890s, the radical Christian politics of the 1920s, and the radical democratic move-ments of the 1960s) but that, second, it is also distinct in some important ways.

Historically, Christian antiliberalism has been decisively shaped by the political watershed of the 1960s, when liberal political order, in its appar-ent triumph, first began to fracture. By liberal political order, I refer not to the political philosophy of John Stuart Mill or John Rawls but the *institu-tional* order that emerged in the era of corporate liberalism and culminated in the postwar Keynesian state. According to Alan Brinkley, "liberalism was the set of political ideas that had descended from the New Deal and that had shaped the steady postwar expansion of federal social and eco-nomic responsibilities."[4] Postwar liberalism became identified with the planned economy of the welfare state and with judicial and legislative ac-tivism. Beginning in the 1960s, this arrangement was assailed from a num-ber of quarters and for multiple reasons. Its underlying principles were charged with insensitivity to morality and community; it was denounced for its structural obstacles to democratic participation; it was seen as pa-ternalistic and excessively regulatory; and it was judged increasingly un-able to carry out its primary tasks of managing the economy and creating social equity.

In Christian antiliberalism, the challenge to political order contains three analytic components (convictions about the purposes and conse-quences of politics) that guide its practice. These are, first, an aversion to the centralization of power; second, a sense that politics has become hostage to elites, which prevents the participation of everyday citizens; and finally, the conviction that politics and the state are out of line with, or even an affront to, Christian morality. Practitioners often draw different conclusions from these basic analyses and gear their critique toward differ-ing normative ends. Some hope to reform the political process and to enact an immanent critique of American politics, intoning before the citizenry that it has strayed from its own democratic ideals. These reformers decry liberalism because the encroachment of state bureaucracy, coupled with the philosophical norms underlying these institutional forms, limits the democratic autonomy of local communities, the ability of citizens to shape the state and its activities, and the cultivation of free spaces in civil society. However, other Christian antiliberals cultivate no such hopes for salvaging the wreck of American politics; there is no buried treasure to be brought back from the critical voyage but only the hope that local and autonomous forms of authentic community can be constructed in ways freed of the taint or corruption of a political process in decay.

These forms of Christian antiliberalism share similarities with libertarianism and populism. Yet although all these philosophies possess a fear of "bigness," of the encroaching institutional powers of the state bureaucracy, Christian antiliberalism does not contest these forces with the populist profession of the rights, wisdom, or virtues of the "common people." Populism is an important antecedent to Christian antiliberalism, but both its historical context and its motivations are distinct, as I demonstrate later. Libertarians object to the state insofar as it limits their individual liberty, yet their shared aversion to state power does not necessarily extend to sharing Christian antiliberalism's religious sensibility or its yearning for community.

The historical lineage of Christian antiliberalism clarifies and further sharpens these distinctions. Religious protest has manifested itself to varying degrees in each of the key moments in the construction of the modern liberal state: the Jacksonian era, the Gilded Age, the Progressive Era, and the New Deal. Postwar liberalism owes its character in part to each of these moments, which together have yielded what James Morone calls the "unwieldy system" of the liberal state, aimed at "checking the mobilization of public power to a single national end; breaking up policy into narrow, poorly coordinated areas; preserving the inchoate public administration still marked by Madison's intricate checks and balances."[5] This "unwieldy system," which intended to provide citizens with access to public power and with the opportunity to reform the state, has developed mechanisms that render political change difficult: the specialization of knowledge such that political discourse becomes a matter of technical proficiency unavailable to average citizens, the growth of bureaucracy, the increased power of policy "experts" to manage political affairs, the state's tendency to co-opt people's movements, and its use of the judiciary to regulate public activism. The mechanisms that the Progressives and the New Dealers implemented in order to secure democracy for the people are seen by many as having ironically problematized this very possibility, yielding a system hostile to grassroots participation, community activism, and the people's consensus.

As Morone put it, "A great irony propels American political development: the search for more direct democracy builds up the bureaucracy."[6] This irony began to take shape in the Gilded Age, the heyday of corporate liberalism. Lawrence Goodwyn notes that American politics before this time had not been overly preoccupied with democratic participation. Instead of being vexed by democracy's absence, he claims, most citizens took for granted the local scale of politics and enjoyed a limited degree of participation. A country of sectional alliances and local solidarities, the United States was once able to nurture belief in the power of humans as cooperative beings whose self-understandings were as democratic citizens.[7] Hence, even in a period of history fraught with conflict and social dislocations, the problems of carving out space for political participation were not as drastic as they would later become.

The decades immediately following the Civil War marked the first of several waves of centralization that have contributed to the growth of the federal government. The relentless drive to expansion of U.S. territory ended with the closing of the frontier in 1872. In its wake, the drive was turned inward, eventuating in the centralization of political power, banking, and law. As the government extended its reach into new territories, it was forced to contend with change and uncertainty in American life more broadly. Huge tides of immigration and urbanization transformed the shape of American society and culture at an even more rapid rate in the late nineteenth century than they previously had. America was now an urban, industrial, pluralist country, with all the difficulties and dislocations these massive shifts entailed.

Religions were both instrumental to these changes and at their mercy. Intellectually, mainline Protestant denominations—the majority of which were still in disarray owing to the splits that had opened up over slavery—became ever more divided by new science, philosophy, and biblical criticism. Further, significant conflict existed among religious groups. During this period, the Nativist and Know-Nothing groups were only the most visible participants in religious conflicts, as the dissipating Protestant majority grappled violently with the growing numbers of Catholics, Jews, nominally freed African Americans, and immigrants from Europe and Asia. Additionally, new religious voices arose during this time period, some promising new revelations and others offering heightened engagement with social problems and reform issues.

Amid this great change, the state attempted to create cohesion by systematizing the law, expanding bureaucracy, and standardizing the economy. It was thought that centralized state power alone could make large-scale industrial and financial organization possible.[8] Reactions to this growth, and the cultural changes it wrought, were varied. Local political organization at times sat awkwardly amid the increased presence of government agencies and new legislation crafted by political "experts." Political religions, too, were destabilized by the new social problems with which they had to contend. Old protest idioms that vaunted free markets, back-to-the-land ideologies, religious freedom, or libertarianism were woven together in a populist critique of state power, much of the energy for which was supplied by religion.

Populism "appeared at almost the very last moment before the values implicit in the corporate state captured the cultural high ground in American society."[9] In contrast to the managerial and administrative politics that necessarily accompanied the centralization of power, populists advocated localism and popular participation.[10] These goals could never have been attained in the Gilded Age, but they became important elements of a protest idiom that still resonates in American political culture and in political religion specifically. The state was blamed for transferring economic power from local merchants and yeoman farmers to shadowy institutions or corporations far removed from communities. American capitalism thereby became identified by its detractors as a moral and political failure that demanded to be challenged or overturned. This critique, with its deep roots in the popular folklore of American democracy, is in many ways an important forebear of Christian antiliberalism. It recognized the perils facing mass democracy in the industrial era: either the tyranny of centralization or the undemocratic prospect of a passive citizenry, neither of which mirrored the activist yearnings of so many religious practitioners of the era.

These new features of American politics shaped the practice of earlier Christian activists and protesters, who saw only compromise or fallenness in accepting the political terms of the state. In a new context of interdependent institutions, cultural conflict, political radicalism, and industrial capitalism, new voices arose calling for change. From the 1890s through the 1930s, political religionists drew on their devotional languages to criticize the state. Socialist-influenced Christians such as the Knights of Labor or the Christian Labor Union, based largely in the urban industrial Northeast, fused biblical writings about equity and social justice with Marxist analyses of society to warn of the turmoil that would surely follow the unequal distribution of wealth.[11] Later, in the 1920s and 1930s, fundamentalist firebrands such as Gerald L. K. Smith decried the moral laxity of "melting pot" culture and worried that the new industrial society would forever undermine Christian values. Among other notable figures operating during this period was Father Charles Coughlin, who, influenced by traditional Catholic social teaching about the priority of local community over centralized power, used the language of his tradition along with populist rhetoric to heap scorn on what he saw as an authoritarian state, captive to special interests and hostile to local communities.[12]

The basic impulse behind these varieties of antistatist (and, to a somewhat different degree, antiliberal) protest has been further altered in the long and tortured history of American politics in the past century. The rise of new economic forms in the first decades of the twentieth century was interpreted by many as jeopardizing small production, local communities, and the democratic process. And the collective protest against these developments often carried a distinctly religious voice, as farmers claimed that the freedom granted them by individual salvation forbade them to be commanded by distant government institutions.[13] Disorderly conduct and political radicalism, in the name of self-determination as well as righteousness, were ways of voicing grievances, of both defying the claims of the federal government and seeking better representation in it. Yet with the Progressive Era and the New Deal, both the state and antistatism were transformed. Each of these historical eras witnessed the further centralization of political power and expansion of the government. Progressives, who had initially hoped to remedy the "bigness" of the state through "scientific" reform, became split between those who despaired of transforming the larger society, eschewing government in favor of local reforms such as settlement houses and houses of hospitality, and those who eventually came to seek entry into the state apparatus.[14]

By the beginning of the 1930s, the government grudgingly came to recognize the political rights of workers and their unions, ending an era of wrenching political radicalism.[15] Promotion of centralization as a means of resolving conflict between labor and ownership led to the atrophying of political activity among workers and, in the eyes of some activists, to the need for the government to take radicalism of any sort seriously. "Corporate liberalism" thrived by co-opting the radical rhetoric of the socialists and the neopopulists, substituting social engineering for participatory politics. This approach "started with the assumption that problems were essentially technical, that the framework of the political economy need only be rationalized and that 'experts' applying their skills in the assumed common interest could best do the job."[16] Dissenters and radicals, too, came grudgingly to accept the reality that their claims would be heard only if brokered between existing actors in the system. Radical rejection of the assumptions of corporate politics gave way to the acceptance of piecemeal reform; the creation of new forms of social legislation and government programs took the place of citizen activity; and the public welfare was defined through a consensus of leaders inside the government system.

By 1945 the state had crafted "an accommodation with modern capitalism that served, in effect, to settle many of the most divisive conflicts of the first decades of the century."[17] Postwar America, for the most part, enjoyed a consensus that presumed that the United States had "gotten things right": that representative democracy was the closest approximation to citizens' participation in the process of governance and that the principles of New Deal liberalism, combining growth politics with the welfare state, were the best economic arrangements for such a political order.[18] The New Deal had fused the market and the welfare state, which would be kept financially solvent by the affluence and growth politics of the postwar period. This influx of capital in the postwar economy thickened the American middle class and rendered systemic challenges more or less moot. Where religious communities had, for the first half of the century, been involved in social and political struggles, the stabilized society of postwar America had a similarly tranquilizing effect on American religious life.

During the 1950s, however, fractures became visible on the surface of state power. Liberal political order continued to enjoy general consensus and growth, but a popular animus against it was also beginning to resurface. Neoconservatives called attention to the specter of Stalin in order to generate fear of state-sponsored social initiatives. The very idea of big government was linked in the popular imagination with fascism and Stalinism.[19] This imagined collusion did little to diminish the growth and power of the state, which was also seen as the guarantor of political order and a bulwark against dissent. A growing number of critics, however, worried that this very focus on order and stability could be at odds with the importance of democratic participation. An increased use of the courts to resolve political conflicts, alongside the seemingly unassailable power of state and federal bureaucracy, appeared to endanger the political participation and activism that many citizens began to crave. Ironically, then, liberalism's strategies began to foment the very radicalism they were intended to curtail.

The Sixties and Their Aftermath

It was in the 1960s—with that decade's two great galvanizing causes, the civil rights movement and the protest against U.S. military presence in Vietnam—that Christian antiliberalism began to emerge from this growing discontent as an impulse distinct from other forms of political religion. Among the many critics of American liberalism active during the 1960s (pacifists such as A. J. Muste and Dorothy Day and Martin Luther King Jr.'s Southern Christian Leadership Conference), the student-led New Left embodied many of the concerns now articulated by Christian antiliberals. The America of 1960, in ways both similar to and different from the contemporary context, was ripe for the emergence of the New Left and its flagship, Students for a Democratic Society (SDS). In a time of unprecedented affluence and political stability, the university students who went on to create this organization felt beset by political disillusionment and power-lessness and by a sense of alienation and anxiety. The New Left and SDS strove, in ways both brave and misguided, to empower citizens in their everyday lives and to provide a sense of meaning through direct political action rooted in community life.[20] The members of SDS craved, in contrast to the political process as it had evolved in post–World War II America, a politics that affirmed the value of human ingenuity and the desire for au-thentic social existence. Such a politics, which SDS referred to as "partici-patory democracy," had two aims: individuals would share in the decisions that affected their well-being, and society would be organized to encourage both independence and common participation. These aims were meant to challenge the individualism, quietism, and materialism so loathed by SDS members.

This democratic subculture emerged in a period when religious figures such as Dorothy Day (as she urged her Catholic Worker movement to ab-stain from the payment of military taxes and from participation in the Civil Defense Act), King (whose Christian message and direct action un-dermined the segregationist establishment), and the Berrigans (whose dra-maturgical politics ritually exposed the abuses of state power) were creat-ing challenges to many of the same conditions that SDS was targeting. The student organization and its projects were marred by impracticality and technical difficulty, and factions of the movement had degenerated into violence by 1968. But the ambiguous legacy of the New Left nonetheless generated what James Miller calls "a valuable, operative reality" for future social critics addressing similar issues.[21]

Although there may currently be no distinct student movement employ-ing direct action,[22] the New Left's update of the populist protest against "bigness"—which was fused with a repertoire of radical direct actions such as sit-ins, trespassing, and building occupations, some of which were new at the time and others of which were indebted to the pacifist Left of the 1930s—has lasted. This combination of political styles, including its em-phasis on local organization, was ironically to prove extremely influential to the resurgent conservative movement (dubbed the New Right) from the 1970s into the present. The New Left's organizational tactics—from direct action to grassroots community organizing—were quickly appropriated by New Right strategists such as Paul Weyrich and Richard Viguerie, and its quasi-Jeffersonian rhetoric has been adapted by figures such as Newt Gin-grich and Ralph Reed. This kind of political "crossover," a widespread feature of contemporary American politics, is precisely the kind of reality that complicates conventional thinking about political religion.

Not only did the political styles and tactics of 1960s activists shape Christian antiliberalism, but so too did the political and cultural fallout from this divisive time period. Three political trends, emerging from the early 1970s, are particularly important for understanding the political world that has shaped Christian antiliberalism. The first is the growing crisis, practical and normative, and subsequent weakening of the welfare state, itself the institutional outgrowth of liberal democracy in the West.[23] Postwar liberalism's success depended on consistent economic growth. As this growth began to decline in the early 1970s, so too did the prosperity and political legitimacy of the state. By the early 1970s, the United States had lost its ability to provide the goods and the services that once served as the basis for the welfare state compromise of the New Deal era and thereafter. The rising demands and expectations of postwar society have outpaced the means of production and distribution. This crisis was compounded by the weakness of organized labor and by increased imbalances in the national economy.

These economic transformations seemed to portend the death of what Peter Clecak calls liberalism's "covenant with the future."[24] Liberalism's legitimacy has suffered further as a result of the rise of economic globalism since the 1970s. The postwar liberal social contract was predicated on the mutual promise between the state and the citizen that participation in the economic and political mainstream would be rewarded by equitable distribution of basic social goods, increased life opportunities for successive generations, accountable and responsible government, fair pay, job advancement according to seniority, job security, and so on.[25] As America has shifted from an industrial to a service economy, capital has become ever more mobile, increased power has been granted to independent bodies such as the World Trade Organization or the International Monetary Fund, and multinational corporations have come to steer the global economy. The result has been to undermine many of the long-assumed features of the liberal social contract and to deepen the crisis of confidence in democracy.[26]

Because of these changes, social reality has been fundamentally altered for both the rich and the poor. New developments in technology appear to render citizens less easy to educate politically and to organize. The decentering and mobility of capital do likewise, as nations relax labor and environmental rules and standards in order to compete. The spaces of work and economy are increasingly charged with accumulating social tensions in the largely unregulated market.[27] These transformations in the economy have affected government policy as well, as funding formerly reserved for social services, many of which were key planks in the social contract, has come increasingly to be invested in the market (through, among other mechanisms, reduced capital gains taxes, increased power for the Federal Reserve, and market incentives for investors). This sea change in domestic policy is even more significant given the steady decline in real wages since the Carter administration.[28]

These shifts have contributed to a fundamentally altered political landscape.[29] In this context, the crisis of liberalism has made it easier for conservatives to appropriate the language of populism and to decry the liberal state's incompetence and false reliance on centralized planning and administration. This reclamation of power by conservatives—from the so-called silent majority invoked by former Alabama governor George Wallace in the 1960s to the power of the New Christian Right as it has grown since the 1970s—is the second major development that has shaped the political world of Christian antiliberalism. Reacting partly to the economic failures of the postwar liberal state but also to liberalism's open embrace of race and gender issues in the 1960s, conservatives began to deemphasize economic or distributive issues. Instead, "social" or "moral" issues came increasingly to define political or ideological differences, whose conventional meanings began to erode in this era. It was the resonance of appeals to tradition, identity, and religion that made it easier for neoconservatives to build a political coalition around lower-middle-class resentment and disdain for the 1960s "left." Public figures such as George Wallace or Campus Crusade for Christ's Bill Bright used "hot button" moral issues such as school prayer or abortion rights to dismantle New Deal constituencies, even as liberalism itself stepped cautiously away from the working class. This conservative backlash created deep confusion about "traditional" left and right positions, as Wallace and others fused traditionally "left" themes of economic democracy with conservative aims and populist political styles. American conservatism began to exchange its stuffy, William Buckley–esque appearance for a souped-up populism, geared toward issues of identity, political insecurity, and anxiety over the increasing obsolescence of industrial or agricultural labor. Like other critics of political order, the New Right spoke loudly of its moral aversion to the "bigness" of the state, to the extent of the government's reach into the lives of "everyday Americans." But, unlike other antistatists, the New Right initially focused on policy as a means of reducing state power.

In time, however, the growth of conservatism would also generate smaller, local struggles to preserve traditions and shared histories, to become politically self-determining, or to protest the "intrusions" of the state. In many of these instances, as in the 1974 Christian Right struggles over public school curricula in Kanawha County, West Virginia, the activists were religious practitioners motivated by the structural changes in the American economy and society at large. These trends help explain the final characteristic of the era of Christian antiliberalism: the growth of identity politics and new social movements. Since the 1960s, "traditional" political identities—affiliated with work, state institutions, or political party—have been frequently supplanted, as many citizens have come to organize on the basis of identity, as manifested in race, gender, sexuality, or religion.[30] These issues have become more politicized since the 1960s, following the impact of both the civil rights movement and the first wave of feminism, and identity politics has taken on wider political currency. This represents a turn away from "universal" narratives, such as those of liberal democracy or socialism, and toward specific forms of political engagement, rooted in the lives of citizens and geared toward problems they can address in a direct fashion. This era has also seen the rise of "new social movements," whose concerns are particularist but often oriented more toward policy issues such as environmental waste and nuclear deterrence than toward issues of identity. The boundaries between these two political forms are often fuzzy, yet they share an aversion to older modes of citizenship and an inclination for direct action that is provocative and frequently confrontational.

These three sociopolitical trends are partly indicative of the changes that have taken place in American public life over the past several decades. Together, they have helped shape the heterodox protest culture of Christian antiliberalism, a culture that is bound up with the changing fortunes of the liberal state in postwar America. Christian antiliberalism's significance, however, is not weighed by what it reveals about a particular period in American history, about a particular religious group, or about a single political constituency. Rather, what stand out are the dynamics of its responses to a particular constellation of political and cultural issues—the crisis of liberal democracy, the rise of confrontational political tactics, the growth of identity politics, a deepening mistrust of political authority, and a widespread desire for community control and local autonomy—emerging from the 1960s.

This brand of challenge to political order has been insufficiently analyzed, despite the broad impact of its basic impulses. Although there has been extensive commentary on, for example, the influence of libertarianism on contemporary conservative thought or on the antiliberal themes in the 1994 congressional elections, scant analysis has been accorded to political religions and religious protests that have contributed to the growth of these political developments and that are evidence of a widespread desire for new forms of public life and political energy.

Theory as Usual?

Much has been said about the contemporary crisis of American democracy, yet surprisingly little of it acknowledges the connection between this crisis and religious protest. Christian antiliberalism is clearly one sign among many of this crisis. Political apathy and cynicism are often attributed to citizens' frustration with "politics as usual," which is seen as an impenetrable web of elite representatives, remote party structures, special interests, and mass media. Sentiments disputing the legitimacy and efficiency of the political process have been buttressed by the material changes documented earlier.

This sense of crisis has shaped all facets of American public life, from electoral politics to religion. However, in its limited engagement with this crisis, our public discourse continues to rely on terms such as "liberals" and "conservatives." Each of these terms refers to a basic orientation toward politics and culture that shapes the institutional life, policymaking, and moral direction of its constituents. Yet in recent decades, as E. J. Dionne and others have written, these labels have become increasingly unreliable guides to politics. Liberals, and the "left" more generally, once championed shared or "universal" human qualities, whereas conservatives, and the "right" more generally, staunchly defended "tradition," "culture," and "particularity." Today these tables have turned: the "left" defends particularity as the "right" seeks to avoid these issues through a rhetoric of commonality.[31] The distinction between "left" and "right" still matters, but it is of decreasing use for understanding the new forms of politics emerging in the United States, forms that are often less defined by their ideological proclivities than by their moral character or their relationship to conventional political culture.

From these new political territories Christian antiliberalism has emerged. It is both symptom of and response to the legitimation crisis of democratic politics in the United States. It is not an outright aversion to the norms of democracy, the rule of law, or the very existence of a political system. It is, rather, a critique of the American liberal articulation and institutionalization of these arrangements. As such, Christian antiliberalism is distinct from civil disobedience for a number of reasons. First, Christian antiliberalism goes beyond civil disobedience in practice. Although various activists do participate in civil disobedience, they also are involved in actions and patterns of life that are not necessarily illegal or "disobedient" in any conventional sense. The very presence of resistance communities and the use of local and school board elections to voice grievances are among the many legal actions in which Christian antiliberals engage. Second, Christian antiliberals do not simply possess an aversion to particular laws, functions, or policies; rather, behind their protest are biblical teachings on government authority and political order as a whole. Civil disobedience is inseparable from public witness and from more generalized forms of resistance to the liberal political order. Finally, as Jonah House activist Elizabeth McAlister succinctly put it, "Even the term [civil disobedience] . . . less and less describes what we are about. Civil disobedience implies a basic faith in a system that needs changes in certain areas. . . . I think it dangerous and misleading to use the term, to talk about constitutional rights, first amendment, etc. . . . [They] never speak about the real powers that control human life."[32]

Actions such as the Berrigan protest described in the introduction must be understood in all their complexity if the wider phenomenon of Christian antiliberalism is to be addressed. What motivates such actions? Which theologies are at work in them? To what political or communal forms are they related?

It is difficult to locate a theoretical or comparative language that can answer these questions and help to make sense of such a phenomenon. Recently academics have found popular sport in the notion that we live in a postideological, postmetaphysical, even a postpolitical age. This notion has been pressed into the service of all manner of theoretical programs. Cultural studies has aimed to track resistance to cultural hegemony in struggles over representation and interpretation. Second- and third-wave feminist writing has focused attention not on totalizing accounts of gender but on more "micropolitical" gestures of resistance to patriarchy. Postcolonial studies has investigated the strategies for resisting power generated by the so-called subaltern classes of society. Cultural anthropology has focused on local and particular constructions of meaning.[33]

Pundits and think-tankers have drawn from this intellectual energy as well. Following the revolutions of 1989, Francis Fukuyama proclaimed that centuries-old ideological struggles had finally eventuated in the triumph of liberal democracy and that we now lived in a postideological era.[34] Social theorists from Daniel Bell to Jürgen Habermas have addressed this political moment.[35] Historians such as Alan Brinkley have charted the complicated fate of New Deal politics and the ways in which their wane has affected postwar America.[36] And philosophers ranging from poststructuralists such as Jean-François Lyotard to pragmatists such as Richard Rorty have described the erosion of the philosophical or conceptual "metanarratives" that once guided and oriented our society.[37] Each of these approaches reveals important features of the turbulence and the fractiousness of our times. It is clear from this constellation of theoretical references that ours is a time of transition and that such reflections on the nature and meaning of these transitions can be tentative at best. Theorists in the humanities write and speak with caution, sensitive that the larger philosophical or political projects of the modern era have been so discredited that language itself risks implicating us in a totalizing worldview that effaces particularity, diversity, heterogeneity, and so forth. With the obvious exception of political theorists such as Rawls or Habermas, both of whom still argue passionately for the construction of a common political language and project, it is common for contemporary cultural or social theorists to excavate simply a small patch of intellectual territory, a niche fairly insulated from larger questions. And yet broader questions about political legitimacy, equality, and morality have hardly disappeared from our culture; they are simply not addressed with as much confidence by academics. They are, however, of concern to American citizens, particularly to religious practitioners who engage political realities in the ways Christian antiliberals do.

There have been some attempts, within political theory particularly, to come to grips with religion's role in public life. For example, Stephen Carter writes that "democracy is best served when the religions are able to act as independent moral voices interposed between the citizen and the state."[38] This well-meaning statement echoes Alexis de Tocqueville's belief that the intermediate institutions Carter refers to are the lifeblood of American democracy. It also means to challenge the conventional wisdom of political liberalism that, buoyed by the influence of John Rawls and his followers, worries that such "moral voices" may jeopardize not only the individual liberty of the citizen but the political legitimacy of the state, as well.[39]

Liberalism fears that religious "zeal" could undermine pluralism, and it responds by situating religion in the private, rather than the public, sphere. The communitarian rebuke insists that liberalism unfairly burdens religious citizens by requiring their "moral voices" to be silenced in order to participate. Yet neither of these responses, which together have dominated conversation about political religion, generates a theoretical language or comparative framework sufficient to grapple with complex forms of political religion such as Christian antiliberalism, which challenge the assumptions of both schools.

Theoretical debates about religion and politics require redirection. Political religion has evolved into new shapes that do not conform to the standard portraits found in either liberal or communitarian writings. Each conception is rooted in historical conditions and philosophical presuppositions that can no longer chart the errant courses of politics. Liberalism has historically sought to protect moral and political pluralism by distinguishing between individual liberty and what Rawls dubs "comprehensive doctrines," particular religious or philosophical commitments that may be too inflexible to work within the procedures of public politics.[40] From this, liberals have developed a corollary distinction between the public sphere (the site of rational deliberation among citizens and also of institutions such as the courts) and a clearly demarcated private one (where civic associations flourish and where religion and morality have purchase on our political lives).[41] Communitarians have criticized liberalism for undermining the very pluralism it seeks to protect. They claim that liberal aversion to "comprehensive doctrines" actually constrains participation, that it is excessively suspicious of the influence of culture and morality, and that its concern for normative issues often entails inattention to the realities of culture and identity. They conclude that any vision of public life lacking attention to the complexity and significance of values and identity will be impoverished and impractical.

The grounding, terminology, and ideological commitments of both liberals and communitarians are of limited use in attempting to understand Christian antiliberalism. It is unclear that the Christian antiliberal practices of disobedience, disruption, and conflict and, most important, a Christian religious sensibility that is purposefully contrasted with conventional understandings of politics map easily, if at all, onto theoretical constructs such as "moral voice" or "comprehensive doctrine." Extant theories do not contain categories that are supple and specific enough to make sense of the various protests and critiques in this "coalition of resentments." The theorists who have most frequently positioned themselves in relation to political religion, namely, liberals and communitarians, operate for the most part at a significant distance from the historical and cultural terrain where political religions thrive. In part because of such detachment, these theories have helped to enshrine a set of categories that prevents interpreters from the fullest possible engagement with phenomena such as Christian antiliberalism. In short, in order to understand Christian antiliberalism's challenge to the institutional order of American liberalism, there must be a move beyond the categories that often frame theoretical debates about political religion.

My project is to fill this gap in our understanding of political religions. Toward this end, it is vital to put the worlds of religious studies and political theory in dialogue with each other, for the story of Christian antiliberalism exemplifies the need to rethink what democracy means in the United States and what a more democratic politics requires. A more robustly democratic politics helps to make sense of the problems raised by political religion, just as the study of Christian antiliberalism clarifies some of the problems facing democratic politics today. Among the conclusions made evident in this study is the reality that, for increasing numbers of religionists in the United States, the terrain of the political is inseparable from the terrain of religion. This blurring of boundaries has profound implications for reconsidering the role of religion in democratic culture. It is my belief that the study of American religion can only benefit and inform this reconsideration by distilling what is at stake in the culture of Christian antiliberalism and what challenges this culture presents to contemporary American politics. In the gap between the worlds of political liberalism and the worlds of American Christianity lies a domain of religiously charged dissent, ritual protest, communities, and institutions, all condemning the direction of the political order. It is into this gap we now go.

Chapter 2

Christianity Faithfully Lived
Is Politics Enough

Prophetic Politics in the Sojourners Community

Woe to you that are rich.
—LUKE 6:24

In the fall of 1978, daily life at Sojourners Community House—in a poor, largely African American section of Washington, D.C.—was engaged with local issues such as food distribution, fights, redlining by banks, or evictions. Affluent white churches in the city's northwest quadrant or even more affluent gated communities in the outlying suburbs rarely consider these concerns—usually tucked away safely in the *Washington Post*'s Metro section—the stuff of Christianity. But in Columbia Heights, Sojourners have spent the better part of three decades bringing these realities into their devotional lives, refusing to keep them safely abstract. On any given autumn afternoon in 1978, they may have been busy preparing for publication the magazine that bears the community's name; working in the food co-op, the day-care center, or the children's school; or preparing sermons. They may have been planning one of their many protests. It was in the midst of such activity that Jim Wallis heard Katherine knock on the door.

A neighbor from across the street, Katherine was a young, African American single mother living with her son, Ofon, in one of the neighborhood's old row houses. She was frantic and had come to ask for help from the mostly white religious community. Katherine's building had recently been purchased by a group of wealthy real estate investors who hoped to begin gentrification in the Columbia Heights neighborhood, just east of the "riot corridor" left after the April 1968 uprising following Martin Luther King Jr.'s assassination. Most of the other families in the building had already been evicted for failure to pay the increased rent. Only Katherine and Ofon remained.

Katherine pleaded with Wallis to help fight the developers, and he agreed. The most visible figure in the Sojourners Community, Wallis had long asserted that the Bible was on the side of the poor and the peaceable rather than what he invariably called, invoking Pauline language, "the powers and the principalities." It was because of this conviction that Sojourners had been established, in 1975, in the heart of poor, black Washington, D.C., where dilemmas such as Katherine's are familiar to the city's poor African American citizens. Wallis used her plea to galvanize the community into a demonstration of the Christianity its members professed.

Over the following weeks, Wallis and others canvassed the neighborhood raising funds and enlisted the aid of other local religious communities, eventually putting together enough money to buy the building back in a no-profit sale. The developers refused to abandon their claim on the property. Undaunted, Wallis put the money in an escrow account, and, on a Friday afternoon, Sojourners threw a party to celebrate what they saw as the inevitable neighborhood ownership of the building. Outside the building, Ofon's friends from the Sojourners Daycare Center planted a tree while local parents marched with signs reading "Let Ofon Keep His Home." That night Sojourners held a sleepover in the building, and the following morning, Wallis and a few others were arrested. After his arraignment, Wallis met with a public defender, who suggested he plead insanity, reasoning, "Anyone who thinks they can stop real estate gentrification in Washington, D.C. is crazy."[1]

Since 1971, Wallis and Sojourners have maintained a communal life and witness that, although explicitly political, appears "crazy" according to conventional political logic. Throughout its eccentric existence, the Sojourners Community has been involved in public witness against what it regards as injustice, frequently trespassing the boundaries that define political order in its city. Sojourners have steadfastly denounced war, racism, cultural imperialism, and the inequities they believe are wrought by capitalism. They believe the United States a fallen nation in need of spiritual and communal rehabilitation. A primary cause of America's moral and spiritual degeneration, they believe, is the ossification of the nation's politics in rigid political categories of "left" and "right." The group believes that no extant political categories or conventions can generate the appropriate moral response to American social ills; hence, its members seek to craft a politics that is "beyond politics," a socially engaged practice that is politically illegible.

In an era when civic participation is often reduced to an occasional vote, Sojourners exercise what they believe is a more robust form of political agency that is both morally sound and practically efficacious. Opposed to what they see as the abstraction and watered-down political moderation of liberalism, they seek to enter the political sphere with a distinctly Christian practice, rooted in the prophetic writings of the Hebrew Bible and the communal witness of early Christian communities. They insist that the fierce moral poetry of biblical social justice is appropriate for our time, an era Sojourners believe is fallen in ways that are reflected in their own neighborhood: in the dwindling economic abundance that disproportionately affects urban African Americans, in the widespread distrust and cynicism toward the political process, and in the deep moral fragmentation in American culture.

Faced with these realities, Sojourners have hoped that the very existence of a radical Christian community would serve as a challenge to liberal political order. They have developed a community life, a series of neighborhood outreach programs, and a repertoire of protest tactics explicitly designed to expose and undermine the moral shortcomings of conventional political language and practice. Through nonviolent direct action (tax resistance, pickets, sit-ins, witnesses at defense institutions) or neighborhood organizing, Sojourners have addressed issues—poverty, racism, militarism—that they believe liberal political order obscures. They claim to embody a religious sensibility whose categories, logic, and meaning not only contrast with those of the political system they feel obscures injustice but also cannot be "read" according to conventional political registers. Only in a climate of deep moral agnosticism and numbness, Sojourners contend, can obvious injustices flourish as they do in the United States; only through the tepidness of liberal thought and policy, perpetuated by the reductive logic of "left" and "right" or "liberal" and "conservative," can such moral enervation exist.

Sojourners' political illegibility contains three primary elements, which together help generate what the group often calls "prophetic politics," a mode of religiously grounded action that marks its distance from conventional political logic by expressing and justifying itself solely in the evangelical Christian terms Sojourners prefer.[2] First, the state and liberal order are criticized as amoral; Sojourners argue that the conventional political logic of this regime obscures this amorality or limits the range of our possible responses to it. Second, they capitalize on recent changes in social and cultural history that have blurred the political distinction between "left" and "right." Formerly stable ideological and cultural positions are reversed, upended, blurred, or restricted. In these circumstances, political analysis of a particular group is aided less by attending to that group's or movement's position on a left-right political spectrum than by examining the degree to which that group or movement recognizes the legitimacy of the spectrum itself. Finally, the political logic of "left" and "right" is rejected insofar as it makes no room for the religious self-understanding of Christian antiliberals such as Sojourners. Not only do they assert that the logic is inhospitable to the moral concerns that occupy them, but Sojourners also feel that such logic registers religion as "other" in an a priori fashion. The group's history reveals a consistent rejection of ideological labeling, a renunciation Sojourners believe is itself a countersign to liberal political order. Dispensing with what they see as liberalism's shopworn ideologies and explanatory schemes in these ways, Sojourners set out to reclaim the voice and heritage of American evangelicalism from the New Christian Right (NCR)—which Sojourners believe has monopolized the tradition—hoping that the voice of their tradition will lay bare liberalism's spiritual impoverishment.

Rankled by the apparent constraints and closures of liberal political order, these activists have sought to forge a public praxis that is "illegible" to the liberal eye, a protest idiom that cannot be grasped using conventional categories and sensibilities.[3] This adoption of "illegibility" is designed to protect their normative commitments or practical goals from co-optation by ideology or state power. James Scott describes "legibility" as the state's desire and ability to normalize and arrange its population through taxation, conscription, prevention of rebellion, codification, and classification. These and other tactics and procedures constitute a form of cultural or cognitive "mapping" that only barely represents a population's social and cultural complexity; when allied with state power, these maps can in fact remake the social reality of everyday citizens and communities.[4] Submitting to the understandings of the reigning political order entails a kind of existential reductionism, whereby not just one's belief systems but one's practice is limited and flattened. In the context of the postwar liberal state, this has meant that those citizens who think and act in categories outside liberalism have been at odds with the narrowness of liberalism's political vision and with its tendency to impose that vision on social reality. This is not to suggest that liberalism is similar to the authoritarian statism of the former Soviet bloc or to a dictatorial regime; the reality is far from either of these arrangements. Nonetheless it is frequently charged that liberal political order seeks to quell political passion in the name of civic order, that it aims to codify and "normalize" social identities and practices that are inhospitable to these efforts.

Without efforts to resist normalization, Sojourners believe they would risk losing both political autonomy and religious integrity, since "legibility is a condition of manipulation."[5] Wallis rails against the need to make "false" political choices between liberalism and conservatism, between personal responsibility and economic justice, between big government and no government. Not only does "normal" politics trap one in this game of false choices, but it also makes neighborhoods such as Columbia Heights invisible. Clearly, Christian antiliberals such as Sojourners hope to capture public attention in order to disturb taken-for-granted political sensibilities and conventions. Illegibility furthers these ends insofar as it constitutes a visible contrast with extant modes of political thought and action. Although all Christian antiliberals speak publicly of their aversion to the political logic of "left" and "right," specifically to the tendency to abstract moral issues from their lived contexts and its insensitivity to religious devotion, this disdain has been expressed most consistently and eloquently by the Sojourners Community.

The religious sensibility and practice of political illegibility are evidence of the breakdown of old political markers: the identifying characteristics that used to mark the "left" and the "right" have been switched, upended, or erased altogether. The distinction between "left" and "right" politics has its origins in the French National Assembly of 1789, where conservative nobles were seated on the right of the assembly's center and new democratic classes on the left. The "right" has typically been associated with individualist or libertarian espousals of rights and the "left" with more social or egalitarian rights.[6] Yet cumulative developments in the West, and particularly in the United States, have rendered this distinction problematic. The "left" celebration of universality and the "right" defense of particularity have become problematized and their positioning destabilized.[7] To all but the most ardent proponents of these hoary old ideologies, these terms and parameters of political debate no longer make the sense they once did. Christian antiliberals reject the very idea of this political logic, which in its dualism reduces the multitextured character of their religious commitments to a shopworn series of ideas, disembodied and decaying. In contrast, Sojourners hope that their prophetic politics bears little resemblance to such conventional political markers.

Faced with a whirlwind of social and political change, the brunt of which they claim is borne by economically marginal citizens such as the

African Americans of Columbia Heights, Sojourners feel that moving beyond conventional political understandings is morally imperative, particularly for Christians. They attempt to break from ideological reductionism by taking seriously the concerns of the poor and the oppressed, which is precisely what Sojourners claim liberalism fails to do: the "right" is too dismissive of protections for the poor and disenfranchised, and the "left" is too bureaucratic and reliant on the courts. Although Sojourners have roots in the political and religious "left" of the sixties, they distance themselves explicitly from sixties models, largely because conservatives have had success mobilizing against the sixties.

The Sojourners Community's self-contained hermeneutic of prophetic Christianity thus avows its political illegibility, claiming that its very Christianness is already marked as politically "other" according to the logic of liberal political order. One might be tempted to see such assertions as evidence that Christian antiliberals exemplify the "postmodern" or "postmaterial" condition of collapsed boundaries, blurred identities, or any other of the keywords so often used by contemporary cultural critics. But to graft onto Sojourners this rhetoric would be to miss much of what drives prophetic politics: faith in a redeemer God who will deliver the poor from bondage and bring judgment to bear on the powers.

Roots and Relations

Sojourners occupy an often overlooked space in the history of American evangelicalism. Many historians focus exclusively on evangelical conservatism, particularly the NCR. The very broad tradition of evangelical Protestantism in the United States has always been associated with a certain "cultural traditionalism," a desire to distance itself from the domesticating or perhaps leveling influences of the modern world. Historically this focus on the maintenance of boundaries between religious and worldly identity, this concern for purity and freedom from corruption, has led many evangelicals to view not just their fellow citizens but the social order itself with a skeptical and judgmental gaze: just as the individual regenerate could not progress as a human without the bestowal of God's grace, so would culture itself remain morally incomplete without the influence of religion. This mixture of separatism and engagement has proved to be of great appeal to conservatives in the post-1960s era. Yet although the reemergence of public conservatism has certainly been the most visible recent trend in American evangelicalism, it accounts for only a part of the spectrum of evangelical life. Like many other American religious idioms, evangelicalism has been affected by increased mobility and intercultural communication beginning in the twentieth century. It has been commodified and dispersed through migrations, new media, and conversions. Mark Shibley claims that it is partly as a result of this diffusion that evangelicalism has come to experience tensions with secular society and has frequently opted to retreat.[8] Yet this response is only one of many, adopted largely by cultural conservatives.

The story of American evangelicalism is far more complex, one of shifting identity and self-understandings, particularly with regard to social action. The term "evangelicalism" usually refers to the historical mainstream of theologically conservative American Protestants, shaped by several defining characteristics. These include the affirmation that all people are born sinners; the profession of the truth of Scripture; an intense dedication to spreading the gospel; confidence in reason and intellectual processes, when used in the service of faith; a commitment (at least for some evangelicals) to millennialism; and a strong tradition of social action that emerged primarily following the Second Great Awakening. None of these characteristics necessarily links evangelicals with varieties of fundamentalism, which is a specific subset within this tradition, or with charismatic Christianity such as Pentecostalism, though there is some overlap between evangelicalism and specifically charismatic beliefs and practices. Histories of American evangelicalism generally begin with the explosions of popular piety known collectively as the First and Second Great Awakenings (the former a series of revivals and traveling circuits by itinerant preachers between the 1730s and 1750s, the latter a proliferation of camp meetings and tent revivals from the tail end of the eighteenth century to the middle of the nineteenth century). Chroniclers of this religious creativity tend to focus, as Nathan Hatch does, on the religious freedom and pluralism that evangelicalism purportedly brought to colonial America or that overlapped with extant forms of social egalitarianism.[9] They cite the influence of Jonathan Edwards, Gilbert Tennent, or George Whitefield, whose emphasis on individual piety, biblical orthodoxy, and evangelism helped popularize this religious idiom. The evangelicalism of the Second Great Awakening, under the influence of Charles Finney and others, emphasized social as well as personal transformation. In each of these revivalist moments evangelicalism emerged as a religion of the "ordinary people," whose emphasis on personal experience and enthusiastic devotion constituted a challenge to established Anglicanism, Presbyterianism, or Congregationalism in the young republic.

Histories explaining the contemporary political forms of evangelicalism

generally place great emphasis on the Civil War. Major Protestant denominations had split over the issue of slavery, and the rifts initially opened
here deepened as mainline communities struggled in their responses to
new social, political, and intellectual developments. In the late nineteenth
century, theologians and laypeople debated the orthodoxy of biblical criticism and recent developments in scientific thought (notably the rise of
the Darwinian theory of natural selection, which seemed to many evangelicals a direct affront to traditional understandings of creation). It is
customary, therefore, to view the evangelical landscape around the turn
of the century as one divided between "traditionalists" such as J. Gresham
Machen, whose staunch defense of religious convention pitted them
against the manifold changes overtaking American culture, and "mod-
ernists" such as Walter Rauschenbusch, who contended that the future
of Protestantism depended on a tentative embrace of certain features of
modernity. It is possible, thus, to see a shift from the primacy of denominational affiliation to political affinities taking place as early as the 1880s. For
several decades activism occurred along the entire political spectrum, and
progressive evangelical social action was a relatively common feature of
American life (common enough, at least, for evangelical conservatives to
have denounced it and its intellectual foundations repeatedly) alongside
the fairly conservative majority.

Around the turn of the twentieth century, then, American evangelicalism was characterized by internal division and multiplicity as it struggled
to define itself in relation to modernity. This shifting identity has shaped
the self-understandings of contemporary evangelicals, particularly with
regard to social action. This time period is generally described by pitting
the heirs of conservative evangelical organizer Dwight L. Moody, whose
Moody Bible Institute of Chicago trained legions of preachers and organizers in addition to disseminating conservative literature, against the liberal theologians associated with the Progressive movement or the Social
Gospel, who attempted to generate modern interpretations of the New
Testament that could inspire activists to work toward the amelioration of
social injustices. Following the 1920s liberal Protestants and fundamentalists both split off from the evangelical mainstream, and these two factions
squabbled over American entry into the First World War, temperance,
unions, and subjects practically innumerable. Many writers see the Scopes
"Monkey Trial"—in which Dayton County, Tennessee, schoolteacher John
Scopes became the center of a heated legal battle after he taught the then
illegal subject of evolutionary theory—as the culmination of this period of
struggle between liberals and conservatives, the latter having been roundly

mocked by the media during this trial.[10] Following this episode, fundamentalists did not retreat but instead shifted their focus from control struggles within mainline denominations to the formation of various subcultures and organizations, each with its own complex relation to modern secular society. Liberal Protestantism achieved considerable moral authority during the Great Depression and World War II, eventually attempting to reclaim the mainstream through a strategy of coalition building.

This narrative becomes complicated, however, when considering the "new evangelicalism" of the post–World War II era, which combined elements of both liberalism and conservatism. It is this subsequent blurring of evangelical boundaries that serves as the historical backdrop to the emergence of both Sojourners and the NCR. During the 1940s, the National Association of Evangelicals (NAE) was formed with calls for a "cooperative evangelicalism" that could heal denominational ruptures and forge a tentative rapprochement with modernity. Opposed to the NAE was the ultraconservative American Council of Christian Churches, headed by Carl McIntire, who also opposed the "apostate" Federal Council of Churches. Each organization differed in degree of militancy, but both saw evangelical unity as a way to combat the perceived threat of liberal ecumenism. Postwar evangelicals were thus increasingly willing to enter the public sphere in order to distinguish themselves from both liberals and fundamentalists. Robert Booth Fowler suggests that the mainstream evangelical journal *Christianity Today* was the voice of this emerging evangelical postwar coalition, which distanced itself from extremists such as McIntire and linked itself with public figures such as Billy Graham, who popularized this new brand of evangelicalism. The journal sought to shy away from political controversy or criticism, implicitly communicating to its readership that such avoidance of scandal was the cost of gaining a voice in the public sphere. Only by the Vietnam and civil rights era did social concern return to contemporary American evangelicalism, though by the 1970s evangelicals had once again split over which direction this concern should take.[11]

Recently, the standard way of shaping this story has been along political lines. In the hands of sociologists or political theorists such as Matthew Moen, James Davison Hunter, and Clyde Wilcox, historiography of evangelicalism since the 1940s has focused largely on the decline of the "liberal mainstream" and the politicization of conservatism. There is evidence to support this interpretation, but this narrative nonetheless obscures the ways in which the evangelical heritage in recent decades has become still more complicated. Much of this complexity has resulted from the persistence of concerns about social injustice and which methods, if any, are appropriate for addressing it. Amid these concerns and debates, from the thick of these factional squabbles among postwar evangelicals, Sojourners emerged in the early 1970s.

In the autumn of 1970, a handful of students met at Trinity Evangelical Divinity School just north of Chicago. Dismayed by American involvement in Vietnam and by the increasing racial tension and economic misery of America's cities, these young people sought to craft an "authentic" Christian response to political crisis. Dissatisfied with the evangelical center's response to the challenge of American social needs, which the students felt violated biblical norms of social justice, and with "left" movements they considered to be insensitive to religious concerns, the students began to publish a journal called the *Post-American* (ironically subtitled "The Voice of the People's Christian Coalition"). These Christian activists felt that an evangelical voice that was critical of the political status quo could serve as an alternative to limited political choices. They soon established a community that they hoped would embody the aims of the journal. Like many of its religious contemporaries, the new community was inspired by the galvanic politics of the 1960s, which largely condemned the injustices of American society. Yet unlike some of their contemporaries, these young evangelicals felt that their own religious heritage contained adequate resources for addressing injustice and for a religious social criticism that was both meaningful and relevant. This fidelity to tradition led them to be fairly conservative theologically while still crafting a dissenting political voice, extending their disdain for the political system into protest, direct action, and community building that contrast evangelical language and meanings with conventional modes of political understanding and action.

The group sought to be more authentically and radically biblical than other evangelicals; and since its members believed that the social and theological legacy of their tradition stood in judgment of contemporary America, this initially led them also to an "almost Manichean belief that America and the gospel were in nearly irreconcilable opposition."[12] Like the Berrigans, whom they greatly admired, the students complained that churches—in their silence—were implicated in war, racism, and economic oppression. Like the Catholic Worker movement, they followed the downwardly mobile path of voluntary poverty as a sign of resistance. They wished their community to be defined not only by institutional structures but by caring relationships.

In 1973, Sojourners brought their ideas into debates among evangelicals about social action. Disagreements among evangelical leadership came to a head at the 1973 Conference of Evangelicals for Social Concern, where Ron Sider and other prominent public figures produced the Chicago Declaration, which spoke of the social crisis and an evangelical hope for social justice. The document was essentially an apology directed by the signatories to God for not adequately furthering the cause of justice. It was signed by a wide array of evangelicals, but Wallis declared this insufficient and used the event as an opportunity to declare his nascent community's radical opposition to the state (and to any form of political compromise). Reform-minded evangelicals such as Paul Henry and Republican senator from Oregon Mark Hatfield expressed unease with Sojourners' radicalism and oppositional rhetoric, accusing the group of extremism. More debates followed, concerning appropriate styles of activism, how best to understand evangelical history, and how to relate to the state (either as an accommodationist or as a separatist).

At these debates, one characteristic that distinguished Sojourners from other evangelicals of the day was their self-conscious habit of constructing fairly eclectic genealogies for their community. Apologetically, almost desperately, they looked to the Anabaptists, abolitionists, charismatics, the Catholic Left, and a motley assortment of social justice activists to establish their legitimacy and credibility. They have also spoken at length of the need to "recover the evangel," to get square with the evangelical commitment to announce the good news, which for Sojourners means a message of opposition to ruling political and religious authorities. Wallis has lamented that "a movement which once fought to free slaves, support industrial workers, and liberate women now has a reputation for accommodating to racism, favoring big business over labor, and resisting equal rights for women."[13] Sojourners contend that the evangel should dispel, not promote, the myths of American empire; instead of exalting political order, evangelicals should humble it by bringing the "real" evangel into ghettos, barrios, and unions.

In the fall of 1975, filled with this sense of mission, twenty members moved to Washington, D.C., to explore the "juxtaposition between making community with the poor and powerless while having a relationship to those in power."[14] Still sensing that allegiance to the nation was disobedience to God, the group abandoned the separatist moniker *Post-American* and became simply Sojourners when they relocated. This change in nomenclature mirrored an epistemic shift that placed less emphasis on liberation from the oppressor state and more on building community. In the remainder of this chapter, I explore how these projects constitute Sojourners' antiliberalism.

Inner-City Koinonia

Since their arrival in the nation's capital, Sojourners have focused on koinonia, a communal life of resistance they saw rooted in the Book of Acts. This is an impulse they share with other Christian antiliberals, and one that I address in my concluding chapter, but for Sojourners it is wrapped up in larger concerns about political illegibility. Their choice of location was motivated by a desire to live in solidarity with the poor. By its very Christian witness, the community hoped to call attention to the deficiencies of a political order they believed had abandoned its poorest citizens. The group believed that living in the Washington ghetto would itself constitute a challenge to a political system that was too limited to recognize either its own moral obligations or the limits it placed on its citizens. Like the early Christian community of the apostles, whose steadfastness in the face of imperial Rome's persecution Sojourners take as a model for life in the American city, the community's "prophetic politics" sought to transform its world (in this case by focusing on neighborhood or city-wide struggles over economic and racial issues).

Community itself was to be authoritative, governed by collective decision making and not tied to an external institution.[15] Members saw commitments to community, justice, and solidarity as consistent with the discipline and obedience of Christian life, a kind of self-determination that still answered divine commands. Central to this theology was identification with the poor, the recognition that community life should labor on their behalf (a view accompanied, to varying degrees, by contempt for the privileged), and insistence against looking to the state for aid. These positions strike at the heart of the ancient tension between institutional Christianity and radical biblical faith, in which the heteronymy of the Word cannot be accommodated to worldly realities. Rather than submitting to a faith of what they denounce as conformity, allegiance, and order, Sojourners aimed to disturb and contest political order with their very religiousness, to interrupt the harmony of the liberal ethos with discord. The evangelical principles of the community would serve as a warning to liberal political order, Sojourners claimed, to summon it from egoism, nationalism, capitalism, and bureaucracy. The group has nurtured this presumption against government, worrying that political order threatens the achievements of both koinonia and the regenerate self, whose success they believe rests on exactly the kind of religious social criticism they practice.[16]

By 1977, Sojourners had settled in the Columbia Heights neighborhood, an inner-city area with comparatively little real estate speculation and few prospects for economic vitality, where they could move in on the ground level and help protect the neighborhood by working on housing and education for the poor, among other issues. Settling a mostly white community in a largely black area would also, they hoped, constitute a sign of racial reconciliation and of resistance to the false divisions that thrive in liberal political order. This desire to live in service to the poor was rooted in their interpretations of the Book of Acts, the Beatitudes, and Isaiah 58:6–7, among other texts, which they claim directed them to live amid the injustices they sought to challenge. In a neighborhood of stark poverty, barely a mile away from the center of political power in the West, the small community accused the reigning political order of idolatry and sinfulness, of moral corruption that lingered in the city like uncollected trash.

Pastor Eugene Rivers of Boston's Azusa Christian Community, an old ally of Sojourners, described this "mission" as biblically imperative, intoning that "if the church doesn't go out into the streets, the streets will come into the church."[17] Rivers's warning gets at something central to Sojourners' theology, the notion that there is no religious authenticity outside of that lived on the streets of the city. No mere reflection could challenge political order; lived experience and engagement with the reality of "Babylon" were necessary. Together, experience and reflection would yield a public Christian discipleship that they believed was consistent with the theological commitments, injunctions, and standards of the evangelical tradition. Again citing the early Christian communities persecuted by Rome, which severed dependence on political power in order to create a new corporate reality based on religious values seen as deviant by the larger culture, Sojourners pronounced that the fecundity of tradition yielded sufficient resources to challenge injustice; faithful devotion required no politics.

Translated into the contemporary context, Christianity faithfully lived would oppose the centralization of power in corporations, state bureaucracy, or the wealthy few. Power rooted in any of these realities, rather than in God, undermined faithful practice and communal spirit. If koinonia could resist these realities, however, it could also serve as "a basic challenge to the world . . . a visible and concrete alternative."[18] A "prophetic" community could thus be shaped only by the exigencies of the Gospels, which required engagement with the realities of the city. As longtime Sojourner activist Kari Verhulst put it, these commitments were not ideological but "just about relationships with people and things that are going on"; they demanded that the hungry be fed, the homeless sheltered, the sick healed, and the disenfranchised organized and that justice be advocated.[19]

These acts were understood as constitutive of fellowship in the image of the Body of Christ, a way of institutionalizing a vision of the good that was illegible to ideologies or political abstractions. Neighborhood action, however, had to emerge from reflection on the meanings of the Gospels in a particular place. Reflection and prayer, in other words, were aids in assessing a neighborhood's needs (e.g., housing rehabilitation, public school work, or aid to refugees). Sojourners read the Book of Acts as a cautionary tale against the abandonment of the needy and as a model for a communal sharing of resources, labor, recreation, and worship. In short, Sojourners believed that the Scriptures revealed basic divine demands, constrained in a liberal regime, that all humans have basic social goods, that the needy receive special care, that people be free from threats to their health, safety and dignity, and that human life be enriched by love, equality, and community.

Beginning in the mid-1970s, the District of Columbia faced a severe economic blight. Lacking the fiscal security of statehood, the city had barely a safety net to protect it from the budgetary fallout of the immediate post-Vietnam era or from the drying up of local industry. These factors—combined with crumbling infrastructure, soaring inflation rates, and a decaying black business community—hit hard in Washington's poor neighborhoods. Hoping to revitalize the city with an influx of capital, the new Barry administration doled out tax breaks and incentives to real estate speculators and businesses willing to purchase and revamp property in poor neighborhoods.

Yet in the name of this physical and fiscal revitalization, longtime low-income residents such as Katherine and Ofon were being put out of their homes. By the time Sojourners settled in Columbia Heights in the late 1970s, countless poor black families had been and were being displaced by these policies. At this juncture, the National Capital Housing Authority had a five-year waiting list for available low-income housing, and families were left in the meantime with little protection under the law, a shrinking rental market, and wild inflation.[20] The result was that nearly everything in Washington's less affluent neighborhoods, from blood-stained Anacostia to Columbia Heights, was inadequate: education, health care, sanitation, police protection, and housing.

Sojourners did something "crazy" and began to challenge these conditions in the name of their understanding of Christianity. The community condemned the city's housing policies and established a household for the homeless with the help of local poor people's cooperatives such as Jubilee Housing and Community of Hope. At times Sojourners served with other local religious groups and activists on "task forces," as with the Community of Hope Church of the Nazarene in the early 1980s, asserting that they could "hardly do less without tragically mistaking the mission of Christ in the world."[21] The work of building koinonia extended beyond the walls of Sojourners Community itself and into the neighborhoods of poor Washington, D.C. The group strove primarily to protect poor people and neighborhoods from redlining by housing and rental agencies and, more broadly, to argue for expanded public access to basic social goods such as education and health care. They worked with local citizens in organizing community meetings, lectures, day care, food co-ops, worship and teaching, and nightly "roundups" of homeless people.

As the community's activism grew, so too did its tendency to speak publicly in "prophetic" terms. The group frequently denounced the wealthy and the powerful for undermining divine justice in their rush to overtake and evacuate of the poor the very neighborhoods that the wealthy had once ignored both socially and politically. Even though the city administration and housing authority labeled neighborhoods such as Columbia Heights "transitional," crime rates soared, and quality of life dwindled for Sojourners' neighbors. The community worked to develop an infrastructure that could help local residents in the same way they were being assisted by Jubilee and Community of Hope. Wallis excoriated local government for using transfer payments and subsidies for local investors or multinational corporations while the poor went hungry. He blamed the excessive individualism of the political culture for its hostility to change and lack of empathy for the poor and the dispossessed, charging that "the urban underclass has been made economically expendable by a system that needs and creates an oppressed class of people."[22]

The community described its conflict as one between God and Mammon. Sojourners believed that, in addition to their efforts to form community in the image of the apostles, resolution of this conflict would require the gift of God's grace. But humans remained, they believed, under an obligation to build economic solidarity by generating more equitable arrangements and distributions of goods. The first of their efforts in this regard had been made with the opening of the Sojourners Daycare Center in November 1977. The center was offered as a space where children were nurtured individually and relationally, prepared for public schools and for the world at large. Students enrolled in the center regularly uttered maxims such as "it's good for people to live in communities and tell people that fighting's not right."[23] The daily routine included singing, dancing, playacting, learning about other cultures, art time, and a modicum of playtime. From its inception, the day-care center was run by an all-black nonprofit corporation (it closed in February 1982). Around the same time as the founding of the center, the Euclid Food Club was established as a neighborhood food co-op, an outgrowth of community household needs. Membership dues were only twenty-five cents, and members included university students, low-income neighbors, and supporters. In 1981, the community made a further institutional move by incorporating the Sojourner Truth Child Development Center, which boasted a school-readiness program (focusing on cognitive and social development), job and skills training for the unemployed, affordable all-day child care for Columbia Heights children, and a leadership structure that included parent participation.

In addition to more programmatic efforts such as those just described, many individuals in Sojourners sought to craft lives of simplicity that they hoped would contrast with the acquisitiveness of American culture. Many community members were fond during these years of sleeping in shelters with the homeless. Cathy Stentzel noted that they came away feeling a sense of identity, community, and peace. David McKeithen breathlessly called them "night[s] with the street saints," though one wonders if those whose presence in the shelters was not voluntary felt this same sense of wellness.[24] Most members of the community proudly walked or used public transport rather than driving cars, though a few beaten jalopies were on call for community emergencies.

Eventually the food co-op, Daycare Center, and Child Development Center were coordinated into the Sojourners Neighborhood Center, completed during Lent in 1984. The Neighborhood Center was to serve emergency food to three hundred families, house tenant-organizing offices, and be the site of after-school programs and nutrition classes. Sojourners activist Barb Tamialis later, around the center's tenth anniversary, described the venture as one in which the community became "partners in ministry with [its] neighbors . . . [to] battle racism and its personal and economic consequences . . . [and to] share leadership."[25] The center claimed to embody norms, values, and practices illegible to conventional politics: helping children through the school system, providing a residential alternative to housing projects, sponsoring food programs, offering parent support groups and computer training, and all in all representing a sort of "freedom school."

By the mid-1980s, Sojourners were still able to support these institutions and to use them as bases from which to organize and pressure the city council about redlining and gentrification. The Sojourners Housing

Ministry frequently established partnership ventures with the Southern Columbia Heights Tenants' Union to help local families who were being forced out by gentrification and real estate speculation. In February 1986, for example, a family in the area received a writ of possession from the city. The family had protested a 28 percent rent increase on the grounds of "hardship" and had been snubbed. Sojourners helped the family force a successful appeal. As the community lost membership during the late 1980s and early 1990s, it naturally became more difficult to mount these sorts of defenses. But by the mid-1990s, when the group was back on its feet, Sojourners tried to further the cause of nurturing and educating neighborhood children, almost all of whom fall below the poverty level, with the Sojourners Freedom Schools. These schools constituted a summer school program that tried explicitly to connect to the educational ethos defined by Bob Moses, famed from Mississippi's freedom summer, an ethos that prized reading support, technical training, "conflict resolution," and community service as central to democratic citizenship.[26]

From the simpler gestures of everyday community life to organized statements to the media, Sojourners worked to enact their vision of Christianity, which they claimed should be oriented toward the basic human needs and social goods they saw as threatened by consumerism and by vast disparities in wealth and power. The drive toward overconsumption and accumulation would pull against biblical community, Sojourners feared, and would make more credible mainstream Christianity's accommodation to the values, spirit, and structures of the age. If the exigencies of the Gospels demanded more equitable economic arrangements (including decentralization of wealth and economic self-sufficiency), Sojourners reasoned, then they also demanded engagement with the related problems of limited housing options for the poor, the inaccessibility of social services, and the poor's lack of political empowerment.

It was in the crucible of these early struggles that Sojourners first denounced the limits of conventional political logic, which they sought to replace with the language and presuppositions of prophetic Christianity. Over time, however, their activities manifested a recognizable drift toward realpolitik. Where they had once insisted that the principles of citizenship in liberal political culture were mutually exclusive with those of the Kingdom of God, the stringency of this proclamation was steadily relaxed from the late 1970s through the 1980s. But they remained wary nonetheless of Christian social action that, in their estimation, followed standard political logic. They believed that by establishing a witnessing community and withdrawing political consent, they were embodying religious truths ignored by political power. Their discipleship was meant as a countersign to the liberal regime and a harbinger of the Kingdom.

Hence, Sojourners gradually became less separatist and came to focus more on outreach, coalition, and building new communities. Perhaps sensing their own marginality to the American political and religious mainstream, they began to establish connections to other intentional communities (such as Bill Kellerman's parish in Detroit, Atlanta's Open Door community, and Boston's Azusa Street community) as a way to amplify their critical voice. In the mid-1980s, the Sojourners Community consisted of a number of houses that served thirty-seven adults and ten children full-time. Yet though the 1980s were a time of the enlargement of both religious concern and practice, they were also a time of crisis. In this period Sojourners began to experience great pressure from government authorities, including frequent FBI surveillance, one result of which was a marked rise in internal strife. Although the community remained morally committed to challenging Reagan administration policies, it began to lose members steadily in the 1980s. Financial woes accompanied these departures as fewer people were asked to accomplish the same tasks. Sojourners responded by reaching out to a broader Christian audience and softening some of their harshest political charges. Nearly half of the remaining community left around Easter of 1990 "over differences in theology and vision," leaving twelve adults and a plummeting circulation for the magazine.[27] Kari Verhulst described this crisis as entailing a number of issues "wrapped up in each other: theological, personalities, how you understand your role and leadership."[28] This move was doubtless an expression of concern over what many saw as the group's growing political centrism. Within a few years, however, the community had revamped, cemented some important coalitions, and attracted new members with Call to Renewal, its organizational alternative to the NCR.

This history of this inner-city koinonia, self-consciously aimed at establishing an alternative to stale political vocabularies, reveals the Sojourners Community to be Janus-faced. Its dual nature, illustrated further below, can partly be captured in an examination of the figures and groups included in one of Sojourners' many genealogies (the construction of which is a recurring activity). One side of the group is localist both in its religious genealogy (in which it places itself squarely in the evangelical tradition of American revivalism) and in the forms of its community service. Indeed, despite growing prominence in national politics, Wallis continues to pastor to the small community, most of whose members serve as teachers, counselors, and social workers. But there is another side to the group: in their deep desire to challenge and confound the political logic of the liberal order, Sojourners trade in ambiguity, multiplicity, and paradox. This side of them constructs a more wildly eclectic religious genealogy, including Dorothy Day and the Catholic Workers, Clarence Jordan and the Koinonia Partners, black activist churches in the United States, South African resistance churches, Latin American base communities, the confessing church in Nazi Germany and the former Soviet bloc, Thomas Merton, nineteenth-century radical evangelicals, Wesleyan revivalists, Franciscans, and sixteenth-century Anabaptists. The sensibility of this face of Sojourners is broader and more global. With this set of references Sojourners aim to underscore the primacy of their commitment to "prophetic" social justice, which they believe supersedes denominational concerns, and thus also to undo the equation of evangelicalism with political conservatism. However, the doubleness of the community fosters confusion in observers. Is the community of Sojourners a conservative or a radical one? Is it "left" or "right"? The community declines to answer such questions, opting instead to play across these gaps, challenging the confines of everyday understandings. Its members contend that they are simply Christians attempting faithfully to emulate Christ in a fallen world.

Establishing Judgment in the Gate: Prophetic Theology

Community practices such as those described earlier are understood by Sojourners as exemplary of an evangelical Christianity that is resolutely opposed to political programs. Any principles articulated or actions taken in the public or political spheres must, for Sojourners, harmonize with their understanding of the "prophetic" tradition. Central to this tradition are several theological constants—that Jesus is squarely on the side of the poor and the peacemakers, for example, and that Christians must engage in acts of resistance to militarism—which Sojourners insist must be verified through exegesis, prayer, and community reflection.

Out of this continual exchange between reflection and practice, two fundamental scriptural insights have shaped the religious self-understandings of the community. First and most basic is the insistence that Christian communities are defined by their resistance to worldly power. The second emerges from Sojourners' understanding of discipleship, as articulated in the Book of Acts. For Wallis, Christian discipleship requires a radical inversion of worldly priorities; as he writes, "if Jesus is Lord, then Caesar is not, the Pentagon is not, ITT, Gulf Oil, Exxon and GM are not, national security is not, the bomb is not, consumer society is not, the good life is not."[29] According to this logic, an ordinary Christian life is discrepant with the world; its difference from the logics of state and economy serves as a critical principle. Christian roots, this worldview suggests, must be ripped from worldly power and political order and replanted in a witnessing community.

The most cogent statement of Sojourners' dissent from political order is found in former member Bob Sabath's exegesis. Sabath premises his observations on Paul's claim in Romans 13 that earthly powers can be obeyed only if ordained by God. In surveying other New Testament teachings on the state (specifically 1 Timothy 2:1–7, Titus 3:1–3, 1 Peter 2:13–17, and Mark 12:13–17), Sabath concludes that Paul never submitted to government authorities. The New Testament may recognize the political order as an expression of God's will that human life be protected from chaos, but "it is also aware of the demonic possibilities inherent within the state."[30] The tension between these manifestations of political order shapes Sabath's interpretation, which is basically suspicious of the state's demonic potential. In a reading of Revelations 13, Sabath declares that John's view of the state as evil holds the keys to a politically responsible contemporary discipleship. As a refusal of the obedience that empire demands, witnessing to Jesus' kingship is itself a political affirmation; only God is to be feared, not civil authority. The state is to be tolerated if it is properly limited in its power and requires nothing antithetical to a witnessing faith. The limits of political power, then, are dictated by a faith that is under no obligation to submit categorically to state demands. Since Sojourners so frequently link the state to military aggression and economic injustice, acquiescence to political power is relatively rarely enjoined.

In what way, though, do they envision political life beyond these circumstances? Sojourners generally claim that the New Testament contains four basic prisms through which to consider political order: the life of Jesus, the Acts of the Apostles, Paul's descriptions of duties (Romans 13, 1 Peter 2, Titus 3:1–2), and the Revelation to John. According to Sabath, Jesus' disregard for political order was nearly total. Seeing himself as a messenger from an authority higher than the state, Jesus cleansed the Temple as an act of defiance toward the Sanhedrin, Pilate, and Herod. And in Luke 19:1–10, Jesus refuses to let God be identified with national cause, intimating that political legitimacy of this sort comes only through coercion. The earthly prerogatives of the state are appropriate only relative to God, a maxim that Sabath sees reflected in Jesus' disregard for temple tax (Matthew 17:24–27) and in Mark's injunction to give our lives to God (Mark 12:13–17).

In the Book of Acts, according to Sabath's reading, the hostility of Roman political authority to the early Christian community was evidenced in its failure to protect believers, effectively prohibiting their self-determination. Christians understood their community to be higher than any human system and thus ignored state law when it restricted them from carrying out God's will. True justice, they believed, would be found only in the eschatological kingdom presided over by Christ. Sabath acknowledges that Paul was considerably more ambiguous about political order. Paul admitted that there were positive aspects to the state and that it possessed the potential to be a part of and reflect the divine order. Paul and Peter both recognized that the state's purpose was the establishment of public order, to which ideally Christians ought to submit. But Christian political obedience depended on certain conditions being met (i.e., that the church remain autonomous and that the divine will be reflected in political laws); neither apostle commended unconditional loyalty or obedience to the state. If the conditions are met, Sabath explains, then the Christian may refrain from protest against the state, should pay taxes, and might respect the state and its officials. In other words, the injunction in Romans to "render unto Caesar what is Caesar's" represents the recognition that both the state and Christians are under God's providential order and that God uses the state to create conditions favorable to Christians.

The Book of Revelation, on the other hand, depicts the state as persecutor and tyrant and looks to the Kingdom alone for redemption. This book demands that the state be ignored if it professes that its power is greater than God's, going beyond Pauline theology to assert that the core controlling power in the state is evil. It is still admitted that political order can provide services for the people of God, but it is also noted that God regularly calls on servants such as Amos, John, and Jesus to unmask state evil, hoping for a new state when Jesus returns.

Sojourners exegetes such as Sabath acknowledge that their audience, mostly American Christians, does not live under regimes of the sort described in the New Testament (monarchies or empires of Rome's scope). They insist nonetheless that these teachings form a political template for citizens of democratic orders. As Peter Davids put it, the "main issue faced in 'democratic' government is that it claims to represent the people, including the Christian. Thus . . . it seems legitimate for Christians to try the claims of the democratic ideal and to request the government to truly represent their point of view . . . to try to change [the government] on behalf of justice; and . . . to unmask hypocrisy and falsehood (this latter being part of the prophetic calling in any society)."[31] In other words, although

Sojourners value the political goods a democracy might achieve, they feel these achievements are continually threatened by powers that exalt themselves above the divine, trampling the meek and doing violence to the causes of justice. So the typical exegesis presumes that the state is hostile, proceeds to acknowledge that political order can and should be respected under certain limiting conditions, but concludes by asserting that these conditions are unlikely to be met in these times. This argumentative procession leads naturally back to the conviction that the "prophetic" tradition must fill the political void. Thus, when Sojourners oppose international commerce, nuclear weapons proliferation, imbalances in education funding, or the presence of pornographic theaters in their neighborhood, they claim to do so on strictly theological grounds.

As theology generates actions of resistance, the most commonly cited biblical precedent is Jesus' entry into Jerusalem. The community sees this action as an inspired piece of street theater, entering into a military occupation and talking about "audacious" topics such as freedom and faithful history. Further, they believe that Jesus' presence at the Temple (the most visible site of public power) exposed the complicity between the occupying forces and religious authorities, a collusion Sojourners claim characterizes most American evangelicals. Jesus' acts here are not seen as civil disobedience in the classic sense of breaking an unjust law in order to change it but rather as the enactment of a different sort of truth in a place that is protected by an established law and authority now seen as illegitimate. Where Roman law was exalted above God's law, Jesus risked personal security to engage in direct public action that challenged the economy of the Temple. Sojourners believe that since this is the example established by their savior, then confrontation with power and established order must be central to Christian life and self-understanding. The fact that Jesus was eventually crucified for these confrontations situates the Christian's engagement with political authority in a larger soteriological narrative, as well. Evangelicals, by this account, are not saved solely in order to experience a personal infusion of God's grace; if one is saved, it is also by entering into a radical form of discipleship that marks one as politically and socially "other."

Longtime Sojourners writer Ched Meyers identifies another central text of resistance in Mark 1:30–4:35, which Meyers interprets as Jesus' first campaign of nonviolent direct action. Meyers reads Mark as a call to break with business and politics as usual: he conflates Roman Palestine with contemporary America, arguing that both rely on illegitimate political authority, injustice, and aggression. Indeed, Meyers also believes that the text exposes the gap between domesticated American Christianity and the actions of Jesus. Meyers asserts that close reading of the text will "upset the reader by subverting their discourse and challenging recognized authority structures through dramatic action."[32] But such subversion is necessary, he claims, since only through such Christian resistance can true freedom be realized.

Resistance is thus singled out as exemplary of the alternate social reality that Sojourners claim is described in the literature of their tradition. The new order is ideally meant to approximate the coming Kingdom that will be inaugurated with Christ's Second Coming. This alternate vision of reality further fleshes out their understanding of discipleship. The Book of Acts emphasizes holy poverty, redistribution, and mutual care, all understood as media of proper service to the resurrected Christ. For Sojourners, community must devote itself to the *imitatio Christi*, the imitation of Christ and the willingness to suffer for the other. Sojourners judge these acts to be the ethical core of Christianity, and they accordingly find mainstream churches deficient in these acts. The willingness to suffer is itself subversive in this worldview, calling attention to the moral shortcomings of the powers and principalities.

Sojourners seek to use the very publicity of their practice to suggest that "prophetic" Christianity needs to meet certain activist standards: churches and religious communities that engage in charity work and volunteerism without criticism of the dominant culture are, according to Sojourners, cozying up to Caesar. Sponsoring weekly meals-on-wheels plans might provide temporary relief to the poor, for example, but it does nothing to challenge the social and political conditions that create poverty in the first place. It is precisely here that the work of community building becomes crucial for the group. Columbia Heights is filled with destructive forces that erode the material and cultural bases that sustain community. The neighborhood and the city confirm for Sojourners the urgency of biblical response to social misery; social reality shapes the nature and the occasion of both reflection and practice; and urban history teaches them about the disenfranchisement, isolation, and marginalization of the poor. If Christians seek to address these injustices, Sojourners claim, they must cease modeling themselves after secular institutions and powers and must emulate, instead, the witnessing community portrayed in Acts. The community they envision would work from the ground up to foster solidarity with fellow citizens and would begin by challenging the abuse of private property rights, as Sojourners themselves did with Katherine and Ofon.

In such actions, Sojourners enact a different model of social existence, one that "does not recognize the developer's or landlord's right to displace simply because he or she holds title to a particular property."[33] Their conviction is that the whole world, poor neighborhoods included, is part of God's goodness. In witness to this goodness, the community condemns the injustice of these practices and the rigid political thinking that prevents creative responses to these realities. To Sojourners, the Cross condemned the political order, and they hope that through community they may likewise contribute to the world's redemption by serving as a countersign to the complacency they feel obscures the plight of the needy. For them the very principles and practices of "prophetic politics" are "offensive" to the sensibilities of mainstream Christians and political order.[34]

This theology of community bears an obvious debt to Latin American liberation theology, which emphasizes the plight of the working poor and seeks to ground religious authority in "base communities" rather than in church hierarchy. Liberation theologians such as Gustavo Gutierrez, Juan Sobrino, and José Miguez Bonino proclaim that the Bible is unambiguously on the side of the poor. They believe that the Body of Christ is anointed for the purposes of justice, liberation, and reconciliation in the world and that a community is Christian only if it serves these purposes. These principles are also linked with the radical communitarian theology associated with John Howard Yoder, which argues that Christian ethics and social life should be modeled on the "radical reformation" of communitarian groups such as Mennonites, while maintaining that every communal or institutional arrangement is fallible. Yoder claimed that his articulation of these principles was not a type of sectarian or "ghetto" theology, which would constitute a flight from pressing worldly realities, since the institutions of modernity represented a threat to the distinctiveness of Christian identity and required biblical critique.

In their desire to avoid the false choices, costly abstraction, and limits of mainstream political thought, Sojourners root all dissent and activism in practice that, by its visibly Christian nature, they hope will contrast with recognizable and available modes of political action. The consistent themes that emerge from this reflection are economic justice, grounded in the notion that God is on the side of the dispossessed, and opposition to illegitimate power, rooted in the imperatives of the prophets and the early Christians. These presumptions and convictions—which seemed "crazy" to the public defenders who aided Sojourners and to the housing authorities the community had challenged—are to the community the sanest response to this city of power and are a way of dealing with social circumstances that they consider alien and unreal themselves. Where conventional political logic abstracts the plight of needy black children, Sojourners denounce this logic with the words of Amos and Isaiah. Where ordinary citizens are forced to choose from a narrow range of political choices, from one side or another of a political order many citizens find alienating, Sojourners dismiss this set of options by living a life that they believe exists independently of these alternatives.

A Local Geography of Christ's Passion

Sojourners' community life exists in a dynamic relationship with other forms of practice, specifically protest and dissent. As social movement theorist Faye Ginsburg describes it, "the activities of daily life out of which consciousness and intentionality are constructed . . . [lead] to more dramatic forms of expressive culture (such as media or social protests)."[35] Throughout its history, the Sojourners Community has engaged in symbolic actions against "the powers," attempts to worry the government, to provoke liberal political order, to vex the categories that guide social and political understanding. These efforts, modeled on Sojourners' interpretation of Jesus' actions in Jerusalem, might be seen as apolitical according to conventional interpretations: they do not conform to standard modes of interest-group politicking, lobbying, seeking representation, or even commonplace forms of public protest. But Sojourners insist that Jesus' own actions were symbolic in ways that were politically illegible; likewise, they hope that either the public manifestation of their actions or the theological underpinnings thereof will serve as challenges to reigning political discourse. They additionally see these actions as attempts to remap public space—through vigils, pilgrimages, public liturgies and prayer services, symbolic actions, war tax resistance, sit-ins, direct-action campaigns, arrests, court appearances, and jail terms—in ways inflected by their brand of evangelical Christianity.

These actions have addressed local, national, and global issues. The issue that has most preoccupied the Sojourners Community has been peacemaking. If their communal lifestyle has been intended as an antidote to the systemic violence of racism, capitalism, and a political order that is considered remote to human concerns, Sojourners' persistent critique of war making has been a similar attempt to repair the breaches wrought by the more obvious violence of militarism. Here, too, they have taken recourse to Scripture to guide their actions. Noting particularly the injunction to beat swords into plowshares (Isaiah 2:4) and Jesus' insistence that Christians should "turn the other cheek" to violence (Matthew 5:39), the community has challenged state-sanctioned military establishments as violations of divine law. Not only do Sojourners contend that the presence of weapons of mass destruction is sinful in its own right, bordering on a kind of idolatry insofar as it attempts to usurp from God the powers of life and death, but they also claim that the budgetary priority given to military matters in the United States sucks money from social programs that might otherwise aid the poor.

Inspired partly by the Berrigans' practice, Sojourners have often used protest action to challenge militarism. One of the earliest such actions involved a trip from Washington, D.C., to Seabrook, New Hampshire, to protest a proposed nuclear power plant. On April 30, 1977, more than 250 people gathered in Seabrook and hiked five miles to the plant's gates. Blocking the entrance, the crowd engaged in direct action throughout the day, including sit-ins, songs and chants, waving banners, and crossing police barricades. Singing a peace song in front of a nuclear plant may not seem like a significant action, but the goal of such action was to occupy space that protesters felt was being occupied by illegitimate power. Seen in this light, these actions constitute a kind of religious reclamation of space and power from a political system whose authority was seen as illegitimate. The protesters sought actively to be arrested so that the cost of food and lodging for hundreds of prisoners would get factored into the plant's costs.[36] During Holy Week of that year, Sojourners staged what they called the Washington Torture Action, a mass demonstration against U.S. foreign policy support for regimes guilty of torture and repression and against the use of tax dollars for such support. For six days, the community engaged in prayer vigils, marches, and other protests, erecting a "Torture Tableau" in front of the White House, the Capitol, corporations, and international banks wherein community members acted out the suffering they attributed to these powers.

The late 1970s were ripe with opportunities to protest militarism. When a moratorium amendment was proposed for the SALT II treaty, Sojourners gathered at the Capitol on December 3, 1979, to support the amendment. They rejected the typical options of rhetoric, polls, and petitions, choosing instead to stage a drama satirizing the upcoming SALT debate in the Senate. Such actions—the Torture Tableau, the public satire, and so on—purposely sought to go beyond the discursive conventions of political order, not only incorporating forms and actions that fall outside the abstract language generally characterizing public discourse but also challenging the prevailing options for participation by enacting a morality that was visibly, viscerally different (even from other forms of political theater staged in the nation's capital). During this time period, the community sponsored annual candlelight vigils in front of the White House on the anniversary of Hiroshima, following which many members were jailed. In addition, the late 1970s marked the beginning of the now annual Pentecost Peace Actions in Washington, D.C., gatherings of witnessing Christians in the Capitol rotunda to turn the sterile space of public politics into a spontaneously inhabited cathedral. The community also began to harbor fugitives and immigrants from Central America, allying itself with the Sanctuary Movement and seeking to contest the "false" boundaries thrown up by nations that run counter to the interests of humans in need. Most frequently, there was nonviolent civil disobedience to challenge nuclear weapons. Beginning in the early 1980s, Sojourners linked up with the Trident Nein group, which staged a Berrigan-style invasion of the shipyard in Groton, Connecticut, to damage a Trident sub armed with nuclear missiles. They followed this up with a Good Friday, 1982, pilgrimage, which processed from the Trident base in Bangor, Washington, and involved participants walking from there to Bethlehem, Pennsylvania.

The community was slowly beginning to enlarge its self-understanding, seeing itself not only as an activist community but also as a witnessing presence in resistance to the prevailing norms of cultures beyond its own neighborhood. The community understood these activities not as normal political ends but instead, as Wallis put it, as activity modeled on Jesus' "tendency toward disobedience and resistance to the demands of repressive political authority . . . to obey or disobey based on a higher loyalty."[37] This emphasis on crossing ideological boundaries, on paying no heed to the "false" limitations that political order imposes on morality and conscience, was seen as a bridge between localism and the more global concerns that Sojourners began to cultivate. Yet such actions were simply, they claimed, part of their existence in a community whose aspirations and actions were politically illegible.

Sojourners' direct action can be seen as a lived theology of trespass. The group claims to draw on Ephesians 5:11–13, which claims, "Take no part in the unfruitful works of darkness, but instead expose them." Its members believe that by bringing Christian symbols, narratives, and practices into a public space normally absent these things, they are contrasting legitimate and illegitimate norms while also exposing injustices that are hidden in liberal political order. For example, on September 15, 1983, Central American Independence Day, a group of community members got together and drove a "tractor for peace" to the steps of the Nicaraguan Embassy. They wanted to call attention to the economic and agricultural sanctions the

United States had then imposed on Nicaragua and to express their solidarity with the Central American poor, who were being victimized by alien ideologies. Beginning in 1982, Wallis and fellow peacemakers conducted the first in an annual series of trespasses on the grounds of the Department of Energy's Nevada Nuclear Test Site. Sojourners convened several dozen sympathizers each year at these events, soon dubbed Lenten Desert Experience, and conducted prayer, reflection, and direct action.

Indeed, significant dates on the holy calendar were soon adopted as occasions for challenges to liberal political order. The community had routinely called on churches to set aside Holy Week for daily vigils of prayer to end the arms race. But significantly, it began also to organize the aforementioned Peace Pentecosts, gatherings in Washington, D.C., to worship and to protest the "idolatry" of violence. By substituting a religiously significant narrative for the traditional nationalist or militarist story of the concurrent Memorial Day, Sojourners are able to use prayerful direct action to strengthen their identity as Christian pacifists. Through such actions, the community aimed to establish control of its identity independent of "the powers" by acting in politically illegible ways: confessing its complicity in the arms buildup, intercessions on behalf of the world at risk, celebrations of Christ's victory over death, or circulating a Pledge of Resistance document that honors the spirit of Pentecost as a saving power in the nuclear age.

Direct action of this sort was understood as "resistance to human sovereigns," a refusal to abide by conventional political decrees, and a prophetic challenge to particular authorities that was "biblically justified and at times even imperative."[38] As the 1980s ground on, Sojourners grew more despairing that money spent on atomic weapons was money that ought to be spent alleviating poverty and injustice. Community friend Bill Kellerman suggested that the only appropriate religious response to these realities was to bring Christian morality into the street even more intensely than the community had previously, to transform public space into a religious landscape. Kellerman called on Christians to stop at "sites of oppression" such as draft boards, the IRS, and multinational corporations for prayer and witness, particularly on high holy days. His idea was that in the absence of genuine political dialogue on these issues the only Christian option was to "expose a local geography of Christ's passion" whereby the actions imply the existence of a different time, a different life, and the new order of the Kingdom.[39]

In the years since, the community has continued in its preoccupation with such undertakings. It has organized to protest the development of the

Strategic Defense Initiative, resisting this and other military proposals with demonstrations, organizing, civil disobedience, nonpayment of taxes, and so on. For example, prior to the Reagan/Gorbachev summit in December 1987, Sojourners organized a four-day vigil in Lafayette Park across from the White House, during which community member Joyce Hollyday argued with none other than Phyllis Schlafly about the merits of disarmament. During the 1990s, the community did not lack for occasions to engage in nonviolent direct action, which it did with regularity in response to events such as the January 1991 commencement of the Gulf War (when Sojourners helped organize seven thousand people to march from the National Cathedral to the White House) and the early months of 1999 (when they protested first the United States' bombing of Iraq and then the NATO bombing of Kosovo). They continued to criticize the state for relying on militarism (among other moral evils) for its legitimation and of paying little or no attention to deliberation or consent by the governed. In the absence of a government responsive to its citizenry, Sojourners contended that the Gospels themselves could provide alternate models of social justice and participation.[40]

Sojourners protest has not been limited to peacemaking issues. In recent years, Sojourners have increasingly extended their concerns beyond the geography of their immediate neighborhood. For example, on the twenty-first anniversary of Martin Luther King Jr.'s assassination, the community participated in Justice for Janitors, a gathering of civil rights activists, church and community organizers, and labor activists at the World Bank to support janitors' efforts to have their union recognized. The community's Pentecost actions throughout the 1990s often protested nonmilitary issues, such as the former Clinton administration's "welfare reform." During welfare-related protests, Wallis often cited Acts 4:35 as a demand that distribution of goods be made according to need. Wallis likened "reform" to inviting a hurricane to descend on one's home; the storm, he claimed, would hit you regardless of whether you're "left" or "right."[41] Churches should not simply clean up the policy mess after the fact, he claimed, but must organize and articulate their concerns directly in the political process itself. In the fall of 1996, Sojourners participated in the Religious Working Group, an interdenominational organization that challenged the World Bank and the International Monetary Fund (IMF) for lack of accountability and complicity in putting poor people at risk by weakening markets through arcane borrowing and lending procedures. Each autumn, when World Bank/IMF operatives gather in Washington, D.C., the group holds prayer services. And in the spring, on Good Friday, the group conducts a Way of the Cross procession through the city, stopping to witness at centers of economic power. In this way, Sojourners have anticipated the post–Cold War politics that has since come to light in the Seattle and Washington actions against the World Trade Organization, the latter of which included a strong Sojourners presence. Most recently as of this writing, the Pentecost events of May 20–22, 2002, were titled "Speaking Truth about Poverty" and sought to tie the Bush administration's "war on terrorism" to the economic causes Sojourners believe are at the root of terrorist action.

In addition to the intercessions on behalf of economic justice and the witness for peace, Sojourners have witnessed against other forms of violence. Out of their local struggles for racial justice, they helped in the 1980s to organize a series of Soweto Days, grassroots protests against South African apartheid. They had long since organized similar events in protest against U.S. involvement in Central America, and they opened the community to political refugees from the region (in so doing, they established ties to the Sanctuary Movement). More recently, they have turned their attention to gang violence and violence against women, which are seen as symptoms of a social order that is damaged. Sojourners' response is to witness against the immediate forms of violence while at the same time calling attention to the larger systemic breakdown of which they are a part. On June 3, 1990, the annual Peace Pentecost focused on ending violence against women. Sojourners organized a procession from Luther Place Memorial Church to McPherson Square Park, stopping at a women's shelter, at the *Washington Post* building, at an alley where a rape had recently taken place, and at a pornography store. On their return to the church, a bell was rung every three and a half minutes (the rate at which women are targets of rape in the United States).[42]

Considerable energy has also been devoted to the dangers of gang violence. Stemming largely from Sojourners' commitment to the concerns for the poor in their own neighborhood, which has been ravaged by gang violence, Wallis in particular has gone to great lengths to raise consciousness about this issue. The precipitating cause may well have been the riots of early May 1991 in Washington's Mount Pleasant neighborhood, when local Latinos and African Americans clashed with both police and each other. During several days of violence, Sojourners and other churches attempted to organize marches for nonviolence and to give voice to the grievances that they felt were underlying the riots. Subsequently, in response to the June 1992 murders of two neighborhood children, Joyce Hollyday enlisted other local children to write letters to President Bush. From April 29 to

May 2, 1993, Wallis participated in the National Urban Peace and Justice Summit in Kansas City, the site for a gang summit and truce that religious figures such as Wallis helped to maintain with frequent visits and consultations to ghettos around the country.[43] In June 1993, in response to skyrocketing murder rates in Washington, D.C., Sojourners helped organize a series of noontime vigils outside NRA headquarters and a huge Mothers' Day antigun rally at the Lincoln Memorial. These gang-related activities can be seen as attempts to transfer tactics from the peace movement into other settings of violence.

What unites these activities is, in the community's estimation, their dissimilarity to traditional interest-group politics whereby groups petition the state for the redress of grievances. Sojourners see their actions, in contrast, as attempts to question conventional ways of understanding social issues. Moreover, these actions occur at a critical moral distance from the state, in what Sojourners judge to be a position of noncompliance. They contend that to accept standard political discourse and modes of action in a political order in which nuclear energy supplants faith in the environment, funding is diverted to the military rather than to the needs of the poor, and multinational corporations receive more benefits than the average citizen is to compromise Christian belief itself. Instead, Sojourners demand a discipleship to the "hard messages" of the gospel's demand to give up material and intellectual security. When liberalism fails to hear the cries of the poor, radical Christianity can speak loudly; when liberalism loses the moral impact of its arrangements in a sea of abstractions and bureaucracy, prophetic Christianity can act concisely.

Through these actions, individuals believe or hope an alternate future into being. Not confident that the political system will even recognize their demands for greater morality, accountability, and participation, they enact lived biblical critiques of the exaltation of political order, the preeminence of money, the concentration of power in the hands of the few, and the marginalization of the poor. If politics is to be redeemed and decision-making power restored to everyday citizens and communities, then this new type of political practice must be centered around repentance, judgment, and righteousness.

These are the jarring, disturbing themes of the prophets who are Sojourners' models. Using their imperatives, Sojourners call on conscientious Christians to remap political territory so that "the geography of worship and prayer is being relocated, moving beyond the confines of church sanctuaries and crossing the lines, fences and boundaries that read 'No Trespass.' By so doing, the evil done in secret at such places is exposed to the light of public scrutiny, of conscience, and of God."[44] This is a movement out from the darkness of conventional political logic into a new community and activism that is politically illegible in a liberal regime.

Call to Renewal

Sojourners entered a new phase of their existence when Call to Renewal (CTR) was founded. On December 7, 1995, Sojourners organized the Capitol Witness, gathering fifty-five urban clergy members and community center workers in the Capitol rotunda to kneel in prayer for the poor. Included in the gathering were Wallis, Ron Sider, Tony Campolo, and Eugene Rivers, among other prominent figures. More than one hundred evangelicals came together that morning to sing, pray, and discuss logistics for organizing a mass movement. They had entered the symbolic heart of the American political system and challenged what they charged was its indifference to the plight of the poor, its abstraction, and its reductivism. They read from the Bible and spoke of love for the poor and the divine judgment they believed would come if this love was not realized. All were arrested, although neither the police nor the detainees expressed any hostility to each other. Two months later, Sojourners convened the first CTR conference with many of the same people from the protest in attendance. Now operating out of a brownstone in the 2400 block of Fifteenth Street NW, just across the street from Malcolm X Park, the group has juggled since its inception both local community issues and the more national foci it hoped to address with a mass movement.[45]

Call to Renewal touts itself as embodying the "prophetic" alternative to liberal political order, seeking to generate community activism and dialogue that can transform the political mainstream. Markedly different from Sojourners' early aversion to mainstream politics, CTR has served since the mid-1990s as an umbrella organization that is also an ecumenical forum for progressive Christians. It challenges the monopoly that its members feel the evangelical right (specifically the NCR) holds on public religious discourse. But the organization also contends that such a challenge does not require that the faithful commit to liberalism, either theologically or politically; if there is to be a challenge to conservative Christian hegemony, it is to be made on religious, not left-liberal, grounds. Call to Renewal hopes that this approach fosters community-based political and economic solutions that bring people together. At bottom, Wallis believes that neither liberals nor conservatives are empowering the poor, helping community, or securing a common good among squabbling citizens.

The Sojourners Community had rebounded from its crisis by the early 1990s. About twenty-five people worked on the magazine, another fifteen to twenty (some of whom were volunteers) helped run the neighborhood center, and the core group of about a dozen lived in the community itself.[46] The local and neighborhood activities have continued since then with great energy, but more work, time, and funding have been devoted to CTR's activities. Wallis justifies this shift in focus by noting that over decades of neighborhood work he and his fellow devout have discovered a widespread hunger in Americans for more substantive moral dialogue and political common ground. Citing general political trends such as low election turnouts, institutional corruption, and disenchantment with "politics as usual," Wallis concludes that the citizenry is ready for a "third way" beyond "left" and "right." For example, in Orange County, California, an old conservative stronghold, a CTR chapter has attracted considerable support from local citizens, even though CTR advocates economic justice, rights for recent immigrants, and a less draconian policy toward local gangs.[47] Throughout the 1990s, Wallis organized speaking tours, national conferences, and study programs with greater frequency, often participating in "gang summits," as well. He and his colleagues believe that, because they couch their approach to social issues in language other than liberalism or conservatism, they are able to gain a hearing from otherwise frustrated citizens.

Call to Renewal was initially conceived as a rapid response to the conservative retrenchment of the 1994 midterm congressional elections. More specifically, many saw the gathering as a counterconvention challenging the Christian Coalition. This first meeting brought together nearly five hundred church and community leaders to discuss strategies for progressive Christian social action. Recognizing that the 1994 elections marked a sea change, embodying a healthy concern for localism but with a language dominated by conservatives, CTR participant Marian Wright Edelman called for churches to be the "locomotive for social change, not the moral caboose," and Tony Campolo (then the "spiritual adviser" to President Bill Clinton) called for an "irrigation" of the political "desert" with love, justice, and compassion.[48] Notably, CTR was embracing the very kind of political sloganeering and reductionist sound bites Sojourners had for so long criticized. Perhaps because of this turn, inconsistent though it may seem with Sojourners' history, CTR has proved extremely popular. Local chapters have sprung up throughout the country, evidence of the kind of support Sojourners never had on their own. Rallying around the antislogan "Not from the Right, not from the Left, but from the spirit," CTR positions itself as a localist movement with global concerns (if not aspirations). Wallis sees the organization as a culmination of twenty-five years of Sojourners Community. Claiming that where the state is too large and the political order has severed its connections to the poor and marginalized, CTR touts itself as "value-centered, community-based, and committed to a spiritual vision of racial and economic justice . . . [and to undoing] the wall between 'public' and 'private' solutions."[49]

These phrases reflect the organization's desire to exist as an inclusive forum that can discuss issues in a way unhampered by labels (either religious or political) and build relationships across the polarities. It claims to evaluate policy and practice not according to established ideology but only by their fittingness to the spirit and teaching of the Gospels. It is striking, though, that the earlier specificity of Sojourners' writings and practice is absent. Where once Sojourners publications would excoriate American foreign policy based on a specific exegesis of Paul or Amos, the group's literature now only evokes a "spiritual vision." When the phrase "values-centered" is used, we are not told which values are included or toward which ends. Likewise the phrase "community-based" is not unpacked, leaving the observer to wonder whether its model is the community that dissolved in 1998 or some as yet unnamed community. There is the assumption here, however well meaning CTR's aspirations, that the Gospels are unidirectional in their implication and meaning.

To be sure, CTR represents a more organized presentation of older Sojourners themes. By stressing the connection between personal belief and political participation, Wallis is proposing a politics of spiritual commitment (which he claims often to be ecumenical and religiously inclusive but is in fact advocating a very specific Christian vision with deep roots in the evangelical tradition). This politics is marked by a self-professed outsider status in relation to political power, a rootedness in particular readings of the Bible for social direction, an overriding concern for the needs of the poor, an uncompromising moralism with regard to economic questions, and a global, rather than narrowly national, perspective. Wallis hopes that this way of thinking about these issues, bringing them out of the cubicles of K Street think tanks and into the streets, constitutes a biblical move from political exile to moral reconstruction, for, as he so pithily writes, the spiritual crisis of American democracy cannot be addressed simply by "voting Christian."[50] An alternate to the religious "right" is not, in other words, a religious "left."

A Very Unexpected Place: Meanings and Interpretations

The jazz pianist Thelonious Monk once said that he wanted to play music that white people would not understand; that way his music could not be stolen. A similarly protective desire is at work in Sojourners' political illegibility. It has become fashionable, after the revolutions of 1989, to speak of our political moment using terms such as "postideological" or "postmaterialist," rhetorical constructions that suggest that the apparent political certainties of the Cold War era have blurred and left us without analytic moorings. If this is true, then Sojourners are a community that exemplifies—indeed, has anticipated—these political trends. They have been shaped by, and have responded consistently to, the transformed political realities of the era that spans the end of the Vietnam War, the Reagan years, and the post–Cold War politics of the late twentieth century: the substitution of identity politics for old forms of political agency determined by party affiliation or ideology, the destabilization of traditional working-class modes of protest, and the blurring of conventional categories such as "left" and "right."

In an age when attacks on liberal politics are widespread, bemoaning either the moral failings of the system or its intrusiveness, it is clear to many that old political narratives are falling apart. Rather than relying on such narratives, I have interpreted Sojourners on their own terms, unpacking the specifically evangelical qualities of their writings and practice. Now it remains to be seen what implications these particulars have for thinking about the broader significance of Christian antiliberalism. In their claim that only by breaking from ossified patterns of thought and action can the pressing moral issues of the day be addressed, Sojourners exemplify Christian antiliberalism's political illegibility. Theorists might reasonably wonder of Sojourners' illegibility whether it opens up into new areas of political participation on behalf of justice, as Sojourners contend, or whether it instead produces the opposite effect of obscuring moral or political issues even further. Norberto Bobbio, for example, asserts that claims about a postideological age are overinflated. The historical traditions of both "left" and "right" are very much alive, says Bobbio, despite the ways in which these traditions have fractured and despite the proliferation of events that threaten to supersede their political efficacy. Not only do political parties throughout the West carry these traditions along, albeit feebly at times, but they also persist as still recognizable orientations toward the social world and as modes of inquiry and interpretation.

So although the "left"/"right" distinction is being challenged by theorists and by changes in political reality, the distinction not only makes sense to Bobbio but must be invoked if we are not to give comfort to a centrist pro-business consensus. He reminds us that the "postpolitical" mentality in Europe is an expression of frustration after the demise of Marxism, but he cautions against the temptations of postideological politics. Abandoning the clarity of this fundamental political distinction, Bobbio warns, effectively erodes the ability of citizens to bring the ruling parties to task on the basis of traditional "left" norms of egalitarianism. Absent this critique, the ruling parties will recognize that traditional possibilities are met with rancor and disgust, and they will simply try to reinvent themselves as something outside traditional categories. Bobbio thus believes that the "left"/"right" distinctions must be maintained and that the natural human propensity to think in dyadic terms can adapt to changing political realities. So rather than conclude that these terms have no relation to new social and political problems or identities in the post-1989 era, Bobbio insists that the "left"/"right" distinction will be reproduced in these new identities and issues.

In the United States, Bobbio's defense of the distinction is supported by social democrats such as Mitchell Cohen, whose "Why I'm Still 'Left'" defends the cogency of a "left" politics in a time when such a politics is feared to be outmoded (or when all political ideologies are seen as relics of an age of political certainty that finally ended in 1989).[51] Cohen, too, rejects the "end of ideology" thesis as too complacent in the face of upheavals such as globalization and ethnic conflict. "Left"-based support for social egalitarianism can contend with these new realities, Cohen maintains, as long as history is not forsaken for the easy conclusions of theory.

In other words, Bobbio and Cohen worry that the postpolitical move is a cover for elite will to power. This defense has both theoretical and practical merit, yet it cannot adequately explain the political illegibility of Sojourners, whose social position one could hardly call elite. Bobbio and Cohen are surely correct to point out that "left" and "right" have hardly disappeared from our world. Although the certainty with which these positions and ideologies are invoked has eroded markedly, the values often assigned to these positions have surely not disappeared. Nonetheless, the political realities of our era are themselves increasingly illegible, and these values often appear in surprising or unrecognizable forms or configurations. Not only are the fixed political certainties of the ideological continuum dissolving, but the issues and identities that animate lived politics continue to fall away from conventional modes of understanding. Political developments in culture and society have contributed to a narrowing, even a dissolution, of standard political discourses and interpretation. As Jeffrey C. Isaac put it in a response to Cohen, "These developments either are outside of the horizon of the historic left or cross-cut the left-right continuum in complex ways."[52]

Perhaps it is owing to these still emerging political realities, in addition to his religious commitments, that Wallis disregards categories such as "left" and "right." In rejecting these older political orthodoxies, Wallis nonetheless adheres to his own brand of religio-political certainty, one that responds to concrete actions and contexts in ways informed by his understanding of evangelical tradition and history. His concern is to address what Jean Bethke Elshtain calls "the stubborn quality of truth and experience" with the moral languages of prophetic politics, which Wallis believes can be more responsive to the complicated and multivalent experiences of contemporary political culture, generating strategies and solutions to our political problems.[53] What Wallis often identifies as the prophetic tradition is envisioned as an alternative to both secular humanism and religious fundamentalism. Its goal is to bring "moral values" and "social conscience" to the public square in order to challenge political orthodoxies. Those acting from the prophetic tradition claim to have spiritual guideposts and roadmaps; they do not need the "false" certainties of conventional political logic. Sojourners thus occupy what Wallis calls a "very unexpected place."[54]

The unexpectedness, however, does not always work in the group's favor. Despite their many avowals, it is unclear that Sojourners always engage the political logics they reject. Are all "conventional" answers simply formulaic and lacking any political or moral merit? Are all habits of political practice merely shopworn and unable to provide guidance? Sojourners do not always take care to provide a biblical "code" for social analysis, naming and elaborating specific biblical principles, nor do they generally establish why the biblical is a self-evidently desirable alternative to conventional models. Rather, we are simply left to conclude that "moral values" and "social conscience" are clear in their meanings and that these meanings are politically unconventional.

When accused in this way of withdrawal from "real" politics, of blanket dismissal of the world of public policy and lobbying, Sojourners contend that there is a great distinction to be made between politics that works within extant explanatory systems and institutional frameworks and a broader sense of biblical political witness. If American Christians too easily accept the terms of political debate, they risk "seduction both by the culture and the state."[55] If Christians are to be Christians, Sojourners claim, it is through independent political witness (as in the community's staunch opposition to the city of Washington's housing policy) rather than accommodation to the state. Such witness implicitly damns the institutional arrangements of the liberal state and, so Sojourners hope, makes explicit the need for the kind of interpretative framework they are commending. The fallen nation, in other words, still needs conversion from affluence and apathy to solidarity and compassion. Sojourners claim that this cannot be aided by cheerleading for one political faction or another, which they judge a concession to worldly power and an abstraction from the needs of the poor and the oppressed. Until American values are transformed, then, Sojourners insist that prophetic politics is necessary.

There is, however, a real ambivalence to these convictions, despite Wallis's protestations. Still present are "classic" Sojourners themes such as Jesus' threat to economic elites, the need to dismantle the "false" wall between public and private (which tends to support moneyed interests), and the urgency of challenging liberal political logic in the name of the common good.[56] But these foci are now couched in values talk that recalls the very New Christian Right that the CTR aims to challenge. Further, Sojourners' new rhetorical strategies seem to rely on the sort of sloganeering emblematic of the political culture they claim to contest. For every statement denouncing liberal order as little more than "a tightly closed political system," there are vague claims that "we need to recover . . . the language of personal moral values."[57] The insight that programmatic liberalism is flawed may be sound, but when Sojourners respond with romantic slogans, this seems equally insufficient to the problems at hand.

Call to Renewal may clearly reject conventional political logic. But amid the rhetoric of "prophetic politics" is a new willingness to play the cards of family and community, a greater willingness to appropriate the popular tropes of the NCR in order to challenge its claims. For example, CTR's recently articulated "Covenant to Overcome Poverty" is composed of a list of prayer points, as it were, a tactic highly favored by contemporary NCR organizations such as Promise Keepers. The "covenant" includes the commitment to "organize across barriers of race, denomination, and social boundaries." Call to Renewal's mission statement also touts its "four primary values (overcoming poverty, dismantling racism, affirming life, and rebuilding family and community)." The language in both statements very nearly mirrors that found in the "Seven Promises of a Promise Keeper."[58]

Some longtime supporters have worried, despite their eagerness for Sojourners to have a voice in national debates, about the growing "political centrism" underlying these aspirations to national visibility.[59] Yet this move may also simply be a canny bit of strategy, designed to position the group more favorably against the "extreme" tactics of radicals such as the Berrigans. As Kari Verhulst put it, "We need the Berrigans out there [to make us more palatable]."[60] Press coverage of CTR has emphasized the former interpretation, however, as when the *New York Times* dubbed the group a more ecumenical "alternative to the Christian Coalition."[61] This is precisely the sort of agenda that worries longtime supporters, who fear that in a roundabout way it accepts conventional political parameters by focusing on opposition to Christian conservatism.

There is something to this worry. Sojourners contend that their aversion to the NCR is rooted not in ideological differences but in the conviction that the NCR is out of synch with the Gospels. They have long been opposed to the NCR, whose ideological conservatism they see as a form of religious imprisonment, a tool of big business, and a comfort to the political status quo. Wallis has often accused the NCR of lacking an authentic social discipleship and of teaching a "false gospel" of militarism, wealth, and power.[62] Wallis thinks the NCR ignores the real conflict between the Gospels and American culture while clinging to "trivial" separations from the world such as creationism and sex education. In other words, Wallis finds the NCR all too legible. His implication is that radical Christians such as Sojourners are in touch with evangelical tradition and seek to renew the religious life at the local level, influencing the wider church by denouncing reigning idolatries and providing the foundation for prophetic social witness, promoting grassroots activism, changing consciousness, and broadening the framework of political and economic conversation. These positions often get confused, however, when Sojourners reiterate NCR claims about community and use similar tropes.

Reporter Colman McCarthy notes that progressives such as CTR have been working without the benefits of the Family Channel, the 700 Club, or the Christian Broadcasting Network, with its revenues of $237 million a year. Wallis shuns these media capabilities and professes a desire to make CTR simply a "Christian alternative to ideological religion." He contends that liberal religion, like liberal politics, has lost its "spiritual center"— faced with this, the worst thing CTR could do would be to reclaim Christianity in the name of "the left" or "liberalism." Members of CTR have little desire to "fritter away their energy uselessly arguing that the . . . left is superior to the . . . right," an endeavor that saps attention from more pressing material issues.[63] But at the same time they do see themselves as antagonists to the NCR, claiming that they want to "win back the word Christian."[64] Although they endorse no candidates and produce no voter guides, they do seek to start conversations about biblical politics through candidate forums, town meetings, and so on. They see this as justified because they feel that neither "left" nor "right" really reflects the messages of the Gospels. As Wallis says, the NCR's "ideological conclusions have really debased the kind of spiritual values many Christians care about."[65] So if there is opposition to the NCR, it is not on the basis of "left" principles but out of antipathy for the political system into which the NCR has sometimes been absorbed. More important than opposing the NCR is working toward "partnership between churches, local governments and businesses to combat problems such as unemployment, poverty and violence."[66]

Sojourners' focus on concrete problems in the community is consistent with other recent trends in community and grassroots activism: community development corporations (CDCs), tenants' rights groups, and localist organizations such as the Industrial Areas Foundation or the Local Initiatives Support Corporation (LISC). These other community activists have, like Sojourners, been working since at least the 1980s to empower local citizens and transform their immediate environs, thus debunking the myth that inner-city neighborhoods are "incurable concentrations of poverty and pathology."[67] Although Sojourners have never been active in overhauling municipal budgets or debates over infrastructure, their concerns with housing, crime, and neighborhood betterment link them with the rise of community-based movements such as these.

At stake in this type of activism is the creation of democratic communities more appropriate to the contemporary political landscape. Sojourners claim that the problems of the inner city are not the fault of the residents of the city themselves (the case often made by conservative moralists) or a result of the paternalist stance of the government. Instead, the moral lacunae so glaring in American politics and the problems of American society persist because of the limited political options available under a liberal regime. Sojourners do not go so far as to suggest that religious communities hold the key to the future of American politics. Rather, they believe that the liberal ethos reduces the complicated texture of religious community life to a moral drama at the margins of American society, a move that not only depoliticizes the crucial problems of community building but also notably fails to respond to them in anything like a democratic fashion. When religion erupts into public life, liberal political order's standard response cautions that "it is dangerous to become too religious. The best advice is to stay as 'normal' and mainstream as possible."[68] Sojourners believe that they have been "remaindered" by liberalism's tidy schemes of ideological organization and explanation.[69]

The group claims that these are unfair circumstances not because its voice should be allowed to dominate but because it believes that American social problems are so intractable that they demand attention from the widest possible array of traditions and communities. In addition to their programmatic recommendations—about different models of community or the more equitable distribution of social goods such as food, housing, and medicine—Sojourners continue to insist that the limits of contemporary social and political visions will be transcended in the coming Kingdom. Wallis claims also that citizens yearn for this kind of transcendence of "normal" categories, that there is a call for conversion and democratic participation coming from the streets, which he claims must be heeded on behalf of "our endangered children, who have become the chief pawns and victims of our absurd bifurcations."[70]

In their political illegibility, which they claim helps stake out a new spiritual and political geography, Sojourners demonstrate the tendency of Christian antiliberals to lock in on the key political struggles that are the legacy of the 1960s. Yet in their desire to awaken Americans to the daily realities of poverty, violence, and despair, Sojourners all but ignore the social fragmentation that could be occasioned by their brand of evangelical politics. Their rhetoric and their practice could be far more divisive than they realize. Highlighting social injustices through Peace Pentecosts, direct actions, prayers, marches, jailings, and economic boycotts may be consistent with democratic norms such as publicity, accountability, and freedom of expression. Yet though Sojourners frequently engage in conventional political action within the liberal system, their rhetoric and action attempt to call attention to what they believe are flaws in the very logic, lexicon, and authority of political order itself, not just particular laws or functions within that order. At the very least, it seems reasonable to expect that prophetic politics engage more fully the discourse and culture it dismisses and, indeed, that prophetic politics explain more fully its own self-proclaimed strengths relative to other moral discourses. Like other Christian antiliberals, Sojourners also vacillate in public statements about their goals. At times they claim simply that the constitutional system is not operating properly, but elsewhere they may deny the very legitimacy of the system of legality. It is a Christian antiliberal trademark to play across the gap between these two goals.

So although the group is clearly comfortable with the practice of a destabilized, nonstatist politics of civil society, whereby religions can be practiced in the streets and attention focused on concrete issues of community, questions remain about the unpredictability of Sojourners' practice. Their resolute use of the languages of Christian self-understanding is meant to undermine the authority of liberalism and in a sense also to "save" law, morality, and politics by reimagining these spheres using familiar tropes of religious dissent. Yet their political illegibility generates questions and difficulties, as well.

Do Sojourners employ the rhetoric of "family," "virtue," and "community" to regain lost political ground from the NCR, or are they compromising their radicalism? Wallis speaks of the benefits of illegibility, praising its ability to render the political sphere a "very unexpected place."[71] But what precisely is this unexpected place? Does it involve a new reformation, a quasi-populist economic program, a politics of conversion? In other words, Sojourners' rejection of liberalism through the strategy of illegibility often entails a frustrating lack of specificity about their own vision. It is not always so obvious what Wallis's key concepts designate, what he can say to Christians who disagree with him, or that the values he supports are so self-evidently transformative. As evidence of this indeterminacy, in the 1998 quarterly newsletters CTR began ironically to replicate the Christian Coalition's turn away from localism. Wallis recommended the formation of "national boards" for organizing local communities and actions, as well as to guide policy development.[72] Indeed, in recent years Sojourners and CTR have more frequently taken to commentary on specific legislation (such as Senate revisions to welfare bills), a clear engagement with the political order they elsewhere question so sternly. Call to Renewal also states explicitly its desire to influence public policy and to craft "a new partnership with all sectors of our society—government, business, labor, the nonprofit sector, and philanthropy."[73]

These moves may be construed as concessions to the liberal state strategy of interest-group bargaining. But even if one contends that this might not compromise Sojourners' antiliberalism, it nonetheless raises questions about the effectiveness of their local action. Kari Verhulst has professed some vexation about these issues but has also clarified some of them. Referring to Sojourners' intense localism, she remarks that "it's a difficult level of energy to sustain . . . there is still a neighborhood center which is very active . . . but to some extent [CTR] has participated in taking energy away."[74] Indeed, one might argue that the neighborhood organizing, national boards, and so forth are paradigmatically legible to a liberal political regime (though Sojourners certainly continue to be energized by, and to some degree are shaped by, the contention and self-understanding that they are illegible).

Despite these conceptual difficulties, though, Sojourners remain paradoxically consistent (or consistently paradoxical) in their Christian antiliberalism. Changes have been made, so all in the group profess, in order to further the ideals with which they have traditionally been identified. Many have come to realize that, despite the importance of local action, the centrist pro-business agenda of the liberal state must be met on more fronts than one. They feel that political and religious reactionaries have achieved their success because "liberalism, which constituted the political center of gravity for the last 50 years, has largely reduced public life to the value-free balancing of interest groups accomplished through self-perpetuating and faceless bureaucracies."[75] Although the scale of their focus has been broadened in recent years, Sojourners still continue to engage in local work on national problems (as with the now annual Pentecost Against Poverty) and have supplemented this work with a national speaking forum in CTR.

In our political context, activists cannot hope to undo the entrenched power of liberal political order in one revolutionary stroke; they can only engage in partial and piecemeal struggles defined around specific communities and concerns. Sojourners' antiliberalism is part of a growing trend among local communities toward challenging the dominant understandings of politics by living out more local and particular meanings (in this case evangelical Christian) and putting these idiosyncratic meanings in the service of reinvigorating American democracy. Their practice is similar to that of other Christian antiliberal groups who express discontent with the political order of the day. In this way, Sojourners attempt to challenge the taken-for-grantedness of our social reality, presenting an alternative view of how things can and, to them, must be. Politics then becomes a process of envisioning this new reality, of living and hoping this reality into being.

As yet, it is unclear if Sojourners and CTR have put any chinks in liberalism's armor. There are no legislative successes or duly elected candidates to which one can point as indicators of "success." These ways of thinking politically may, however, make little sense. What seems like lack of impact according to traditional electoral or policymaking criteria may be simply an expression of the paradoxical character of Christian life. Since the Sojourners Community was founded in 1971, liberal political order has become even more unstable, global economic trends have raised questions about the role of average citizens in the political process, and political apathy in the United States has mushroomed. Faced with these overwhelming obstacles, many members of Sojourners admit that long-term change might be impossible to realize. Yet alongside these realizations, there is also the sense that this mode of assessment "seems to be irrelevant."[76]

Through the early 1980s, the community often spoke in highly "prophetic" language, invoking the spirits of Amos and Paul's Epistle to the Ephesians in order to rebuke the state. That language has now disappeared almost entirely, and in its place is a more modest, chastened Christian criticism. What remains, though, is the desire to reform political order. Community members insist that, though some of the recent conceptual shifts have been difficult to make, they are not moral or religious compromises. The idiomatic shift is not viewed as a concession to liberal political order but rather as a shift within the Christian tradition that places community members no closer to mainstream political logic. According to this rationalization, one need not demand that followers "give up [their] cars and move to the inner city" in order to remain a religious radical.[77]

The strategies have changed, but the group remains openly guided by its understanding of evangelical Christianity. The overriding belief is still that the power of Christian belief can break open the closed world of liberalism. And in the end, Sojourners' distinct practice of Christian antiliberalism turns on an understanding of grace. Evangelicals have always understood this term as a sign for expressing the mystery of God's purposes in the world. Human powers, it is said, are too limited fully to comprehend these purposes, yet people all too often twist God's purposes to suit their own. For Sojourners, grace should not accommodate worldly or temporal goals, which may finally be sinful, but should open a path to discipleship and disobedience. Turning away from political orthodoxy, the faithful remain content with the recognition that "to hope against . . . power is to undermine the illusions and control they depend on."[78]

Chapter 3

The Rootedness of Discontent

Culture and Identity in the New Christian Right

*We don't want approval, because we feel it's a matter of
state control. . . . We believe the head of the Church is Jesus
Christ, and if I let the State become the head of the church,
then I will be removing the Lord from His position, and this
Church is definitely built on the Lord, Jesus Christ.*
—PASTOR OF AN UNAPPROVED FUNDAMENTALIST
BAPTIST CHURCH, QUOTED IN E. VANCE RANDALL,
"RELIGIOUS SCHOOLS IN AMERICA"

U.S. Route 77 stretches and winds its way from the shore of Lake Erie in
Cleveland southward through West Virginia, Virginia, and North Carolina.
It crosses a number of different regions, communities, and cultures, but
its path through the hills of central West Virginia is particularly tortured.
The highway snakes through mountains that loom up suddenly, past old
mining towns perched precariously on steep slopes or nestled in tiny val-
leys between the peaks. Few would suspect that here in Kanawha County
occurred one of the most significant political battles in the recent history
of the New Christian Right (NCR).[1] Kanawha County may seem an unas-
suming territory, remote from the concerns that animate protest movements such as the NCR. But in fact, its bounded landscapes, coiling moun-
tain roads, and stark setting capture both the insularity and the protean
nature of the NCR's identity.

In this setting, secreted away from the intensity and mobility of America's urban centers, the role of liberalism in public education seemed all
the more outrageous to citizens such as Alice Moore, who in 1974 led local
citizens in one of the NCR's most prominent political campaigns of the

1970s, one that captured many of the emerging themes of Christian anti-liberalism. That year, housewife Moore successfully ran for a position on her local school board in order to protest the use of "un-Christian" textbooks in the public schools. What made the case so notable was that it was the most dramatic public attack on liberal political order that the NCR had made in the postwar era. Moore and her backers challenged the purported neutrality of liberalism and charged that public education, endorsed and mandated by the liberal state, was robbing them of their ability to create their own worlds of moral and religious meaning.

For decades prior to this case, the Christian Right in America had prided itself on its moral and cultural distance from mainstream politics, which it saw as hopelessly corrupted by liberalism and modernism. Although a network of organizations had existed through the 1950s, led by figures such as Billy James Hargis and loosely composed of conservative evangelicals and Protestant fundamentalists, the Christian Right during this time had been largely concerned with sustaining its culture rather than with engaging the political sphere.[2] But by the late 1960s, as George Marsden notes, evangelicals were becoming increasingly activist through their "hodge-podge of ad hoc structures . . . personal contacts and small group meetings."[3] Kanawha County was not a particularly politicized environment in the late 1960s, but divisive ideological differences were surfacing even in its apparently homogeneous communities.

In 1969, the Kanawha County school district introduced a federally designed sex education program into its curriculum. Many residents were outraged at what they saw as government usurpation of a traditionally familial task, and Moore attended a school board meeting to protest the materials. She argued that what was most offensive about the program was not the sexual content but "that this wasn't just a sex education course. It dealt with every aspect of a child's life . . . [and] the stated purpose of the course was to teach the children how to think, to feel, and to act."[4] Against the liberal defense of public education as morally neutral, Moore and other critics maintained that public education was actually a comprehensive and non-neutral system that required them to falsify their beliefs.[5] Elected to a position on the school board, Moore was able to alter the curriculum (specifically what she judged to be its graphic content). A further controversy arose when, in 1974, the school system approved the use of new multicultural textbooks. Moore worried that such readings detracted from common educational standards, introduced "non-Christian" viewpoints to children, contained relativist moral outlooks, and increased race consciousness.[6] Each of these charges carries with it NCR practitioners' concern that educational materials may actually, even when introduced as neutral, be "dirty books" that are hostile to their children's beliefs.

The Kanawha County case struck an important blow for the resurgent Christian Right, and in many ways it set the tone for the NCR's antiliberalism in subsequent decades. It may appear that this case was merely a local skirmish over isolated curricula. Yet in important ways, local cases such as these are cultural turf wars over the authority and legitimacy of liberal political order. By focusing on public education, NCR practitioners hope to undermine the socialization of their children in a liberal political culture that, in Moore's words, teaches children "how to think, to feel, and to act."[7] Kanawha County became symbolic of the broader mission of the NCR: to undo the moral and spiritual damage it claimed was wrought by postwar liberalism and to restore power to local evangelical communities by creating a parallel educational culture. Struggles over the meanings and directions of education are contests over the sacred registers of politics; for the NCR, these are nothing less than all-out defenses of Christian identity itself against the intrusiveness and immorality of liberal political order.

In this chapter I discuss Christian antiliberalism's focus on the sacred registers of politics by exploring the recent history of the NCR, particularly as it has engaged public education. Conservative evangelical Christians in America have always been wary of state power. In the era immediately following the Second World War, both the state and the judiciary took a more active role in public education. Much of this activism directly transformed the NCR's wariness about the state, rendering practitioners increasingly likely to see it as a hostile power against which they were obligated to take aggressive action. Since the landmark Supreme Court cases of the 1960s, the NCR has emerged from the political margins to denounce liberalism's authority to instruct its practitioners' children. By extension, this is a denunciation of the very moral and political legitimacy of liberal political order.

The NCR has attracted more attention than other antiliberals. Much of this notice is devoted to the NCR's "shock value" rather than to the complex world of practitioners themselves, their genealogy, or their concerns. Nicholas Lemann warns of the NCR's "foot soldiers," and Isaac Kramnick and R. Laurence Moore claim that the "silly things" that concern religious practitioners (they, like Lemann, were writing in reaction to the Christian Coalition's prominence in the 1996 elections) cannot withstand the more substantive demands of politics.[8] Alternately, Leo Ribuffo is altogether too sanguine about the NCR's resurgence, claiming that it is merely part of an ongoing spectacle that has ever thrived in American culture.[9] There are three broad lacunae in these and other accounts of the NCR. First, most are deeply ahistorical, ignorant not only of the devotional world from which the NCR has emerged but also of the historical sources of its discontents. Second, the context within which many of these accounts are written is framed by an often unstated conviction that religion is not the stuff of "serious" political inquiry. Finally, the term "fundamentalist" is so badly overused that it has become analytically useless; it serves too often to paper over important political, moral, and doctrinal differences among groups in the NCR or simply to ignore the significance of conservative Christianity by dismissing it as "excessive" or "intolerant."

A different set of analytic tools is needed for a sufficiently fine grained account of the beliefs, genealogy, and political praxis of the NCR. It is certainly prudent to be attentive to the dangers that NCR antiliberalism could pose to individual liberty and to public civility were their policy concerns to be realized on a broad basis, but these issues only partly account for the political and cultural concerns addressed by the NCR. A more nuanced interpretation must consider how the NCR is part of the larger animosity toward liberal political order; this is essential for understanding its particular conceptions of society and politics. Further, the NCR's attention to the sacred registers—deep-seated issues of meaning and identity—problematizes those interpretations that focus largely on either the moral or constitutional issues raised by its activism. It is necessary to explore the connections between grassroots campaigns against public education and the intimate concerns of meaning and identity. Only through such explorations can the NCR's antiliberalism be understood.

An Antiliberal History

The resurgence of the NCR has been greatly abetted by the general discontent with liberal politics that has flourished since the 1960s. Aided by organizers such as Richard Viguerie and Paul Weyrich, the NCR has become infamous for its organizational acumen in galvanizing the growing constituency of conservative evangelical Christians to attack what they perceive as the liberal state's moral laxity. New Christian Right organizations are politically connected to the New Right ascendancy of the Reagan era. They are religiously connected to the traditions of conservative evangelical Christianity in America. In the NCR's recent manifestations, however, these religious markers have become publicly manifest in ways that relate it to other identity-based movements that push at the conventional boundaries of the political sphere. By refusing to "bracket" religious belief, and by insisting that its religiosity is what is most politically relevant, the NCR challenges the liberal state's moral and political authority by disregarding the rhetorical and practical limits that are placed on political speech and action.

The religious groups represented in the NCR have their roots in the evangelical Protestantism of eighteenth- and nineteenth-century America. The decades after the Revolutionary War saw not only political conflict and economic expansion but vast religious energy. The new religious idioms introduced to the colonies during the First Great Awakening continued to pose challenges to established churches on the eastern seaboard, even as the Second Great Awakening continued to develop these new idioms in different territories and with different ends. Additionally, many itinerant religious groups flourished and new religious movements proliferated during this period. Decentralized political power and the disestablishment of religion afforded evangelicals the chance to define their religious life and practice for themselves.[10] The transformation of evangelicalism during this era is marked both by its revivalism—whereas the itinerant preachers of the First Great Awakening stuck largely to established colonial urban centers, those of the Second Great Awakening brought the evangelical message to new colonies in the West via camp meetings and tent revivals—and by its elaboration on basic evangelical themes such as an emphasis on a personal experience of rebirth, an individual relationship with the divine, and atonement for sin. During this period, evangelicals began to stress in particular the importance of individual conversion, a suspicion of worldly powers, a sense of unmediated divine activity, and, somewhat later in the nineteenth century, a doctrine of biblical inerrancy. No external or arbitrary powers could make a claim on one's conversion, soul, or status before the redeemer God. Indeed, these powers were often understood as antithetical to one's religion, as obstacles that stood between the worldly individual and potential regeneration in Christ.

Following the Second Great Awakening, evangelical Protestantism adjusted its theological priorities to include not only saving individual souls but also saving the social order, an impulse that was part of and consistent with wider reform efforts proliferating in American society. The impulse to transform society according to evangelical principles was strengthened in the years following the Civil War as American Protestantism became deeply divided. In the late nineteenth century, America was besieged by new anxieties, felt acutely by Christians whose denominations had divided over regional alliance and slavery. After the war, churches were further divided over a host of social issues. In the 1870s, the size and power of the government increased, the frontier closed, cities swelled with industry and immigrants, and new intellectual forces profoundly altered American social and religious life. Evangelical Protestants responded with attempts to Christianize the social order, to reassert old truths in a time of disruptive change.

Although they would later become divided over methods and ultimate ends, it is to this old and multivariate tradition of evangelical Protestantism that the NCR is heir. At once profoundly ill at ease with their culture but also undeniably of it, oppositional groups such as millennialists, dispensationalists, revivalists, and holiness churches multiplied in the latter part of the nineteenth century. Their religious identity was often linked to discontent over social change, driven by an animus against intellectual trends such as evolutionary theory, biblical criticism, and skepticism, as well as against broader social forces such as industrialism, immigration, and urbanization. Many Protestant denominations split over their acceptance of natural science and biblical criticism. Theologically conservative Protestants rejected these, holding fast to old certainties in a time of transition. They were suspicious of the "permissive" spaces of the city and distrustful of a new politics of centralized economics and bureaucracy. Such tensions with modernity did not transform conservative Christianity into a unilaterally separatist culture. Rather, it has been marked by a social ambivalence, identifying both with the "establishment" and with "outsiders."[11]

This ambivalence helps to explain why a decidedly antimodernist religious impulse would find expression in a modern social movement that formed in the early twentieth century. Within Protestant denominations, schools, and local communities, conservative evangelicals disseminated teachings on how best to respond to cultural anxieties. Between 1910 and 1915, the inchoate reactions of conservative Christians were partially codified in a series of twelve pamphlets entitled *The Fundamentals*. The pamphlets laid out a "fundamental" set of beliefs (including the Virgin birth, Christ's power to work miracles, the inerrancy of the Bible, "substitutional atonement," and others) to which Christians disaffected by modernity could assent. More than three million copies were distributed free to students and preachers across the country, greatly strengthening the organizational network of the new "fundamentalist" movement. This acceptance served as a symbolic point of reference around which to organize.

The "fundamentalist" challenge to false doctrine now expanded to include a fair degree of militancy on cultural issues, a move exemplified in figures such as William Bell Riley or Billy Sunday. Sunday was the point man in the antiliberal crusade of early fundamentalism, charging that the liberal state was suppressing the Christian spirit with barely concealed socialism. The betterment of societies had to come through the sum total of individually saved souls and subsequently through religiously motivated social action, not the overbearing legislation of a small cadre of liberal intellectuals promoting neutrality and the disestablishment of religion. This challenge in many ways parallels the rise of populism around the turn of the century, particularly in its tendencies to practice a politics that was grassroots and discordant rather than bureaucratic and conciliatory.[12] Yet there was a sharp decline in activism following the Scopes trial of 1925–26. In the early 1940s, major conservative groups such as Carl McIntire's American Council of Christian Churches and the National Association of Evangelicals divided over whether to be separatist or accommodationist in their efforts to transform the social order.

Through the 1950s, the Christian Right was rather isolated from the political mainstream, condemning communism but having little other public impact. The resurgence of the NCR can be directly attributed to its repudiation of 1960s countercultural politics while simultaneously appropriating many of this era's political strategies. The organizations formed, the causes chosen, and the tactics employed are all expressions of this broader repudiation. Beginning in the 1960s, most major denominations in the United States once again split along political lines. As the religious "left" mounted its own challenge to liberalism, this created a partial legitimation of the discourse the NCR claimed as its own. The collapse of postwar political consensus in the 1960s created openings for latent social conflicts to become manifest and for religious critics to expose the deficiencies of liberal politics. A radical politics favoring more civic initiative, grassroots organization, and decentralization was proposed as a corrective, in much the same direction in which the NCR would soon head. The NCR's strategic shifts were abetted by a larger transition within American conservatism, toward a new populism that fed on growing antiliberalism in ways that aided the resurgent NCR.

The NCR began to appropriate the New Left's practices of participatory democracy and invest these tactics in a new constituency: conservative evangelicals outraged by the apparent permissiveness of the liberal state. The NCR echoed the New Left's claims that liberalism is hostile to robust political participation, that it has fostered a permissive and immoral society, and that it is biased against the interests of religious communities. Certainly, these claims have been given different direction by conservative

evangelicals than they had by neo-Jeffersonian radicals. But these judg-
ments were far from alien to the NCR, which had already begun to decen-
tralize and reorganize at the grassroots level in order to gain the political
ground the "left" was losing.[13] By the late 1970s, a host of new groups had
begun to galvanize widespread public reaction against the 1960s "left," to
provide clarity on issues of meaning in a time of widespread confusion following the Vietnam era, and, as they saw it, to rectify America for the Second Coming. These organizations pinpointed legalized abortion and the
gay rights movement as evidence of growing immorality, a shock tactic
that lured voters from major parties and led to the resurgence of the NCR's
organizational strength.

Although rhetorically committed to decentralization, the NCR's highly
organized national institutions sought a direct impact on public policy and
moral culture. In widely publicized rhetorical attacks, these organizations
charged that liberalism's deracinated view of public politics was directly
responsible for the country's cultural and economic crises. Leaders claimed
that their organizations would help foster "community-building movements in a time of modern individualist anomie."[14] Jerry Falwell intoned,
in *Listen America!*, that "liberal forces such as the abortionists, the homosexuals, the pornographers, secular humanists, and Marxists have made
significant inroads" into Christian America. Proudly defiant of liberal culture, Falwell celebrated the NCR's "burial" of the Equal Rights Amendment, its campaigns to censor sex and violence on television, the wave of
creationism bills in state legislatures, and the role of Christians in the 1980
elections.[15] The resurgent NCR directed its energy against a Congress and a
judiciary it felt had been "stacked" against it.[16]

The NCR used direct mail, television, radio, and support from wealthy
patrons such as the Coors family to expand its organizations, form coalitions between disparate groups, and coordinate voting efforts. Much of the
organization building was accomplished by Robert Billings (a school activist who headed the National Christian Action Coalition) and Ed McAteer
(head of the Christian Freedom Foundation), who recruited Jerry Falwell,
Pat Robertson, and others to join them in strategy sessions that yielded
prominent organizations such as the Religious Roundtable, the American
Coalition for Traditional Values, and the Moral Majority. These organizations enshrined the NCR's commitment to interest-group strategy and lobbying on issues such as abortion, exempting Christian schools from the IRS,
abolishing racial "quotas" in Christian schools, taxation on church property, and government intervention into religious life in general. The very existence of these issues was morally outrageous to the NCR and, in political
terms, was direct proof of the depredations to which liberalism gave rise.

These machinations were hugely important on a symbolic level because they spoke of the NCR's willingness to meet liberalism on its own ground. Rather than remain above the political fray, the NCR sought to "copy the success of the old Left" in dismantling the Left's achievements.[17] The NCR claimed that a liberal elite had seized power from everyday citizens and that "the chief instrument of its rise to power . . . was the state."[18] With broad appeals such as these, the NCR was able to pinpoint sources of discontent and to mobilize support for antiliberal programs geared largely toward education, sexual morality, and taxation. The movement was committed to an activist brand of politics that, like various forms of identity politics emerging in the same period, sought to ground political action in issues of particularity and morality. Unlike identity politics, however, the NCR has generally seen its workings in the sacred registers of politics as defensive, aimed at the protection of religiously unique worldviews from "corrupting" or "worldly" influences that are judged to be unfairly burdensome. By contrast, identity politics often seek explicitly to build mass movements that can petition the state for recognition or for various forms of redress. The NCR's moves were able to capitalize on the "unfocused but conservative political sentiments of many evangelicals" by avowing earlier articles of faith such as anticommunism and folding them into a more broad-based antiliberal movement.[19]

By the late 1980s, however, the NCR's power had decreased radically in the wake of the scandals of televangelists and Pat Robertson's failed presidential campaign of 1988. However, the NCR's desire to articulate its identity, upend the priorities of postwar liberalism, and infuse the public with particular values did not disappear. It began to flourish primarily at the local level, as the NCR developed "a decentralized movement structure, relying on 'umbrella' organizations that brought together grass-roots groups at the state and local level."[20] Instead of incorporating new organizations for immediate mobilization, the NCR focused on the long-term development of political power in communities at the local level.[21]

Keeping Safe from the Liberal State

Like other Christian antiliberals, the NCR seeks, through its religious activism, to transform liberal political order (or its experience of it) through the cultivation of values more conducive to its understandings of virtue, participation in political life, and moral uprightness. The movement seeks to redirect the social order on the basis of a non-neutral conception of the good. The vitality of this form of political religion comes not only from its specific organizational or activist features but from the relationship it posits between its own communities or practitioners and those of the "outside culture."[22] Practitioners believe that liberalism is composed of two linked tendencies: an overly artificial view of public politics and a consequent moral permissiveness.[23] So if the "outside culture" of liberal political order is experienced at the sacred registers as intrusive and omnipresent, the NCR naturally responds with heated defenses of its own culture, of the very registers its feels liberalism challenges. Indeed, Ralph Reed often links liberal neutrality with social ills, rhapsodizing over a lost 1950s composed of strong military, families, and morality. Predictably, he blames the loss on liberalism, arguing that abortion and child pornography have replaced "lower taxes, less bureaucracy, and leaner government."[24] In this interpretation, an overarching, neutral government discourages moral behavior and political participation, since, for example, it does not ask that the recipients of social welfare demonstrate ethical propriety. The NCR feels that it is by bouncing values from the public sphere and absolving citizens of their share in the work of politics and public morality that America has sunk into its cultural morass.[25] Liberalism certainly may not be as totalizing as these claims indicate. Yet the NCR has nonetheless organized and mobilized under the perception that liberalism *has* become all-encompassing and that it *is* hostile to public expressions of religion. The movement's self-understandings and modes of action have largely derived from this perception.

Aside from the marked aversion to liberal politics, there are a number of theological and philosophical concerns that animate the NCR's struggles. First, many of its initiatives are defended in the name of individualism. Although the rhetoric of community looms large in the movement, it is undergirded by a commitment to the dignity and the worth of the individual. Not only is the individual central to understanding the religious dynamic of salvation and God's grace, but the individual is also possessed of unique gifts that she or he can realize only when unimpeded by government intervention. This defense of individualism is invoked as part of opposition to an encroaching liberal state and is linked to the protection of both private initiative in the economic sphere and freedom from intervention in the family sphere.

Ironically, the NCR's quite public claims about religion and morality turn here on a use of the liberal language of rights. Viguerie, for instance, positions the NCR against liberalism by relying on images of a governmental "war on private property, private initiative, private education, public morality, religion, and finally human life itself."[26] This defense, which vigorously defends the public/private distinction so common to most liberal democratic regimes, is importantly connected to the preservation of the nuclear, patriarchal family and of free enterprise. Many of the NCR's most vocal activists, notably including the Promise Keepers, advocate returning to what is remembered as a "golden age" of the American family, a time before the women's movement disrupted familial stability and before parents become unduly stressed by an unfriendly tax code. Figures ranging from the Eagle Forum's Phyllis Schlafly to former Christian Coalition figurehead Ralph Reed have claimed that this dissolution of the "traditional" family has helped to usher in corrosive social forces such as sexual promiscuity, pornography, abortion on demand, homosexual rights, sex education, and profanity in the arts. Such critics see this assault as a detraction from individual opportunity and incentive, contributing to the higher taxes, enforced planning, and social engineering that have threatened family values.

To NCR followers, at the heart of all these convictions is the iron-clad belief that liberal government is, despite its claims to the contrary, decidedly non-neutral with regard to its citizens' conceptions of the good. They believe that liberalism has adopted a posture of neutrality on issues of meaning in order to smuggle a rationalistic faith in bureaucracy into a sphere where values ought to hold sway. In the name of neutrality, the liberal state has become an overbearing administrative apparatus unfairly burdening individuals and families with high taxes, costly expansion, and social programs not to their benefit. Its paradoxical commitment to neutrality has seemingly opened the door for the expression of manifold political, sexual, and cultural affiliations, while at the same time preventing the NCR from articulating its religious commitments—in other words, "neutrality" opens up political space for those the NCR considers deviant while simultaneously placing limits on its own political activity. Dick Weinhold, director of the Texas Christian Coalition, using language that smacks of liberal rights claims, calls this "religious bigotry . . . [an] intolerance and censorship of people of faith from the . . . process."[27]

Through a series of hyperbolic but always pointed characterizations and actions, NCR proponents have painted liberalism as "a set of ideas and values that ostensibly eschews power and upholds equality, liberty and the brotherhood of man but which is amazingly congruent with and acceptable to the political, economic and social interests (the structural interests) of the . . . elite."[28] The NCR contends that shadowy groups of elite secular liberals steer the administrative apparatus of the state, whose intrusive efforts in social engineering have produced not only immoral policies and practices but a culture that the NCR believes is antithetical to its deepest faith. The liberal state has expanded at the expense of small-scale communities, muscling into the domestic realm with intrusive tax codes and family planning. It has coddled transnational organizations that jeopardize American sovereignty. In sum, the NCR believes that despite its much-vaunted rhetoric about neutrality and the common good, liberalism actually disdains government neutrality and favors an activist state coupled with a rationalistic faith in bureaucracy and administrative planning. The NCR sees liberalism as an instrument for the realization of specific moral ends that are hostile to Christians.

Suburban Virginia housewife Karen Jo Gounaud, for example, was outraged that liberalism's guarantee of freedom of speech and press would permit gay periodicals to be stocked in her public library branch. On spotting copies of local gay journal the *Washington Blade*, Gounaud organized a protest group of local parents. They not only sought the removal of gay periodicals from all county libraries but also requested that all library holdings meet with parents' approval, that parents have full information on their children's checkouts, and that gay employees be forbidden to wear "pride" pins. They succeeded only in removing the *Blade*, but their actions exemplify the kinds of incidents that are often at the heart of NCR challenges to the authority of liberalism.

Here the promises of "traditional" conservatism, seeking to limit the power of the state and to deregulate the market, are buttressed with the moral resonance and familiarity of specifically evangelical Christian conservatism. Within this framework, a "coalition of resentments" is mobilized in the name of family, nation, market, property, and God.[29] The overriding fear is that the state is taking the place of God, that liberal cultural elites and an activist judiciary are crowding "traditional values" out of politics. It is for these reasons that the public school is at the center of not just educational but broader political activism, too; public education is often seen by the NCR as a vehicle for indoctrination into liberal secular values, one that operates at the sacred registers of emotion, perception, and reasoning. Since there is tremendous organizational diversity in the NCR, it is not always the case that these activists seeks ultimately to use the state as a tool for restoration. Although all NCR activists share a sense of attack by state expansion, judicial activism, and regulatory agencies, they differ in their response, with some seeking to seize control of the state and others opting for cultural separatism. In all corners, however, the key NCR organizational tactic is to target the self-understandings—the sacred registers—of so-called pro-family citizens.[30]

Local communities and school districts form the arena in which the NCR wages its battles over the sacred registers of politics. In an aggressive reassertion of the public authority of religious belief, NCR antiliberalism works here by invoking oppression from the secular liberal state in order to foster solidarity and cooperation among the movement's constituents. The culture wars, especially those surrounding educational issues, are pitched as a struggle between innocent Christian citizens seeking to live out their piety and the harsh exercise of secular authority. Among the many evils of liberal political order, the NCR has long singled out education as an area of high stakes, for it is in the public schools that the state is most clearly antagonistic to the uniqueness of NCR religion and the vitality of the NCR's public identity. Pat Robertson once claimed, "We used to think that if we stayed home and prayed it would be enough. Well, we are fed up. We think it is time to put God back [in society]."[31] For the NCR, if liberal order is to be undone, it must be tackled first in the schools.

Educrats of Sexology

In the culture of Christian schools and homeschooling, life is organized around the very Christian identity felt to be threatened by liberal political order. Alternate schools are among the most visible and compelling manifestations of this concern for identity. Christian school culture is preoccupied with seemingly mundane matters, such as preserving tax credits for religious schools. But the very existence of such schools carries far wider cultural and political significance. Beginning in the 1960s, fundamentalist churches began to establish private schools. Originally designed to sidestep mandatory desegregation in many cases, they later came to focus on evolution, humanism, and sex education, seeing each of these curricular areas as evidence of liberalism's permissiveness.[32]

The result was the establishment of an alternate educational culture, with specifically "Christian" curricula designed to create and maintain a particular religious and social identity. New Christian Right activists have consistently complained that their schools are targeted by the state; in response, Christian school officials have often challenged state boards of education over the government's right to oversee hiring policies and set curriculum standards. In 1978, a coalition of Christian schools battled the IRS over tax exemption. Seeking to strengthen their position for the future, Robert Billings and Paul Weyrich formed Christian School Action (later the National Christian Action Coalition) to help mobilize antiliberal campaigns on behalf of schools.[33] In 1978 NCR organizations confronted the IRS over the tax-exempt status of these schools, battles that proved instrumental in rallying an "informal network of parents out there in real America . . . [who] weren't on the radar screen of the policy wonks in Washington."[34] Connie Marshner's *Family Protection Report* newsletter, a watchdog sheet on government interference with families, established connections between NCR organizations and parent groups. Marshner spoke for the NCR in general when she claimed that "families are strong when they have a function to perform. And the more government, combined with the helping professions establishment, takes away the functions families need to perform—to provide their health care, their child care, their housing—the less purpose there is for the family, per se, to exist."[35]

In order to combat the state's perceived intrusiveness, the NCR has undertaken grassroots initiatives designed to challenge liberal culture point by point. Christian school board members have had success in prohibiting pornography but have frequently met with failure in their efforts to ban "lesbian" books and to teach creationism. New Christian Right local campaigns to reform or undermine public education use the foci of morality and identity to ground political action.[36] The NCR claims that an enormous groundswell of support exists for opening up public schools for religious education (or for allowing homeschooling in place of Head Start, multiculturalism, and sex education), for implementing a "pro-family" tax code, and, in states such as Oregon and Colorado, for attempts to prohibit antidiscrimination laws that protect homosexuals. In this proliferation of issues and initiatives, one can see the crucial elements of NCR activism: the willingness to combat the state, the propensity for local organizing, and the fluid capital resources stored in NCR organizations.[37] By explicitly mobilizing on the basis of a shared identity, the NCR mirrors the challenge of identity politics in important ways, even as it appropriates these tactics in order to attack other identity-based groups. And by honing such a critique, in particular spheres such as education and family as well as in a broader tactical sense, the NCR has continued to contest the premises and the practices of postwar liberalism.

The NCR's broader goal is to evangelize public institutions with an emphasis on structural issues such as economics, law, and education. Much of this work is seen as part of "the great commission" that Christ gave to the apostles. In an attempt to enact this theology, NCR practitioners have mounted grassroots campaigns around issues such as local school board elections, often charging the liberal state with the violation of their constitutional rights to the free exercise of religion. There are earlier examples of Christian Right opposition to curriculum—from the Scopes trial to Kanawha County—but on a more general level, public education is widely seen as the servant of a hostile liberal state. Thus, the NCR's educational battles are charged by a sense of danger or vulnerability. The NCR fears that the liberal goals of promoting a common civic faith, of ensuring the stability of a democratic regime, will lead to the flattening of particularity, the constraint of religious (particularly evangelical Christian) belief, and the stifling of religious practices that cannot be "normalized." The NCR believes that the seeds of this constraint are sown in public schools, whose operations are overseen by those the NCR believes to be hostile secular humanists who cavalierly ignore the risks that public schools pose to the NCR young.

According to the NCR, this educational decline started when the Supreme Court began to apply the First Amendment to public religion in the 1940s, in particular with the 1940 case *Cantwell v. Connecticut*.[38] During the post-war era—in cases such as *McCollum v. Board of Education* (in which the Court ruled that voluntary "released time" religious instruction in public schools was unconstitutional), *Engel v. Vitale* (which ruled that prayer in public schools was a violation of church-state separation), *Abington v. Schempp* (which struck down state-mandated recitation of the Lord's Prayer), *Epperson v. Arkansas* (in which the Court forbade religious censorship of public school curricula), and *Lemon v. Kurtzmann* (wherein the Court established the infamous "Lemon Test," demanding that public policy have a "secular legislative purpose," a primary effect that neither aids nor inhibits religion and does not foster "excessive government entanglement" in religious affairs)—the Supreme Court has taken on a highly activist role in adjudicating conflicts over the role of religion in public education, a role that has stoked the fires of NCR cultural anxiety.[39]

For NCR education activists, this judicial activism has eased the entrance of "humanism" into public schools. To the NCR "humanism" is a permissive philosophy that renders children tolerant of evils such as pornography, gay rights, abortion rights, and one-world government. It is this sense of imminent threat to Christian identity that gives the NCR its energy. Many conservative Christians cite the presence of humanism in public schools as evidence of a double standard in American public discourse, a formal bias against the faithful. As one charismatic Christian put it, "Schools have completely removed anything that has to do with Christianity or God or the Bible or any of that. And then they will let in books like *Heather Has Two Mommies*, real secular and anti-moral books."[40] If conservative Christian viewpoints are being suppressed by liberals—as a fundamentalist Presbyterian put it, "Values are being tilted against Christians, in the name of neutrality"—then the challenge is to generate an alternate educational system.[41]

This challenge must be understood in historical context. Nowhere in the Constitution was education designated as an issue falling under federal authority. Indeed, the Tenth Amendment dictates that education is the responsibility of the states. From the second half of the nineteenth century to the early 1970s, the majority of private schools were Catholic parochial schools (though other religious traditions routinely formed schools, if in much smaller numbers). Following World War II, federal- and state-level assistance to schools increased, as did the use of national educational standards. Each state already possesses guidelines for the allocation of funds to public schools, but not so for private or religious schools. Thus, methods for recognizing, approving, and funding private schools or alternative schools have traditionally been forged in very different contexts, varying from state to state. Legally, it has been necessary to do so in ways that are consistent with both the First and the Fourteenth Amendments, which together shape the state requirements for private schools that have often proved greatly contentious to the NCR. Although funding and certification debates generally revolve around how best to assist parents in enrolling their children in the school of their choice (e.g., through tuition tax credits, deductions, or vouchers), the NCR worries further that the state indoctrinates students in a worldview that "influences how one perceives reality, what meanings are attached to those perceptions, what social arrangements are legitimate, which personal relationships are proper, and what constitutes moral or unethical behavior."[42]

In response, the NCR has both challenged and detached from state education, through either homeschooling or the establishment of Christian schools.[43] Some would be tempted to dismiss the NCR understanding of these realities as conspiracy theory, but at the heart of the movement's concerns is the very real anxiety that the state has placed too much in human hands, not God's.[44] Key to the NCR's arguments is the charge that the state is actually supporting the "religion of secular humanism," the teaching of which NCR families believe violates their own constitutional right to the free exercise of their religion. The assertion is that secular humanism constitutes a "belief system"—traceable to the *Humanist Manifesto*, the writings of John Dewey, Abraham Maslow, and others—that, NCR advocates contend, posits fundamental beliefs about the nature of reality and our relation to this reality and hence must be recognized as religious in its aspirations.

This argument has been advanced and popularized in the influential and often idiosyncratic writings of Tim LaHaye. Although now best known for his coauthorship of the successful *Left Behind* series of apocalyptic fiction,

LaHaye has long been a key figure in NCR culture, particularly its educational activism. By the mid-1960s, LaHaye had gained notoriety for his proclamations that secular humanism had taken over the media, the government, and education. He called on Christian conservatives to speak out not just in church but in the public political arena. In 1965, he founded Christian High School in San Diego, and by 1975 the institution was large enough to constitute its own school system. In 1970, LaHaye cofounded Christian Heritage College to help train teachers for Christian schools. In 1971, he founded Family Life Seminars to advise families and schools on how to resist the corrosive influences of liberal culture. Participants in these seminars are trained in "biblical principles for family living as a means of counteracting the harmful influence of humanistic education."[45] Along with his wife, Beverly, LaHaye cofounded Concerned Women for America (CWA) in 1979, and based on its organizational strength, he was able to solidify contacts with other NCR organizations during this important period in the movement's growth.

LaHaye propagated his ideas in a series of widely read books, including *The Battle for the Public Schools*. In conspiratorial language, he asserted that schools were no longer interested in learning but in training American youth "to be anti-God, antimoral, antifamily, anti-free enterprise and anti-American." He cites poor student performance in standardized tests and general skills, blaming the influence of Dewey on public education. Using the antiliberal and anti-elite language that is popular with the NCR, LaHaye attributes these trends to radical sixties activists who he believes have invaded the schools to create the proper mental climate for revolution. The state effectively allows this usurpation of parental authority to continue in the name of curricular neutrality, which LaHaye considers a blatant disregard for the "spontaneous outcries of parents and citizen groups throughout the land." The book is replete with elaborate diagrams of the web of organizations that control the schools (including the National Endowment for the Humanities, the Department of Education, the Trilateral Commission, and, of course, the Illuminati) and of the thickets of anti-Christian ideas through which students are unwittingly being led.[46]

Not only are these tangled networks responsible for unorthodox ideas, LaHaye believes, but they are also ineffective at basic education. According to LaHaye, "liberal educational philosophy" promotes grade inflation, a "look-and-say" method of teaching reading (as opposed to his favored phonics method), and outcome-based education, which privileges meeting technical pedagogical requirements over the inculcation of character. To LaHaye, this is all little more than "educrat propaganda" whose falsehood is highlighted by the superior test scores of Christian school students.[47] In his account, humanist education is guilty of greed, brainwashing children, pedagogical inefficiency, and academic arrogance. Two normative issues underlie this litany of accusations. The first concerns liberalism's ironic intolerance of religion, and the second revolves around what LaHaye sees as the state's usurpation of parental autonomy. He believes that liberalism's neutrality actually enforces a narrow conception of personhood and citizenship (both relying on the notion of the rationally disinterested agent) and inculcates these views through an educational program that the NCR claims is a "religion of humanism." This state of affairs, if accurate, would clearly disadvantage the religious, or at least those whose devotion mandates a clear separation from the taint of "worldly" influence.

LaHaye also believes that public education prevents parents from effectively rearing children. He complains that "God has placed in a child's heart a giant shrine for his parents. . . . Because of our national romance with education, we have gradually remanded that place to the public school."[48] State-controlled education has forced NCR parents to pay taxes in support of the very school system that they believe undermines the "traditional" values of conservative Christianity and the patriarchal family. Unlike in the halcyon days of yore, when each student possessed a well-thumbed McGuffey reader and respected his or her elders, liberal-humanist education promotes criticism of the very values that the NCR champions and that it claims were once normative for all citizens.

The story of public education in the postwar era is thus one of decline. Instead of promoting patriotism, Christianity, and free enterprise, the schools now promote multiculturalism, critical thought, and sex education. The last is only the most noxious example of the state's assumption of time-honored parental tasks. For LaHaye, compulsory sex education is a major culprit in the wider moral and communal breakdown that concerns the NCR. Teachers are no longer paragons of virtue but mere "educrats of sexology" who subject innocents to "sexploitation."[49] Liberal culture is actively promoting secular humanism in an effort to "take over" educational institutions and train generations of young minds who will change the legal and political structure of the nation according to their will. Perhaps what is most scandalous to LaHaye is that tax dollars are being "inappropriately" used to wrest autonomy away from Christian parents. LaHaye concludes that parents must take back school boards, imposing order and discipline on their communities in whatever way is necessary to combat liberalism.[50]

Despite the conspiratorial tone in much of this critique, it is nonetheless evident that the NCR has generated an issue that challenges the premises and practices of postwar liberalism. Rooted largely in ideas such as LaHaye's, Christian schools and home schools have vigorously lobbied for tax privileges and exemptions for parents who opt out of the public school system. Most of these schools, if not associated with independent school systems, are part of the American Association of Christian Schools (AACS). Founded in 1972, the AACS boasts well over 1,000 schools and 350,000 students.[51] The organization helped to unite local schools and districts under a national umbrella organization and thereby also to link the AACS to powerful NCR funding organs. The desire to preserve the sacred registers of Christian identity and to destabilize liberalism is clear in the AACS charter goals: "1) to bring children to salvation; 2) to inform children about the word of God; 3) to keep children immersed in the word of God; 4) to keep children separate from the world; 5) to encourage children to proselytize the unsaved; 6) to lead children to enter full-time Christian service as preachers, teachers, evangelists, etc.; and, 7) failing this, to have children become full-time Christians, living their lives, whatever they do, wherever they are, always for the glory of God."[52]

Most Christian schools therefore constitute what sociologists call a "total system," incorporating commitment, discipline, absolutism, missionary zeal, and conformity in all facets of school life (including teachers, curriculum, doctrine, community, and school structure). The formation of these schools is usually aided by a national organization such as the AACS, but it is usually precipitated by the work of a local NCR community. A community member might be outraged by the teaching of evolution in public schools, appalled by the popularity of Marilyn Manson among local children, or distressed by state usurpation of the family's role in education. Generally, a congregation responds by culling teachers from a local church, who are then trained to meet the minimum state requirements for certification. These schools differ from conventional parochial schools by virtue of their antagonistic stance toward liberal society. They are formed in the context of perceived persecution and have strict theological and political requirements for admission. The students are inculcated with an unwavering belief in and obedience to the antiliberal Christianity imparted in their schools. Meditation and prayer suffuse the school day, all intended to establish and preserve students' relationship with the risen Christ. Through the integration of Scripture and subject matter, the Christian school student is cleansed of the "dirty" influence of liberal-humanist public education. The community is thereby clearly marked off from the profaned space of liberal society.

These schools believe that statist education is all-encompassing, recognizing no reality outside itself. In response, the NCR asserts its own reality by removing its children from state education. Where liberal education perpetuates the influence of humanism, the usurpation of parental rights, and the invasion of privacy constituted by failure to convey "traditional" information, the very establishment of Christian schools is seen as an antibody to the liberal virus. Textbooks are evaluated by textbook reviewers Mel and Norma Gabler, among others, as well as by national organizations such as the Creation Science Research Center. The NCR sees textbooks as a particularly powerful vehicle for values indoctrination and in response seeks either to purge objectionable elements from texts or to produce alternate texts of its own (often coupled with "learning guides" from figures such as James Dobson, head of Focus on the Family).

Many of these texts begin by asserting that all religious devotion other than conservative evangelicalism is illegitimate. Asian religions are coolly dismissed as cultic or lacking the substance of monotheism; a firm finger is wagged at Judaism and Islam, monotheisms that have erred; and intense denunciations are hurled at other Christians.[53] American history is cast in a similarly loaded way: one text claims that "every Democratic president departed from constitutional principles of limited government, instead preferring to advance the behemoth of the secular state and a socialist economic system."[54] Generally Christian school advocates rhapsodize over the era of common Protestant schooling and the McGuffey readers, waxing Tocquevillean over the thriving religious context of yore. They link the demise of this culture to the late nineteenth or early twentieth century when the state was centralized and administered by liberal philosophy. In keeping with this interpretation of American history, student movements and protest movements in general (including the civil rights and labor movements) are attacked as anti-American and anti-Christian. These notions are part of these schools' general concern to exclude those behavioral standards and curricula considered inconsistent with biblical principles (as these are understood in the schools).

Christian education seeks explicitly to mold young people in Christ's image. According to veteran Christian schools advisers James W. Dewink and Carl D. Herbster, public schools effectively force students to reject the religion of their upbringing by accommodating to worldly powers and values.[55] Although this aversion to accommodation is also shared by Christian antiliberals such as Jim Wallis and Philip Berrigan, Christian school advocates possess the powerful apprehension that God's will cannot be followed in public schools and that the establishment of Christian schools is a form of spiritual rebirth. The independent, "parent-oriented school" is most common (and easiest to maintain for tax purposes), though many schools are also established as part of a local church.[56] "Spiritual" standards are used to filter enrollment, hoping to eliminate the presence of "unsaved students" or "students from families associated with cults like the Jehovah's Witnesses, eastern religions, witchcraft, and other religions not based on Scripture."[57] Similar standards are used in hiring personnel, so that all levels of school life can be modeled on Christ's action as the organizers understand it.

Thus the average Christian school is quite self-consciously a separate institution, seeking to avoid the corrupting influence of liberal political order while maintaining the long-term goal of revitalizing American society—community by community—according to its beliefs. Theological diversity exists among the schools, but all are explicitly antiliberal.[58] They quite openly seek to inculcate their version of Christian virtues and character traits, a desire reflected in the tripartite pledge of allegiance adopted by many (involving the American Flag, the "Christian Flag," and the Bible). The life of the schools focuses somewhat on individualism and self-actualization but primarily on communal values that will positively shape the self. Christian school educators see mainstream individualism as mere humanism, preferring instead a focus on the person's salvation through grace and imitation of Christ. The Christian self recognizes, however, that nothing is possible through human effort alone and so submits to God's will; this submission involves membership in a confessing community and adherence to strict norms. Hence, Christian schools are of vital importance in the salvation history in which members claim to participate. As the student handbook from Ebenezer Christian School acknowledges, education is intended "to help students realize that there is not any difference between the secular and the sacred."[59]

This culture is a response to the insufficiency of traditional liberal statist solutions to cultural conflict. The schools aim to socialize students by transmitting values, behaviors, and beliefs that are necessary to function in NCR culture.[60] The establishment of separate institutions is a way to restore control to churches and families, whose concerns the NCR feels have been railroaded by liberalism. To maintain control and autonomy at the smallest level of organization, Christian schools seek to limit state regulation to matters such as health care and fire safety.[61] To those who inhabit this culture, public schools are not neutral space where knowledge is presented, detached from any larger worldview, to students; rather, they are spaces where Christian identity itself is subjected to "antifamily" and "anti-Christian" pedagogy. Balancing citizenship in the Kingdom of Heaven with the need for worldly action, Christian schools exist as a countersign to liberal political order.[62]

Drawing the Line

Once more we see how Christian antiliberalism willingly and self-consciously seeks to mark its distance from the deracinated world of liberalism. Like Jim Wallis or Philip Berrigan, Christian schools seek to counteract the "pernicious" influence of the reigning values of the day by embodying their understanding of Christianity in the public sphere. Yet unlike these other Christian antiliberals, the NCR is diffuse in its concerns and decentralized. To sharpen the NCR's concerns, and to establish more parity with the other Christian antiliberals in my comparative framework, I turn now to the practice of Michael Farris and the Home School Legal Defense Association (HSLDA). Farris received his law degree from Gonzaga Law School in Spokane, Washington, where he soon began to accept cases prosecuting abortion clinics and pornographers. Farris's compelling oratory and aggressive practice drew the notice of NCR leaders, and in 1980 he became executive director of the Washington State Moral Majority.[63] He foresaw the organization, which he renamed the Bill of Rights Legal Foundation, as a Christian alternative to the American Civil Liberties Union, which would lobby on behalf of "Christian" causes such as school prayer and outlawing abortion. During the same period, Farris began an association with LaHaye's CWA, in time becoming the organization's chief legal counsel.

Farris became something of a terror within the courtrooms, openly baiting judges and using the public forum of a trial to articulate NCR grievances.[64] Pressured to befriend moderate conservatives, Farris claimed he was unable to do so, since the "mere" economic conservatism they championed relied too heavily on state regulation and in so doing, according to Farris, flirted with communism.[65] During the 1980s, Farris helped maintain the NCR's social movement energy, issuing extreme statements ("we kill off old people to save money for sex education films"), participating in public forums or roundtables, and often organizing protests.[66] His detractors claimed he sought to ban books from schools and libraries, concerned only to apply his narrow interests to society at large. Farris responded that he merely provided concerned parents with legal recourse and a forum to make their voices heard.

The loudest such outcry came with the 1986 case *Mozert v. Hawkins*

County, Tennessee.[67] In 1983, seven fundamentalist families, led by local parent Vicki Frost, filed a joint suit against their public school system. The parents were concerned about the use of a Holt text containing multicultural readings on a number of reportedly offensive subjects, including witchcraft, pacifism, and Hinduism. They claimed that the school system was violating its own claims to neutrality and "indoctrinating" their children with non-neutral values such as tolerance, relativism, and evolution, effectively undermining their religious beliefs by implying that values can change according to time and place. The parents consulted famed NCR textbook reviewers the Gablers, whose regular scrutiny of public educational materials operates according to the following convictions: children belong to parents and not the state; tax dollars pay for books; and Christians can vote school board officials in or out.[68]

The parents tended to vacillate between charges against "illegal books" and calls for "viable alternatives" within the system. Eventually, Farris was called in to represent the families. He charged that the school system was not neutral but was teaching the "religion of secular humanism," thus violating the plaintiffs' constitutional right to free exercise of their religion. Farris argued that the school system was acting as an arm of the state, promoting a "militant religious system" that undermined Christianity.[69] He argued that if it was illegal to teach Christianity in a pluralistic school system, then teaching secular humanism should also be barred.

It is clear from this rhetoric that Farris sees public schools as the site of an intractable opposition between the liberal state and NCR families. Ideally, evangelical Christians could exist as citizens of both the Kingdom of God and the United States. But, according to the well-worn claim Farris invoked, the demands of the state had come into conflict with those of his clients' faith. What was more, he asserted, the state's coercion was illegal within its own constitutional system. The lower courts ruled for the plaintiffs, but when the case came to the Sixth Circuit Court, the majority opinion concluded that, contrary to Farris's claims, "mere exposure" to the values in the reader could not constitute a violation of the free exercise clause.

This case was an important and widely observed legal challenge to the authority and presuppositions of liberal political order. Although Christian Right cultural crusades have often been advanced in the past century, it is arguably with the *Mozert* case that the NCR's preoccupation with defending Christian *identity* against the state first manifested itself, and with it the NCR's most pointed antiliberalism. In the aftermath of *Mozert*, the conflict between the NCR and public schools led Farris to establish the HSLDA. He had long been convinced that "public schools invariably transmit a religious worldview, so they are 'per se unconstitutional.'"[70] Yet with so many NCR organizations already defending Christian schools, Farris chose to focus his new organization on Christian families and communities whose disenchantment with and antagonism toward public education were even deeper. The organization was founded with the intent to grant legal protection to homeschooling families. Membership costs one hundred dollars per year, per family, and guarantees full representation throughout a legal proceeding (with no other attorneys' fees required). In 1990, the National Center for Home Education was created specifically as a watchdog to spot federal and state legislation that is relevant to HSLDA concerns.

The Christian homeschooling movement is related to the Christian schools movement both normatively and practically. Homeschoolers share with Christian schools an antipathy toward liberalism, but most important is their shared outrage over the state's usurpation of parental authority in child rearing. Home schools have thrived in recent decades in part because they represent a concentration of parental authority in the safe space of the home and also because the financial commitment of private education is beyond the means of many NCR families. Practically, many home schools are founded in fallout from a conflict between Christian schools and the state; often, small informal meetings between local parents (almost always mothers) serve as the basis for home-school organization.[71] Longtime NCR leader James Dobson's Focus on the Family radio show in the early 1980s included regular interviews with Seventh Day Adventist educational researcher Dr. Raymond Moore, who had long advocated homeschooling for young children.[72] As these ideas began to influence Dobson and others, the NCR appropriated them as ways in which to promote "traditional" models of the family.[73] Indeed, for many NCR parents the commitment to homeschooling is "an extension of their efforts to live out a faith somewhat at odds with the surrounding culture."[74] Against what is perceived as widespread permissiveness, NCR homeschooling parents seek to craft different models of both educational and personal development for their children, including among other things a commitment to what Farris calls the Twelve Spiritual Goals of Christian Parenting (for example: "My child will be sure of his or her salvation" and "My child will love and understand the Lord").[75]

The NCR is often divided over the extent to which Christian schools should submit to minimum state requirements for test proficiency or teaching certification. When schools refuse to acquiesce, the only available educational option for many is to establish homeschooling. Many parents use set curricula provided by organizations such as Accelerated Christian Education (ACE) or the Christian Liberty Academy Satellite Schools (CLASS). For an annual cost substantially below that of private school enrollment in most areas, a local parent or pastor can purchase one of these curriculum programs for training as a school principal. In each of these programs, the buyer receives a training course, textbooks, workbooks, and general "pro-Christian" materials.[76] The programs place the burden of learning not on the parent/teacher but on the student, who is responsible for her or his own academic growth. Even the most mundane activities are "biblical," as with handwriting assignments that ask children to copy out Scripture verses.

All these strategies are, like those of Christian schools, legal. Home schools are most frequently located in rural areas, and in most states only a high school diploma is required to gain a teaching certificate for teaching at home.[77] Most homeschooling parents boast of the superiority of their children's test scores over those of public school students, while simultaneously expressing their fears over the effects of state regulation. The HSLDA attempts to guarantee parents' rights to educate at home, defending them against "harassment" by the agents of the liberal state. Indeed, Farris claims that it was his constant exposure to "cases in which Christians have been harassed, intimidated, threatened and silenced" that led him to form the HSLDA in the first place.[78] Like so many other NCR activists, Farris is galvanized by the notion that Christians' rights have been ignored (e.g., children are denied the opportunity to be educated at home, a job that requires attendance at a "new age seminar," or children being forced to view "explicit" material in class), their civil liberties attacked.

As with other antiliberals, Farris deftly uses liberal rights talk to advance antiliberal claims. His HSLDA sourcebook, *Where Do I Draw the Line?*, is peppered with such claims, from the state's "growing insensitivity to the rights of churches" to "secularists' efforts to drive Christianity from the public schools" (Farris notes a cancellation of Handel's *Messiah*).[79] Farris sees these attacks as "the consequence of ideas that are being systematically taught in our schools and communicated through mass media."[80] He urges parents and local communities to oppose public education, mixing his justifications by claiming both that parents' rights are being usurped and that the state is immoral. He contends that citizens of a democracy are required to obey the law as long as it overlaps with God's law, but a citizen of the Kingdom of Heaven is obliged to challenge laws that conflict with God's. Further, he asserts that no one is obliged to obey orders from government officials that are not authorized by law.[81]

Farris urges two courses of action, the first homeschooling itself, the second vigilant public activism. The long-term solution to the threat of liberal public education is parent-controlled education. Farris estimates that more than seven hundred thousand children are homeschooled, despite the fact that "humanists" control not only public schools but the legal mechanisms regulating private education. He further claims that in 1982 all homeschooling was illegal but that currently, thanks largely to the efforts of the HSLDA, only Michigan forbids it. Yet the state enforces its norms by "harassing" home schools with requirements that "exceed" those of public schools: official visits to home schools, demanding that children enroll in public schools; obligations that parents obtain state teaching certificates; requiring students to pass state tests; zoning laws preventing churches from establishing schools in their buildings; or requiring parents to submit lesson plans for their home school a year in advance.

Parents and homeschoolers can defend themselves against these challenges by petitioning a number of NCR organizations, including the Christian Legal Society (founded in 1961 to train lawyers "to serve Jesus Christ effectively through the legal profession"), the Christian Action Council (which "exists to raise a biblical Christian voice in the councils of government and courts of law"), and the AACS.[83] The HSLDA itself represents more than twenty-four thousand homeschooling families. Farris also encourages NCR families to become involved in the political process in order to make communities more hospitable to home schools. Learning how the political system works, he claims, is the most effective way of realizing the NCR's goals and principles insofar as it would enable parents and activists to transform the political system from within. In order to determine the state of a local educational system, Farris recommends vigilant parent interrogation of children, teachers, and the PTA. If education is found wanting, Farris advises rigorous engagement with school boards and city councils, focusing on issues relevant to political jurisdiction (particularly zoning licenses for churches, state "interference" with home schools, and "illicit" community presences such as gay rights, pornography, and abortion clinics). He urges the NCR devout to organize, network, protest, publish, and lobby to have their concerns addressed and realized.

Practicing what he preached, Farris himself entered the political arena in Virginia's 1993 elections. Running for lieutenant governor, he used his long-standing contacts with the CWA to mobilize his candidacy. Gearing up for his campaign, which he saw largely as an opportunity to publicize and politicize his antiliberal concerns, Farris had access to the CWA's forty active chapters and seventy liaisons to churches and community groups; its telecommunications tree, which helped to spread word of "hot" issues to its fifteen thousand members; and its legislative hot line. The major issues of his campaign were an outgrowth of the HSLDA. He called for smaller schools, a more activist role for parents in school choice and programs, and an opposition to outcome-based education. But the Farris campaign also initially concerned itself with more "mainstream" issues such as educational and legal reform, tax cuts, and reduced government debt.[84] Farris advocated private tuition and homeschooling tax breaks allowing parents to purchase private education or acquire materials needed to school at home.

He also repeated his frequent claim that public schools taught the "religion of secular humanism," violating Christians' right to free exercise, and that schools are a front for "the state's program of values indoctrination" on racial integration and politics.[85] Homeschoolers, he claimed, should not have to pay taxes in support of an educational system hostile to their faith. This was the first time such a wide audience heard his claim that public education bordered on unconstitutionality: if schools teach values, and "since inculcation of values is inherently a religious act, what the public schools are doing is indoctrinating your children in religion," which violates church-state separation. On the basis of this conclusion, Farris pronounced that it was acceptable to reject state educational standards that conflict with their religious views, even stating, "If, for instance, you believe you have received a mystical communication from God telling you not to use the Standard Achievement Test, then your belief is entitled to constitutional protection."[86]

When it is to his advantage, however, Farris attacks the priority of church-state separation. In his view, the Declaration of Independence deals with the laws of nature (which he interprets as reflections of his God's laws) and should trump the more quotidian concerns of the Constitution (which has a presumption for separation).[87] On economic issues, Farris and his backers believe that capitalism alone is consistent with Christianity and that the United States must return to the gold standard to ensure national sovereignty and autonomy. They support tax cuts and oppose government health insurance or state support for the poor; they endorse the death penalty and advocate an isolationist foreign policy. Throughout his campaign, Farris accused his opponent of "religious bigotry" and "radical feminism," two of the NCR's long-standing key terms for liberal government. The extremism of Farris's views and campaign tactics ultimately lost him the election, yet his initial goal of publicity was more than met.

The antiliberalism of homeschooling has, in the years since 1993, continued unabated. In early 1994, for example, Congress was to vote on H.R. 6, an education bill requisitioning $17.4 billion for the "Improving America's Schools Act." Democrat George Miller had inserted a late amendment requiring all full-time teachers to be state-certified in each subject they taught, on penalty of withdrawal of federal funding. Learning of Miller's amendment, Republican Dick Armey sought an exemption for children taught at home or in nonpublic schools. This proposal was defeated by the House Education and Labor Committee. Armey alerted Farris, and the HSLDA contacted 150 state and regional homeschooling organizations, who used a phone-tree network to contact an estimated nine hundred thousand home-school parents, who in turn pressured their representatives to support the Armey amendment or to quash H.R. 6. Christian radio helped publicize the HSLDA's campaign, and in the eight days prior to the vote, congressional switchboards were jammed with five hundred thousand to one million calls. The campaign was successful: the House voted 429–1 to defeat Miller's amendment and 374–53 to approve Armey's.[88]

These and other incidents testify to the NCR's vitality as an antiliberal movement embroiled in the struggle to preserve identity. New Christian Right identity is, of course, not fixed or static prior to its entry into the political process (although many in the NCR do in fact believe this). But in the contest over the meanings and directions of education, the NCR's framework of religious norms and beliefs nonetheless constitutes an authoritative repertoire for public activism. The incremental construction of NCR educational culture has consistently and self-consciously targeted the fundamental precepts and practices of liberal political order. The growing strength of this educational presence does not simply proclaim the vitality of the sacred registers of politics against the normalizing practices of the liberal state. It also enables NCR practitioners to engage in a continuous enactment and development of their own identity and self-understanding. Christian schools and home schools constitute a sequence of disturbances aimed at liberal order, disruptions that allow the NCR to demarcate and protect an alternate public space where the lived contours of its devotional world can flourish and grow.

The Sacred Registers of Education

In the complicated world of the NCR's antiliberalism, it is clear that for the activists nothing less than their experience of the world as Christians is at stake. Although the NCR, in all its vast organizational diversity, is occasionally prone to functioning in a manner similar to that of mainstream social movements or conventional issues-based organizations, the majority of NCR practitioners (particularly those found on the local level and involved in educational struggles) are involved in a more agonistic contest over the sacred registers of politics. What is most distinct is that the NCR is not always, or even often, seeking redress from or representation in the state. Instead, its antiliberal edge is sharpened until identity itself—and the felt, sensible experience of its world through the sacred registers—is wielded as a countersign to liberalism.

The politicization of identity has its origins in the 1960s, the political moment from which Christian antiliberalism more broadly emerged. Concerns about identity and meaning are, for the NCR, manifestations of discontent with available roles for citizens. Yet as I explained in the introduction, there is more at work in Christian antiliberalism than identity politics alone. I understand identity politics as a reliance on features of the self or community (race or gender, for example, rather than institutional affiliation) as the substance of political organization and action. The sacred registers, however, do not exactly share the terrain of recognition or legislation that accommodates many movements associated with identity politics. The sacred registers are more specifically a religious mode of self-understanding and experience by means of which the beliefs, emotions, sensibilities, observations, and commitments of particular individuals are crafted into a perception, or a register, of political reality. In other words, the NCR's politicization of schooling is not necessarily a demand that citizens with specific identities be included in the political process or be mollified with legislative redress; it is in many ways a dismissal of that very process, one that religiously constitutes both a defense of an extant form of American Christianity and an important innovation within it. Certainly NCR activists are eager to work within this system in many cases; but they do so agonistically, in the hope not so much of gaining entrance as of declaring their religious difference from it, the very difference they experience in the sacred registers of politics. Such declarations forge new connections and modes of organization among NCR practitioners, enabling them both to preserve and to renegotiate fundamental aspects of their identity. These practitioners believe that defense of the sacred registers permits them to make claims to which liberalism has generally been insensitive, linking both activism and education with conservative evangelical faith. Educational contestation by the NCR, then, is nothing less than a sustained project of identity enactment and will formation.

To this extent, NCR antiliberalism bears little resemblance to conventional interest-group politicking, nor does it truly constitute a defensive reaction to some form of social "deprivation." Even though the NCR regards contemporary liberalism as antagonistic, there is little sense that these antiliberals are a deprived or antediluvian minority.[89] As is evident in the NCR, Christian antiliberals are not concerned exclusively with strategy but with meaning, identity, and their experience of their world. Religious identity, particularly when mobilized in opposition to political order, can transect social and geographical boundaries in ways that enable fruitful political action. Yet part of the uniqueness of the NCR, and of Christian antiliberalism more broadly, is their inability to be grasped fully by any single interpretive or analytic model. Their operations and even their own self-understandings are charged by fractiousness, flux, and multiplicity.

The NCR's self-avowed distrust of "mainstream" politics, in particular of the political and cultural boundaries constructed in the post–World War II era of American liberalism, brings with it a preference for mobilization on the basis of local and particular affiliations. In some ways the emergence and restructuring of social identities and political space are responses to the material conditions outlined in chapter 1.[90] Yet NCR activism nonetheless privileges culture over economics as the locus of political contestation; as the movement's educational campaigns make abundantly clear, culture is no mere displacement of class. Religious practice and belief are not categories that can be fixed or essentialized, nor are they neatly bound to the private sphere of the liberal political imagination; rather, both belief and practice are constructed, mobilized, and modified through the specificity of everyday action, community, discourse, and consciousness. The NCR works on and works out its identity through specific challenges to liberalism that are maintained in the emotional registers of outrage at lurid textbooks, concern over the welfare of Christian children, and faith that individual salvation and rectitude guide the development of alternatives to liberalism. These meanings and registers of identity are mobilized at the most specific of levels, in addition to the macrolevels of soteriology and theology. They are deployed in libraries, when hands turn pages thought to be laced with corruption. They are audible in the oratory of NCR leaders such as Farris. They are visible in the Christian flags that are draped from schoolroom ceilings, the murals on the walls of Christian schools, and the familiar sights of home that form the educational horizon of many NCR children.

The sacred registers are cultivated as marks of collective will, operating through vast communications networks, circulating through independent textbooks and curricula, and promulgated in conventions and institutions. Where the NCR differs from conventional forms of identity politics (often discussed under the rubrics "new social movements" or "multiculturalism") is in its refusal to see identity as merely so much "symbolic capital" to be deployed within extant institutions by rationally governed interest groups seeking material benefits. This is a materialist interpretation that sits awkwardly with the postmaterialist concerns and context of the NCR, for which culture, meaning, and identity are far more complex than material resources. For these activists, their identity as devout evangelical Christians is politicized against their will in a liberal regime; they experience this politicization as difference in the sacred registers of politics. In response, they aim to regain control of the politicization of their beliefs and self-understandings, wielding them instead as countersigns to liberal political order.

In this contest for control of meaning, important issues are raised concerning the status or even the desirability of a common constitutional or moral framework. Christian antiliberals claim that liberal political order has, at best, an awkward relationship to cultures and identities that do not admit their own partiality or that do not map neatly onto liberal political schemes. Liberalism seeks to balance demands for cultural survival and recognition with "the established principles of the politics of equal respect," hoping in this way to reduce the fractious presence of identity politics in public life.[91] Yet when one examines religious activism such as the NCR's, it becomes evident that the often intractable issues bound up in culture and identity cannot neatly be limited to "established principles" or common frameworks, however laudable these political goals may seem in the abstract. The NCR's activism—like that of other Christian antiliberals—is proof that the "established" and "common" elements of political culture are still being contested.

It is vital not to ignore the concerns raised by antiliberal activists such as the NCR. Regardless of how these concerns and programs strike us individually, they are signs of discontent that merit understanding; there can be no dialogue or constructive political work without such understanding. It is folly to think that the stuff of Christian textbooks and schools is a distraction from more "important" socioeconomic matters or from more "legitimate" expressions of identity.[92] There are certainly serious concerns to be raised about the NCR's near rejection of "common" civic identity in favor of narrowly defined Christian identity: this may indeed represent, as many commentators worry, a fraying of the bonds of the "common good" or an undermining of the very ideals of publicity and commonality on which democracy thrives.[93] Compelling as this language of the common good is, however, it relies on the questionable assumption that an elusive political "common ground" not only can be achieved but will be a balm for political wounds.

A necessary first step is to avoid making easy assertions about the priority of socioeconomic issues and to attend to the motivations and concerns of those who turn to the sacred registers for their politics, feeling that the system has abandoned them. Only on the basis of understanding can dialogue proceed; and without such understanding, there can be no hope of addressing the concerns of these activists. Culture and identity have a political weight and value of their own; the claims of Christian antiliberals are both civically interesting and politically significant. If there is to be any engagement with the NCR in a democratically legitimate fashion, there must first be a more substantive reckoning with its theological and cultural concerns.

Not for a moment am I suggesting that NCR theology deserves to be represented on local school boards and legislatures, since many citizens would be understandably concerned about the social policies often advocated by affiliates of the NCR. The NCR has supported legislation such as Colorado's Amendment 2 (1992), for example, which sought to overturn a ban against homosexual discrimination, and has advocated replacing evolutionary theory in the classrooms with "creation science." One may disagree with the NCR on these issues for reasons that have little or nothing to do with religion; but regardless of reservations about these matters, it is hardly prudent (much less would it embody the liberal virtues of respect and tolerance) to dismiss such claims as fanatical or tyrannical. One of the key lessons to be learned from the NCR's antiliberalism is that a democratic culture must not waver on its commitment to tolerating the intolerant.[94] In other words, though one may find the NCR's views "frightening" or "shocking," this is precisely how the NCR views the commitments of its critics. Neither liberal nor antiliberal viewpoints have any priority antecedent to the political process itself; both are equal participants in the culture-sustaining dialogues of a democracy.

Yet this very contention, that the NCR is or should be an equal participant in conversations concerning the shape of democratic culture, raises questions about just what shape these dialogues or conversations should take. The trenchant issues raised by Christian antiliberals (and, indeed, by identity politics more generally) are not easily accommodated by methodologies oriented toward disinterested dialogue, rights of recognition, and neutral cultural evaluation. The NCR goes beyond such concerns in its suspicion of the very legitimacy of liberalism. So a formal methodological emphasis on dialogue or evaluative politics is part of the very procedural liberalism the NCR seeks to contest: the NCR appropriates the language of recognition to subvert the political system of which this language is a part; and it frequently rejects the very concept of equal respect on the grounds that it gives license to social practices the NCR finds abominable. The notion that critical reason can effectively counter political power— whether wielded by governments or sought by social movements—is a conjecture that seems flimsy when measured against the complicated practices of Christian antiliberals. How does one simply convince agonistic identity groups to embrace a national culture or a critical ethos of dialogic rationality? It is difficult to imagine that these demands would be embraced by NCR homeschoolers. This is not to suggest that the NCR should form the horizon of a theory of identity politics but only that most accounts of political presences such as these suffer from an unfortunate detachment from their social world. The turn to particular meanings and identities in politics is not simply a cause or a symptom of larger changes in American public culture. As manifested in the Christian antiliberal cultivation of the sacred registers, it is a political phenomenon possessed of its own significance that challenges the restrictions it claims characterize liberal democracies, destabilizes the often artificial boundary between public and private, and strives to pluralize the political sphere with the introduction of forms of participation far more robust than it claims liberalism can tolerate.

The NCR's defense of the sacred registers is no flight from the modern world. Rather, such activism calls attention to the multiple valences along which identity is constructed and to the ways in which liberal political order may privilege a mode of citizenship that, by contrast, is singular. This has clear implications for participation in politics, for critics claim that liberal political order demands the privatization of identity as a condition for public participation. To acknowledge the power of this criticism, made by critics far more numerous than just conservative evangelicals, is not tacitly to endorse NCR educational programs. Rather, it is to acknowledge that these programs are evidence of a need that is not being met in American democracy.

Appreciation of these forms of religious social criticism, and the potentially deep fractures they uncover in liberal political order, reveals not only the closed spaces of incommensurable discourses but also some potential openings for political practice created by the politicization of religion.[95] New social movements that mobilize around issues of meaning or identity are not prima facie inconsistent with liberal democratic norms or with "common" public culture. For example, Jürgen Habermas believes that identity politics, if subjected to the constraints of what he calls communicative rationality, can avoid the imposition of antidemocratic or particularistic values on the broader society.[96] Even when analyzing a political presence as challenging as the NCR's, I agree with Habermas that movements of this sort can promote engagement with and understanding of our own political culture and call attention to political resources that lie untapped by conventional liberalism.[97]

Not all such movements have "liberalizing" impulses—clearly the NCR does not recognize its own fallibility, nor is it willing to integrate into the broader polity on terms other than its own, both conditions of Habermasian public discourse.[98] However, to suggest that only "liberal" or "progressive" movements may enjoy these forms of participation is to replicate precisely the form of liberalism the NCR so hotly contests, privileging only a single register of political experience. This does not mean that we must support the NCR or other identity movements whose motivations and actions we may find disturbing; yet neither must we write them out of our theoretical reckoning prior to an engagement with their concerns based on their own self-understandings.

Without attention to this detail, those who seek to understand the sacred registers of politics may ironically endorse constraints likely to promote the same type of backlash suffered by conventional liberalism. The world is replete with antiliberal impulses, and the contest over meaning does not always point in liberalizing directions. Yet these more antagonistic forms of activity are vital and contain critical impulses that are potentially viable in a democratic culture. This wide range of possibilities for conflict and mobilization must remain open to our understanding.

Identity is not fixed but is enacted in often disruptive ways.[99] If responses to such disruptions entail calls to establish sameness, this may serve only to "convert differences into modes of otherness" in a way that can stoke the fires of political or religious backlash.[100] The perils of these approaches to identity politics can be avoided with rigorous attention to the lived world of religion. The NCR transforms religious meanings and self-understandings from parochial concerns to means of exerting influence on both the state and the economy. Thus the emergence of NCR educational culture has been methodically designed to expose what William Connolly calls the "fundaments" of liberalism. Through the continuous enactment of identity within this educational subculture, and through a continual series of disturbances aimed at liberal order, the NCR has succeeded in creating an alternate public space where the lived contours of its religious world can flourish.

The NCR thus constitutes a challenge to liberalism, both in terms of its grassroots and localist tactics and in its aversion to overly "thin" conceptions of politics and identity. Like its evangelical predecessors, the NCR feels that America is in a state of drastic moral decline, the responsibility for which rests largely on the shoulders of liberalism, which the NCR feels has created an atmosphere of moral laxity by promoting philosophical suspicion of the religious and communal values that should properly guide political life. The NCR's local activism is undergirded by a broader antiliberal strategy wherein activists use the "moral campaigns" of local parents, primarily those concerning the education of their children, as openings onto broader debates about the economy and the political process, as these threaten the sacred registers.

The cultural protest of alternate education addresses existential issues that the NCR believes liberal institutions block out. It is also an attempt to create a substantive emotional alternative to what is perceived as the unflinching logic of liberal culture, an alternative that is deeply meaningful to those who follow it. New Christian Right educational culture is intended to serve as a visible sign of the risen Christ manifested in profane society. The NCR believes that its schools cultivate virtues, tend to souls, and turn hearts toward Christ. Prior to a direct engagement with this culture, my own tendency was to overlook the emotional or experiential meanings of this education. Yet despite the seemingly hyperbolic assertions that NCR leaders make about liberal conspiracy, and though the culture itself can be exclusionary in its theology and practice, it is clear that this manifestation of Christian antiliberalism is a heartfelt defense of identity.

As a mass movement, the NCR has steadfastly charged liberalism with ignorance of the emotional and devotional valences of its citizenry and abetting the rise of social corruption and decay through its reliance on rationalism and neutrality. Both operating within the political mainstream and detaching from it, the NCR privileges grassroots activism as a mode of political empowerment and thus helps, through the establishment of Christian schools and home schools, to satisfy a practical and normative need felt by many practitioners.

This educational and devotional subculture that is so contestatory, so riven with contradiction, and so politically "other" is part of Christian antiliberalism's growing politics of disturbance, ritual protest, and identity formation. Along with the other features of Christian antiliberalism, this politics demands from us a recalibration of our political sensibilities, in a way that acknowledges the blurring of cultural boundaries often taken for granted. The NCR mixes political and tactical goals in order to challenge liberalism and to realize its own theological commitments. Sometimes from without, sometimes from within, the NCR seeks to transform the political order, arguing that the very institutions that gave rise to suffrage and democratic representation now constitute a set of limits on the public. This reconstitution of the political sphere is furthered by the style of politics the movement often employs. Marking the public sphere with religious presences such as Christian schools or home schools constitutes a direct challenge not only to particular policies but also to the way we think about political religion.

When the logic of conservative Christianity is directed against the state, a parallel world of political meaning is established. The gap between these two worlds is exposed in the insurgent, disturbing activist politics of the NCR: demonstrations at abortion clinics, electoral assaults on local school boards, the dissemination of Christian literature, sieges of nightclubs and rock concerts, and primarily its educational endeavors. All this represents a growing repertoire of tactics that aim to destabilize "conventional politics" through the constitution of a visible contrast with its policies and procedures. For the NCR, these tactics enable it to engage in public witness to the power of the risen Christ, a witness that is an act of will formation aimed against the liberal state. By bringing religious meanings into the streets and into the schools, the New Christian Right has challenged what it means to be a citizen.

Chapter 4

The Fracture of Good Order

The Berrigans and Ritual Protest

Saints don't work in a democracy.
    —STEVE SACHS, PROSECUTOR
    OF THE CATONSVILLE NINE

*Our apologies, good friends, for the fracture of good order,
the burning of paper instead of children, the angering of
the orderlies in the front parlor of the charnel house. We
could not, so help us God, do otherwise. . . . We have chosen
to say, with the gift of our liberty, if necessary of our lives,
the violence stops here, the death stops here, the suppression
of truth stops here, the war stops here.*
    —DANIEL BERRIGAN

Everywhere there are graves. Small, unostentatious headstones with Irish names dot the large expanse of grass that is St. Peter's Cemetery. This land belongs to the Archdiocese of Baltimore but is maintained by the residents of Jonah House, the resistance community founded in 1973 by Philip Berrigan and Elizabeth McAlister. For nearly four decades, Berrigan, McAlister, Daniel Berrigan, and others have confronted what they see as the worldly ways of death, have gotten up close to the sources of death to name them and to denounce their power. It is little surprise, then, that they live amid death. Even the surrounding neighborhoods of southwest Baltimore are littered with graves of a kind: dead factories at the horizon, the rubble of old row houses everywhere, and the walls of the city festooned with graffiti that reads "R.I.P. Dontae" or in memoriam to a morbidly long list of names.

But there is life, too, of course. Families tend to their yards and wash their cars, children skip home from school and call to one another from the stoops of brownstones, and small businesses struggle to survive in postindustrial Baltimore. And just over the hill from the projects that line Edmondson Avenue, sharing an alley with Emmanuel Tire Recycling, lie St. Peter's and Jonah House. Susan Crane and Michelle Naar-Obed sit atop power mowers. Greg Obed is weeding. Phil Berrigan is away speaking on the *Democracy Now* radio program. In among the other full-time residents who tend the garden or paint the wall or prepare the latest round of letters and press releases is Liz McAlister, smoking Marlboro Lights and fretting about a fan belt. An idyllic scene, but Jonah House has also been labeled by the state as a site of "ongoing criminal activity." For decades, its residents have organized ritual protests that challenge the legitimacy of state power.

The world of Jonah House is far removed—physically, religiously, and politically—from that of the New Christian Right's (NCR) Christian schools. Gone are the rural landscapes of Kanawha County or the semisuburbs of Michael Farris's Virginia; instead there are blown-out buildings, an old husk of a Montgomery Ward store, and streets peopled by young African Americans with cornrowed hair and vinyl jackets. Where one might hear in a Christian school the sounds of old Protestant hymns being sung or of Scripture read aloud by the evangelical young, at Jonah House one hears the clanking and humming of Emmanuel Tire (staffed largely by Central Americans who send most of their paychecks to their families abroad and who occasionally beg for food at Jonah House), lawnmowers, dogs barking, children shouting. The very idea of establishing a resistance community in such a neighborhood might seem alien to the NCR, though the residents of Jonah House share their concern that the state is hostile to religious identity. But the incarnational, sacramental worldview of the Berrigans is rooted in an entirely different understanding of faith, of community, and of the Holy Spirit than are the communities of the NCR.

In the world of Christian antiliberalism, little is more jarring to conventional political sensibilities than the fractious disturbances created when these understandings are enacted, in the rituals and symbols of Christian faith, and directed against the political order. Like the other characteristics of Christian antiliberalism I have interpreted in successive chapters, the use of ritual protest is common to all practitioners, visible in Sojourners' community activities and the caustic public presence of the NCR. But from their radicalization in the early 1960s through their infamy during the Vietnam era to their later role in the Plowshares Movement, the Berrigans have consistently taken their flair for ritual and spectacle into the well-ordered spaces of the public sphere. They have used the very "otherness" or "out-of-placeness" of religion, as they experience and enact it, as a critical principle used to judge liberal political order. They have drawn on the "prophetic" examples of Isaiah, Jeremiah, Amos, and Jesus to condemn the uses and abuses of political power. Insisting that the state is an abomination before God, that the political logic of liberal order numbs citizens to the violence of late capitalism, and that resistance is the only Christian path, the Berrigans have trespassed, damaged property, and created spectacles and a fantastic dramaturgical presence in public, all in the name of fracturing the "good order" of liberalism.

Blood and the Signs of Contradiction

Much has changed in the decades since Daniel and Philip Berrigan first burst from relative obscurity into state buildings, newspapers, and courtrooms. The political and economic fortunes of the nation have shifted, the precipitant causes of 1960s "left" action have faded from public conscience, and religious communities have been dispersed by shifts in ideology, community, and technology. Meanwhile, the Berrigans have steadfastly continued their witness against the U.S. government (which they also call "Caesar," the "superstate," the "war machine," "Big Brother," or simply "the empire"). Although they no longer enjoy much public support, their activism remains a living thing, which they feel is animated by a rich sense of religious tradition and social teaching and by the blood of Christ.

The Berrigans are keenly aware of their place in very old traditions of Christian social action, particularly Christian witness against the state. In this lineage they include not only those who have literally engaged in direct action and protest but also those figures for whom love of God and Christ was itself a mark of difference from worldly power and custom. Indeed, life at Jonah House is filled with references—visual and spoken—to this "cloud of witnesses," which includes Dorothy Day, Saint Francis of Assisi, Julian of Norwich, Gandhi, Hildegard of Bingen, and Archbishop Oscar Romero, among others. And though the relationship of Jonah House to the church is marginal—it was founded in direct response to Philip Berrigan's and McAlister's excommunication in 1973—there is still, as explained by McAlister, a "very deep sense of our roots and the gifts that the church has given us, especially the Scriptures, the sacraments."[1]

Dorothy Day and the Catholic Worker movement loom large in the Berrigans' personal history. Day was fond of calling on Christians to fill up the jails, and, for a time, from the Great Depression until the end of the

Vietnam War, many Catholic radicals heeded her words. But since the closing of the 1960s, American society has been transformed in a number of ways, one of which has been the steady marginalization of Catholic radicalism. Catholic social protest in the twentieth century was frequently torn between reformism and a frustrated separatism. Catholic radicals had never been terribly sanguine about the ends of the state, but activists such as Day once believed that local actions could help reform both the Catholic Church and the larger political culture. This reformist impulse, however, was chastened by a separatist inclination that held that the state is beyond the transformative power of works of mercy. Shifts between the two idioms have often been a function of the changing relationship between Catholics and the state.[2]

This Catholic ambivalence about the state, and the shift in orientations to it, have been most visible in Catholic pacifist protest.[3] Reformists such as John Ryan, who helped found the Catholic Association for International Peace in the 1920s, urged the hierarchy to articulate and support pacifism more fully. But whereas reformists called the church to realign itself with Jesus' teachings about war and poverty, the separatist impulse slowly evolved into a full-fledged critique of state power, arguing that the church possessed an inner dynamic against the world and a critical language by which to measure human projects and institutions. The only way to resist the corruption of state bureaucracy, so some began to argue, was to return to the simplicity of the Bible's ethical teachings and the communitarian lifestyle of the early Christian communities. One major source of the tension between reformism and separatism was the fact that they both claimed inspiration from the same social teachings, particularly the so-called social encyclicals of the late nineteenth and early twentieth centuries.[4] Thus, while the separatist idiom pulled the church from its complacency and comforts, the reformist impulse enfolded this critique in the everyday life of the institution and communities. This debate has flourished in the American context since, as Gene Burns notes, the American understanding of the separation of church and state dovetailed with the church's self-understandings as an entity "other" than the state.[5] In the era after World War II, though, Catholic blood boiled infrequently over the transgressions of the state. By the early 1960s "there was nothing less dangerous than a Catholic priest," according to Garry Wills.[6] Yet it was from this political moment that the Berrigans began their "ongoing criminal activity."

Raised by an authoritarian father, each of the Berrigans took a different path to embrace what McAlister calls the "gifts" of tradition. Philip Berrigan served in the Second World War, later experiencing a crisis of conscience that led him to join the Josephite order. The Josephites' primary mission was with African Americans in industrial cities, and with this work Berrigan became politicized. He began to denounce the hierarchy's silence on economic and political injustices. When he was himself repeatedly silenced for speaking out on such issues, Berrigan came to feel "that there is no separation of church and state in America. There is merely a collective articulation of power."[7] Working with African American youth, first in New Orleans and later in Baltimore, Berrigan became outraged that it was predominantly poor young men of color being sent to fight in Vietnam. He recalls becoming aware of what he deemed a "cruel irony": "The United States government wasn't lynching African-Americans; it was convincing them to lynch themselves."[8] In Baltimore, Berrigan was beginning to believe that young African Americans were trapped by economic disenfranchisement and allegiance to a system that rendered them outcast, a system that at the time also inflicted violence on the Vietnamese in Hanoi and sought to suppress dissent at home. Sensing that allegiance to the larger project of postwar liberalism was responsible for much of this violence, Berrigan had begun by 1965 to help African American communities to build grassroots resistance to service in Vietnam.

Daniel Berrigan had joined the Jesuit Novitiate in Poughkeepsie, New York, before his brother Philip went to war. There he spent twelve years cultivating his literary inclinations while immersing himself in what he obscurely calls the "radical Gospel." He spent 1954 in Europe and there became attracted to the French "worker priests" who helped organize farmers and factory workers. The decision of these priests to live among the poor struck Berrigan as a pure expression of Jesus' ministry, and he was puzzled when they were denounced by French bishops and then by Pius XII. When Berrigan returned to the United States, he allied himself with the Catholic Worker movement and helped convince Philip that, as representatives of the church, they owed a moral debt to the people they served and to the spirit of the church itself. Daniel began voicing his concerns about American racism and the war in Vietnam, at the same time experimenting with new liturgical forms such as lay-led liturgy. For these experiments he was exiled by the Jesuits, first to Mexico and then to France. When he returned, he helped found the organization Clergy and Laity Concerned About Vietnam (CALCAV) with Abraham Joshua Heschel and Richard Neuhaus. As the Berrigans grew ever more concerned about the war in Southeast Asia, they sought to draw on the moral languages of the church and of the vast traditions of American dissent to highlight the injustices they perceived. Inspired by the Student Nonviolent Coordinating Committee's (SNCC) and the Southern Christian Leadership Conference's (SCLC) integration of theological beliefs about human dignity and justice with innovative organizational tactics, Philip helped organize many of the Freedom Rides. From these traditions, as well as from those of the Catholic Worker and grassroots activists such as Saul Alinsky and the Industrial Areas Foundation, the Berrigans inherited both the conviction that nonviolent direct action was the only appropriate response to state power and the desire to organize on the local level.

This development makes clear that communities such as Jonah House, and the importance of nonviolent direct action more broadly, are unthinkable without recognizing the role of Gandhism in American pacifism. The influence of Gandhism, in particular the concept of *satyagraha* ("truth force"), extends from the actions of the Union Eight to the SCLC and the New Left, a mode of resistance to political injustice that publicly manifests its disobedience to political power through noncooperation and illegality.[9] The tactics, structure, and culture of direct action (rooted in pacifist and labor struggles from the 1930s onward) have been profoundly influential on the Berrigans and on the wider culture of Christian antiliberalism. "Putting one's body on the line," or, as Mario Savio called it, "throwing your body onto the machine," touched on the rage people felt about the abuse of state power.[10] Indeed, many people involved in this culture were committed to new forms of democratic community building that were nonhierarchical and decentralized. Activists such as David Dellinger, Bayard Rustin, A. J. Muste, and others worried that "the modern state, even in the United States, gravitated by its very nature toward becoming a vast prison camp and so their program focused on reasserting political space for individuals by symbolic acts of resistance."[11]

For the Berrigans, direct action aided in bearing witness to the higher law and the higher power they believed conflicted with state militarism. They asserted that American involvement in Vietnam was an expression of the injustice characteristic of the society at large. The inequities of capitalism, the horrors of racism, the quiescence of hierarchy and statespeople, and the abstract logic of political liberalism together, argued the Berrigans, combined to enshrine a national commitment to military adventurism. Christian mercy and the spirit of democracy, moreover, had both been abandoned in the mad militaristic rush of postwar American life. Moreover, the church itself was implicated in this culture of death: Philip asserted repeatedly that the church no longer served as an exemplary community grounded in the dignity of human life, and he accused the hierarchy of exploiting the authority of the Gospels without being subject to it, serving up in its stead a "degenerate stew of behavioral psychology, affluent ethics, and cultural mythology, seasoned by nationalist politics."[12] The American church had too easily accommodated itself to the historically contingent and limited decisions of secular power and thus had compromised the radicalism of its love ethic and its critical stance toward human social arrangements. The hierarchy grew increasingly uneasy with the Berrigans' position.

The Berrigans attempted to demonstrate their understanding of an authentically Christian community and to embody those acts befitting a moral conscience outraged by the exercise of illegitimate power. To this end, they embarked on a course of protest and iconoclasm that led them into confrontation with both the church and the state. First the Baltimore Four, led by Philip, poured blood on draft files in the Selective Service office in Baltimore in October 1967. The Berrigans' infamy reached national proportions when they joined with seven other pacifists to raid Local Draft Board #33 in Catonsville, Maryland, on May 17, 1968. The Catonsville Nine seized more than 600 draft files and burned 378 of them with homemade napalm before they were arrested in the parking lot outside the draft board. The Berrigans accompanied their protest with song, prayer, and laughter, marking their distance from what they saw as the solemnity and lifelessness of the government. Public reactions were quick, widespread, and sharply divided: some called the Berrigans charlatans who mocked their religious orders and priestly dignity, whereas others saw them as authentic exemplars of Christian values.

Since these first two actions in Baltimore and Catonsville, the Berrigans have often used blood in their witness against the state. In Catholic ritual and eucharistic theology, blood is a central sign of purity and redemption, standing for "life, vitality, the identity of the one who gives his blood, and for sacrifice itself. The blood of the Lamb, the body and blood of Jesus, the blood of Christ in the sacrament of the Eucharist."[13] Blood is also the medium of the reenactment of Christ's words at the Last Supper; it recalls the divine sacrifice Christ was to undergo; and it links those who consume it, as consecrated wine, in the Eucharist to the body of the Church. Connected to these uses is the Berrigans' understanding of the sacraments, so central to their ritual protests. They rely not primarily on the meanings of sacraments in their use as sacred signs—persons, places, or objects regarded as holy—but on the role of sacraments as gateways between the human world and the realm of the divine. Liturgy, blood, ashes, and reenactments of scriptural imperatives are all, within this understanding of the sacraments, conferred with the very sacred power for which they are understood to stand. By performing these sacramental actions in the spaces of military and political power, spaces that the Berrigans consider profane, the Plowshares activists understand themselves to be creating an opportunity for divine grace to redeem the fallen world of American liberalism.

The use of blood is for the Berrigans also a visceral reminder that Christ's blood was spilled by an imperial power, that the Son of God was tortured and killed for refusal to submit to Caesar, and that the blood of the innocent runs red in the halls of power. Since October 1967 and the actions of the Baltimore Four, the Berrigans have often drawn their own blood for use in their ritual protest. The two brothers, Elizabeth McAlister, and all who have joined them in what would become known as Plowshares actions (named for the biblical injunction to "beat swords into plowshares") have placed their blood in glasses, gallon jugs, and other containers to be poured on warships, train tracks, missiles, computers, and the sidewalks and steps in front of state buildings. On a moral level, they want the blood to remind the public of both the real blood spilled in American wars and Christ's blood. On a ritual and theological level, the use of blood in ritual protest is intended as a re-creation of the sacrifice of Mass and as a way of consecrating ground that the Berrigans believe the state has profaned. The ecclesial significance of these actions was to suggest that the church had become estranged from its own traditions, stories, and symbols.

These meanings are intentionally performed in the Berrigans' actions: the significance of blood in Catholic cosmology is integral to their ritual protest. In the early 1990s, for example, members of Jonah House staged a "litany" against what they believed was the blood spilled by the Pentagon. They had received information that Pentagon officials had begun exploring the use of "force multipliers," devices that could make local meteorological transformations in order to render military operations more efficient. As McAlister put it, this meant that "we won't have any problems with bombers in Kosovo, in terms of weather, because we'll control that."[14] On the steps of the Pentagon, the Jonah House group performed a version of Bob Dylan's "Masters of War," intoning, "This is the blood of Christ, and this is the blood of the innocent in Iraq, in Yugoslavia, this is the blood of our sisters and brothers." With these refrains, Jonah House members identified the blood they poured on the Pentagon steps as blood seeping from the building itself. For the Berrigans, the Pentagon is spilling Christ's blood just as surely as Pilate did, and to do nothing in the face of this outrage, which they consider a usurpation of the name and the authority of God, would be tantamount to apostasy.

As a countersign to state militarism, blood is poured in sacramental actions and ritual protests. The Berrigans here effectively use the "otherness" of Catholic social teachings and ritual in American culture as a symbolic means of opposition to the inhumanity of liberal political order.[15] As Sister Anne Montgomery, a longtime Plowshares activist, put it, "The very 'offensiveness' of bloodiness is part of the message . . . [but] [b]lood also speaks of human unity and of the offering of oneself, in however small a way, in a new liturgy of life and hope."[16] Blood, the vehicle of the spirit, life, and redemption, is also the mark of injustice splashed on "the portals, porticos, floors, walls, and porches of the 'sacred' temples of our government, as well as at corporations that make the weapons and at bases that store them."[17] Blood is a sign not merely of death, then, but of death's transfiguration into new life.

The use of blood invokes an alternate history. In red splashes across public space, the Berrigans hope to transfigure the world, first by naming the state as a source of violence and war making, then by refusing to pay obeisance to false authority. Without war, without the spilling of innocent blood, they claim, the modern state cannot survive. Through ritual protest, they declare that the blood of the Crucifixion still flows as a gift to humanity, but they also insist that this redemptive blood marks a strict boundary, a moral limit that forbids the spilling of blood by anyone, under any circumstances. Although their initial practice of these rituals was tentatively reformist—dissenting from the norms of the institutional church and American society, to disturb the sensibilities of each in order to return both to their proper ideals—the Berrigans came quickly to articulate an idiom that was more separatist, anarchist, and even scornful of the institutions they had once sought to reform. The Berrigans lament that the gift of Christ's blood has become cheapened by both church and state, its redemptive powers rendered a mere commodity.

"No Man of State Has Seen His Own Heart":
The Berrigans and Caesar

Behind the use of blood and the wider array of ritual protests deployed by the Berrigans is an understanding of the state firmly grounded in Scripture.[18] In Ephesians 6:12, Paul warned the members of the fragile young community at Ephesus to beware the "powers and principalities" that stood in the way of their Christian practice and koinonia. The Berrigans have made a lifetime's work of cautioning that the scepter of power is an instrument of forgetting, of forgetting the blood of children and the cries of the poor. This theology of the state is not inconsistent with Catholic social teaching. The church has often been suspicious of the "inside" of American society; maverick figures such as Peter Maurin or radical pacifist and self-proclaimed "un-churched Catholic" Ammon Hennacy have often linked the state with the "war machine." Not only does the state shed so much blood, but for the Berrigans it stands in radical contrast to works of mercy they place at the center of Christian life. Like the Catholic Workers, the Berrigans have consistently identified themselves with the beleaguered early church and its radical distinction from Caesar's power.[19]

Despite frequent sentences in the late 1960s and early 1970s, the Berrigans and others followed their year-long witness of 1980 (which found them at the White House or the Pentagon every day) by entering the General Electric plant in King of Prussia, Pennsylvania, and damaging nuclear warheads manufactured there by beating on them with hammers. In 1988, Philip was jailed for hammering on cruise missile launchers in Norfolk, Virginia; he was jailed in 1993 for repeating these actions on an F-15 fighter plane in North Carolina and again in November 1998 for the action aboard the USS *The Sullivans* described in the introduction. By 2001, Philip Berrigan had spent more than ten years of his life in prison. He recently finished a one-year sentence for violating a previous parole in a Plowshares action in 1999, in which he and others hammered on warplanes at Warfield Air National Guard Base in Maryland. Apparently the sentences are little deterrent to any of the activists, since Plowshares actions continue. Berrigan acknowledges that many see him as a museum piece, an aging relic from a bygone political era. Yet though he may preach only to the converted, and though the state he condemns may pay him little attention other than at sentencing hearings, Berrigan believes that he must "confront the institutions of injustice" as a requirement of faith.[20]

Central to this understanding is the belief that Christ was crucified by an imperial power. This stark reality has informed the Berrigans' actions since 1967. They contend that the existence of international superpowers is an affront to God, a mark of blasphemy and idolatry. In its disregard for human life, its refusal to submit to the command of love, and its illegitimate usurpation of authority, the U.S. government exists and acts, according to the Berrigans, as did imperial Rome in Christ's day. Many of these assertions are made without argumentation by the Berrigans. In contrast to fellow social critics such as Noam Chomsky or historian Howard Zinn, the Berrigans often proceed simply by assertion. In McAlister's understanding, the story of Christ's Resurrection reveals much about the operations of imperial power. The soldiers who guarded Christ's tomb, she recalls, were the first to witness the Resurrection. In the face of "this truth," Rome entered into "a state of cover-up." McAlister believes that denial of religious truth is endemic to political power, which exists only to perpetuate itself. Like "an aging spider, weaving the same old tired web out of its gut," the state is indifferent to truth except insofar as it threatens its monopoly of power.[21] The mechanisms by which it maintains its power may be unjust (mere plebiscitary democracy, arbitrarily invoked gag rules in court) or destructive (civilian casualties in military operations), yet the Berrigans claim that in either case the state insulates itself from moral petition. They contend, further, that the state requires this opposition to justice, since "death is the moral power on which the state relies," and the Kingship of Christ is a threat to this power.[22]

Although the Berrigans once saw their Christian witness against the sinfulness of the social order as linked to the reinvigoration of American democracy, this concern was never as central for them as was the responsibility of protesting the "inhumanity" of the government's Vietnam policy. Still, they clearly were disturbed that power and moral authority had been wrested from individuals and communities by remote institutions effectively insulated from citizens' petitions. Their early witness was therefore not extrinsic to either the Catholic or the democratic traditions but belonged to an expression of dissent that the Berrigans saw as integral to both. Their conviction that acts of protest were not criminal according to God's law underscored their hope that American politics could realize its own most valued principles: "the behavior of the American government is illegitimate *within* the constitutional terms that it formally accepts."[23] They saw these acts as part of a lost tradition of social criticism, which Daniel linked "to a broad spectrum of dissent that goes back . . . to the act of leaving Europe and settling here, then waging a revolution against England, a colonial power."[24] Philip, citing the Declaration of Independence and Jeffersonian federalism, articulated the connections between democracy and religious social criticism by claiming that "the clerical voice is absolutely essential to promote the democratic process and to give guidance to those whose consciences are searching along those lines."[25]

Beginning in the 1970s, however, these reformist attitudes began to buckle. The Berrigans' hopes and expectations began to change following prison terms, time in the underground, and the trial of the Harrisburg Seven (during which then FBI director J. Edgar Hoover accused the Berrigans and five others of conspiracy against the U.S. government).[26] In the wake of these events, the Berrigans became considerably more pessimistic about the church and American democracy. In their growing antagonism to the state, they began encouraging others to resist state power by withholding taxes, harboring dissenters, preaching to new GIs, and organizing protests. This period marked an increase in comparisons between the state and ancient Rome, with Daniel proclaiming, "I never expect decent activity from great power, whether it be church power or state power."[27] The Berrigans' emphasis on the redemptive power of personal and communal sacrifice, and their living theater of protest, were now directed against the system they once sought to reform. Philip summed up this new attitude of scorn for political and ecclesiastical reform when he wrote from Lewisburg Federal Penitentiary that "Christianity faithfully lived is politics enough. . . . [There is] no time for ideology, or the murderous abstractions of the irresponsible."[28] The distinction the Berrigans had always invoked between conventional politics and Christian obligations was giving way to a distrust of any non-Christian politics. Their sense that the church contained an inner dynamic against the world was evolving into Christian antiliberalism.

Eventually these convictions would be enshrined at Jonah House. Its norms—including nonviolent resistance to state power and a commitment to property held in common—are lifted from the Book of Acts, whose descriptions of the earliest Christian troublemakers guide the community. What is most distinctive about the Jonah House community is the vigor of its separatism, which is exclusively Scripture-centered and vehemently opposed to the institutions and values the Berrigans once defended (albeit in an iconoclastic way). The state has no longer simply strayed from its true purposes and values; it is "the enemy, not the champion of ordinary people . . . [and] laws are written to protect power and privilege."[29] The state is willing to use violent means to protect its interest and will deploy undemocratic strategies to vanquish dissent. Even the church, which the Berrigans once hoped could reform the state, is implicated, since it "enjoys enormous privileges from the state" that it will not risk.[30] Hence, the Berrigans now see the Gospels as inherently opposed to the state—"it is spurious, a human creation in rebellion against God"—and to the depredations of institutional life in general.[31] The nature of the protest has moved from resistance to a particular set of government policies to resistance against the very existence of the government. The very notion of reforming the state is now mocked: "Nothing of that matters; we aren't attempting to reform or overthrow the government. We don't care who sits in the White House or who walks the hallowed halls of Congress."[32]

This separatism is qualitatively different from that of the Catholic Workers, which initially inspired the Berrigans and which still held out hope for reform, in part because of that organization's particular characteristics and in part because the Berrigans have practiced their separatism during an era of significant change within American politics. One reason for the Berrigans' increased marginality is the decline of the antiwar movement itself. By the end of American involvement in Vietnam, the American "left" was mired in sectarian debates that began to dissolve the coalitions that had once united to oppose the war. Much of the former working-class constituency of the American "left" had been alienated by the antiwar movement. Once the movement itself disappeared, so too did the tenuous alliances on the "left." The Berrigans' post-Vietnam focus on nuclear weapons is, however, a continuation of their long-standing focus on the abuse of state power, the idolatry of technology, and the dire consequences of deracinated political thought. They contend that liberalism is unable to redress inequities, unable to repent for its own corruption and lack of compassion; it is profoundly remote from the needs of its citizens, in a way that concretely threatens humanity. As McAlister put it, "the type of money and the kind of human power that's put into the creation and storing of those weapons is all *stolen* from the needs of other people."[33] According to this understanding, then, liberal political order has detached itself from authentic human concerns. Through ritual protest, the Berrigans aim to challenge this reality, hoping to give birth to a new church and new community through ritual and sacramental action.

Plowshares actions challenge the "false" boundaries erected by the state. By constructing these boundaries, protecting them with weapons and remote bureaucracy, the state causes justice to wither away, to play on Marx's famous phrase. The Berrigans are compelled to resist this political order because they believe the state already rejects justice, humanity, and compassion for normalcy, complacency, and injustice.[34] Liberal political order defies God's commandments: "it compels people to acts prohibited by God's law, thus violating our freedom of religion."[35] The Berrigans and their followers do not, however, see such challenges to liberal "idolatry" as disobedient. Rather, as Anne Montgomery put it, "disobedience" is an inappropriate term because it implies a basic faith in a system that they claim does nothing to protect and enhance human life.[36] This system is illegitimate; its laws are not real laws. Instead, Plowshares activists practice "divine obedience," or a transvaluation of values that emphasizes direct action, community building, and faithful life as countersigns to political order.

The "good order" of the liberal state suppresses truth. The tenets of what Philip Berrigan calls the "civic gospel"—"the economy cannot endure without war; doomsday weaponry is necessary as long as our enemies agitate; 100 million casualties are morally acceptable"—are violations of divine sovereignty.[37] The Berrigans believe that if they are to uphold God's law, especially the commandment not to kill, then the false gods of liberal political order must be rejected. No reality, no social arrangement can be spared judgment according to the Word of God. If any of these realities are found to suppress the truth of the law of love and justice, these realities are defied, trampled on, and marked with the signs of a different order of value. Only through visible, unsettling, demonstrably Christian engagement with injustice can the "good order" of the liberal state be fractured, and to fracture public order is, indeed, the goal.

"Pissing on the Dynamite":
Ritual Protest and Sacramental Politics

An enumeration of the Berrigans' ritual protests since Catonsville would run for pages.[38] The range of their responses to what they see as the warlike liberal state is highly creative, methodically considered, but also spontaneously antagonistic. Despairing over the United States' long-term addiction to warfare, the Berrigans call for public resistance to the state. Such resistance, which they dub "pissing on the dynamite," is even more necessary in the post-Vietnam era, when political activism has dwindled (a fact that may account for the increasing virulence of their protest). Jonah House is the base from which most actions are planned and conducted. Scripture is the handbook. Against the taints of power, privilege, and the ravages of consumerism, all of which the Berrigans denounce as mockeries of human life, only the community of saints and Scripture possess the moral legitimacy to subvert human disorder.

Instances of subversion have come steadily since the 1970s, as the Berrigans and others engaged in actions such as protest on the steps of the Pentagon and pouring blood on nuclear warheads at a General Electric plant in King of Prussia, Pennsylvania.[39] These are the most common protests, and I discuss them in greater detail later in this chapter, but they are by no means exhaustive of the Berrigans' disruptive politics. For example, Dale Ashera-Davis, a Jonah House resident, frequently chained herself to embassies and fasted during the 1980s. Sympathizer John Schuchardt, a member of the Plowshares Eight, was once arrested for disrupting President George Bush Sr.'s churchgoing in Kennebunkport, Maine. Philip Berrigan himself posed on one occasion as a fake tourist in order to engineer a protest aboard the battleship USS *Iowa*.[40]

By the time Jonah House was founded, the Berrigans saw little utility in the idea of civil disobedience, claiming that to be civil or obedient to the larger system of American legality was useless, since "our country is no longer (if it ever was) governed by a constitutional system."[41] Actions would instead be rooted in Christian witness against the "powers and principalities" of Ephesians 6. During Christmas of 1973, the residents of Jonah House joined with members of the Committee for Creative Nonviolence (CCNV) to conduct a ritual protest at the White House. They drove from Baltimore to Washington, D.C., and, on Christmas morning, "enacted a medieval morality drama of Herod's massacre of the Innocents," hoping to connect this massacre to the actions of the contemporary state. They "left broken and bloodied dolls on Nixon's front lawn, gruesome reminders of the Vietnamese victims of our war."[42] These intentional actions tried not only to evoke the horror the Berrigans felt was being wrought by the state but also, in ways I discuss in greater detail later, to serve as entreaties to God to enter into profane reality.

The actions strive purposefully to "piss" on the conventions of American politics, respecting no boundary or law. They also manifest the Berrigans' understanding of witness, which involves placing oneself in a position to declare a truth that one believes has been obscured by worldly power. The Christian in the world professes the truth of the Beatitudes, the truth of the injunction to beat swords into plowshares, and the truth of God's solidarity with the wretched of the earth. When these truths are not honored in a liberal regime, the witness "has the authority and the duty to speak on the matter in question."[43] As Philip Berrigan put it, the Christian must stand in the public square and profess divine truth, whether or not this witness creates pain, perplexity, or inertia in others. Laws that have no "base in love" serve only to concentrate power in the hands of the ruling classes, and property that houses the instruments of warfare deserves no security or sanctity. "Unless legality has a base in love and is interpreted by love it can become a weapon to club and cripple people, instead of encouraging them and supplying guidelines for conscience."[44] The Plowshares activists believe that professing these truths, rather than the false truths of state power, is necessary to heal the world and that the violation of laws and the destruction of property are necessary to attract the attention of those to whom the Berrigans hope to speak.

The witness of the Berrigans employs Christian symbols, rituals, and sacraments whose values, presuppositions, and methods contrast radically with those of the liberal state. The radical incommensurability of this devotional voice in the public sphere generates an opportunity to disrupt the normalcy of political operations in liberal political order. In the mid-1970s, for example, Jonah House led a series of actions called "Disarm or Dig Graves!," which sought publicly to dramatize or depict the horrendous consequences of nuclear war. The action was staged on the lawn of the White House, where participants clothed as "Specters of Death," robed in black with painted skeleton faces, attempted to dig graves in the presence of an Uncle Sam figure.[45] The Berrigans called this creative theater a "die-in," and it became one of many such actions they staged as part of their "resistance calendar." On Thanksgiving of 1976, for instance, they posed as beggars and chained themselves to the Pentagon's pillars while others poured blood. Martin Luther King Jr.'s birthday has traditionally been their occasion to witness against racial injustice. On Valentine's Day, they witness against nuclear weapons in the name of love and resistance. Perhaps the most significant dates on this resistance calendar are tax day, July 4, August 6 and 9 (the anniversary of the bombings of Hiroshima and Nagasaki), and the high holy days of the Christian calendar such as Easter, Good Friday, and Christmas. On each of these days, the Berrigans contest the public meanings or commemorations seen on these dates and instead set out to expose the suffering, displacement, and persecution they feel are the result of extant political order. This witness reached its apex during all of 1980, as the Berrigans stood present every day at the Pentagon until, frustrated by the apparent inattention to the peace and justice issues they hoped to raise, the Plowshares Eight invaded the General Electric Plant in King of Prussia, Pennsylvania, in September 1980.

On the morning of September 9, after weeks of prayer and deliberation, the Plowshares Eight entered the General Electric plant to disarm symbolically the nuclear weapons components manufactured there. Security guards were detained with bear hugs while Anne Montgomery, Molly Rush, and the Berrigan brothers slipped in to perform what McAlister calls "symbolic but real disarmament" by hammering on nuclear warheads.[46] Once the hammering was finished, the Plowshares activists waited patiently to be arrested, filling the halls of the manufacturing plant with their songs and prayers (which reportedly disturbed the security guards as much as the hammering itself). Since this first action, scores of other Plowshares rituals have been performed, by the Berrigans and by those they have inspired. On December 13, 1980, Pete DeMott of Jonah House broke into the General Dynamics Electric Boat shipyard in Groton, stole an empty van with keys in it, and rammed the van repeatedly into a docked boat, denting its rudder. On July 4, 1982, the Trident Nein (Nine) returned to Groton to issue a "declaration of independence" from nuclear weapons. Four boarded the Trident USS *Florida* by canoe and hammered on its missile hatches, poured blood, and spray-painted "U.S.S. Auschwitz" on the hull, as the other five conducted a liturgy in the storage yard. On November 24, 1983, McAlister and six others trespassed into Griffiss Air Force Base in Rome, New York, to hammer and pour blood on B-52s and aircraft engines. They left a written indictment of the government for sanctioning war crimes and denying its citizens' constitutional rights by enforcing the "religion" of nuclearism.[47] On Easter morning of 1984, several members of Jonah House entered Martin Marietta in Orlando, hammering on Pershing II missile components and launchers.

This list of Plowshares actions is enormously abbreviated, for there have been scores more both during and since this interval. The list suffices, however, to highlight some basic elements and themes of this ritual protest idiom. The use of hammers is central to the actions, both because they call attention to the scriptural precedent for disarmament (found in Isaiah 2:4 and Micah 4:1–4, as well as in Matthew 5:38) and because of the way they are used. Hammers are wielded not as weapons themselves or as instruments of violence but as creative and transformative tools, evoking the simple carpentry that was Jesus' trade. The use of blood further underscores the transformative nature of the rituals, as well as calling attention to the sacrificial and sacramental overtones of the actions. The Berrigans realize that the use of symbols and rituals may seem irrational or illegible, given that they are transposed from a "private" religious context into the spaces of industry, militarism, or law. Yet they hope to use this irrationality, or better, the out-of-place-ness of the symbols, to their advantage, arguing that what is insane by political or military standards is in fact the only form of sanity. As Philip Berrigan and McAlister wrote, "Restoring symbols and purifying them through suffering and public exposure is part of the renewal of a community of sanity; in fact, a definition of the Church."[48] This symbolic action does not merely inject Christian symbols or narratives into the public—it goes further and purposefully uses the symbols to break laws that the Berrigans deem illegitimate, thereby establishing a rupture or a break in the world, just "as Christ broke into the temple, in nonviolent rampage against those who rattle the missile keys and level the megaton guns."[49]

The most noted rupture of recent years was among the Berrigans' more dramatic. On February 12, Ash Wednesday, 1997, Philip Berrigan and five others convened at 2:30 A.M. to drive through a whiteout snowstorm to the Bath Iron Works in Maine. Arriving at the shipyard, they found that security was heavy. Berrigan had to use bolt cutters to get through the gate adjacent to the Aegis destroyer USS *The Sullivans* (named for five brothers killed on one ship in the Pacific in World War II), which is tooled to fight atomic, bacteriological, or chemical war. Berrigan calls such weaponry "an example of imperial blindness, arrogance, and waste." Mounting the gangplank onto the ship's stern, the group was accosted by military police demanding to see proper credentials. Berrigan lied and said that General Dynamics had sent them to check security, a ruse that stalled the authorities long enough for Susan Crane and Steve Baggarly to reach the foredeck and begin hammering on Tomahawk Cruise Missile hatches and dousing them with blood. The sailors panicked and went on high alert, instantly seizing Berrigan, Tom Lewis, and Mark Colville, taking away their hammers and containers of blood. By this time, Steve Kelly had found the so-called Combat Information Center (fire control room), where he disarmed navigational technology by pouring blood on all the circuitry. Berrigan later wrote from prison that, "with missile hatches and navigational controls tended, symbolic yet real disarmament happened. Praise be to God!"[50]

Berrigan has steadfastly refused to refrain from these actions, despite his age. While he was in prison for the Bath action, McAlister organized numerous protests from Jonah House. Three annual faith and resistance retreats were held during the 1990s: during Holy Week, on August 5–9 (to commemorate Hiroshima and Nagasaki), and after Christmas (to commemorate the Feast of the Mass of the Innocent). These events gather peace activists in Washington, D.C., for readings, reflections, presentations, and acts of resistance. During Holy Week of 1999, for example, McAlister coordinated actions at the Department of Energy (which she calls the "Department of Extinction, which is what it is"), the Pentagon, and the White House. At the Department of Energy, five people strode past security into the secretary of energy's office in order to confront him about department policies. McAlister and others filled the building's lobby, where, she recalls, "we sang, we did a litany, we read our leaflet, we went through some reflections, and then we were escorted out and basically did the same thing on the [street]."[51]

McAlister believes that these actions are sacramental and that, in them, Christ is literally breaking into the world. The actions employ the symbols and the gestures of Catholic devotion to form a ritual that "contains what it points to [e.g., blood] but it points beyond itself, it transcends itself."[52] This understanding of symbols captures the doubleness of blood in the Berrigans' ritual lexicon: blood is both a product of U.S. militarism and a sign of the redemption made possible in Christ. On Good Friday, 1999, for example, McAlister poured her own blood on the steps of the Pentagon. Although she believes this action to be significant in and of itself, she claims further, "I believe and believe deeply that the blood is there and that we just make it more visible."[53] This sacramental politics is an effort to invest the sterile, abstracted spaces of the state with the power and vitality of life seen through the prism of Christian suffering. The symbolic actions aim to achieve the spirit of disarmament, jarring sensibilities with rituals that are "out of place," which is one meaning of profane, and hoping thereby to transform human will and consciousness.

One key principle in ritual protest is the inversion of the values of mainstream society and politics. Where America values militarism, the Berrigans celebrate peace; where capitalism reigns, the Berrigans follow the downward path of holy poverty; where the "sour-faced gorgons" of the state scowl, the Berrigans smile.[54] The rituals aim to provoke crises, not only by creating religious interruptions of public life but also by sharply contrasting the ways of God with the ways and decorum of the state. Such ruptures in the fabric of the everyday, these absurdities in the midst of political logic, are opportunities to direct religious creativity against the state. There is new life to be had in the fracturing of good order. By inverting the conventions and habits of thought that govern everyday lives, the Berrigans are able to mock, scandalize, and rebuke liberal politics. Since traditional forms of legal protest have failed, the Berrigans dramatize their indifference to legality not only in the acts themselves but also as fugitives from political authority, in the courts and even retrospectively in film and theater.[55] The destruction of property and the trespass against political authority help dramatize the crises of the Christian heart in the ostensibly benign liberal state: they are messages to the public that it is "increasingly impossible for Christians to obey the law of the land and remain true to Christ."[56]

The significance of barbed wire and other "false" boundaries is the way they display state power. These boundaries enshrine the principles of political order, and they control the space and mobility of citizens with "state rituals" of security and clearance.[57] Through trespass, the Berrigans make several claims: that the authority of the Gospels cannot be constrained by temporal power, that militarism survives only because it is protected from the scrutiny of the governed, and that political legality is arbitrary in comparison with divine law. Thus the Berrigans are willing to accept the consequences of violating governmental law if this is done in the name of "divine obedience," for they believe that when God's laws are obeyed, even if worldly suffering and sacrifice are necessary, this obeisance contributes to the redemption of the world.

In opposition to the false world of state power, moribund liberalism, and militarism, the Berrigans seek to create a sacred reality that is made tangible through embodied ritual, new modes of social interaction, and political dramaturgy. By pounding hammers on weapons and spilling blood on state property and through prayer and song, the Berrigans act and sound out different meanings, establishing alternatives to accepted conventions and enacting a different world, one in which religious and moral meanings prevent people from resorting to violence.

A kind of religio-political ontology is at work in the Berrigans' actions. They believe that the liberal state masks its intentions and sacralizes idols and myths that legitimate militarism, bureaucracy, and corporate capitalism. This masking draws on the legitimation of mainstream religious groups, on the specialized knowledge of pollsters and lobbyists, and, more frequently, on what the Berrigans call the "religion of nuclearism." The liberal state attempts to position itself as "normal," "necessary," and "rational," and, in response, the Berrigans have practiced a protest idiom that subverts this normalcy in favor of carnival and disruption, which mocks this necessity through playful contradiction and condemns specious rationality with the surplus of meanings generated through Catholic sacraments and rituals.

According to James Scott, such social unmasking and intentional contradiction are long-standing features of the politics of resistance. Scott claims that political power creates "transcripts" for acceptable public conduct and values, thereby confining difference and subversion to "backstage discourse."[58] Resistance to authoritative codes of action and meanings takes place in the gap between the public transcript of the state and the "hidden transcripts" of the oppressed or the resisters. This gap is the space of diverse strategies of resistance such as unmasking, contradicting, or creating a surplus of meaning, all components of Berrigan actions. The Berrigans contend that liberal political order has been achieved by asking its citizens to act and to behave in ways that contradict their beliefs or self-interests: the public transcript of American liberalism contrasts with the hidden transcript of authentic Christian faith, and one result of such contradiction is the emergence of Christian antiliberalism. When the Berrigans spill their blood or pound their hammers on weapons of mass destruction, they castigate citizens for allowing their faces to fit the public mask too easily. The very use of political ritual calls attention to the arbitrariness of the "normal" and establishes that it is not necessary but is the product of particular wills and interests masked by the language of rationality and necessity.

An open statement of a hidden transcript such as Catholic ritual is "a political time bomb," in Scott's words.[59] Ritual is charged with meanings that the Berrigans hope will explode the conventions of liberal political order. Between the "hidden" realm of the private and the "public" realm of state power lies the domain that can be mapped and illuminated through masking and unmasking, paradox, double meanings, and contradictions. Conducting a liturgy over burning draft files, intoning prayers while spilling blood on government property, and hammering on nuclear warheads are strategies of resistance designed to halt the momentum of state power by rupturing the image of unity that power requires, fracturing the good order of its public face.

Part of the construction of political power is the construction of a particular language to describe political acts or moral decision making. The liberal state defines its policies as "rational" and "legitimate" and asserts that protests against these policies are beyond the pale of legal and political discourse. It is this power of political nomenclature that the Berrigans attempt to undermine by infusing the spaces of power with a disruptive religious "language" of symbol, ritual, and narrative. When ritual protest attempts to wrest control of the public stage from political power, it changes what that power wishes us to see and believe of reality. These "offstage rejoinders" to the public transcript create a social domain wherein patterns of resistance can be formulated and negation can occur, often through the construction or dramatization of an alternate ideology or metaphysic.

It would be simple to dismiss ritual protests as ineffectual posturings or fanciful ravings at the margins of political discourse. Yet such dismissals would overlook the richness and the significance of these creations. Recent theory of ritual and the body has reappropriated phenomenology in the service of a broader critique of the notion of culture that has evolved in anthropology, one that has historically depended on etherealized views of the body and culture. Anthropological work on culture—in the classic writings of Tylor, Frazer, Malinowski, and Lévi-Strauss—prioritized social rules, roles, and obligations.[60] These structures were seen as imprinted like patterns on the human body, conceptualized as passive. Social behavior was consequently understood as a series of acquired habits, precepts absorbed from a wholly external culture and subsequently internalized. Classic social theory also failed fully to appreciate embodiment and intentionality, thus compromising its usefulness in understanding ritual protest. The Durkheimian tradition, which includes contemporary thinkers such as

Mary Douglas, more or less reifies society, positing that "the social" inscribes itself on the individual body through dress, ornamentation, comportment, and other external signs of social necessity or determination. Power and authority can be recognized, in other words, by the signs and symbols that people do or do not have. The body is largely passive, in this account, an object on which social power inscribes itself. The celebrated work of Michel Foucault is a more sophisticated update of this tradition. In *Discipline and Punish*, Foucault outlined what he called a political economy and technology of the body, wherein the shift from public punishment to confinement and incarceration also marked a transformation of the body in society. The birth of the modern prison as an institution depended on the functioning of the so-called superintending gaze, which renders bodies into passive objects. In other words, the ways in which institutions and powers are designed and organized are dependent on and establish a political economy of the body. Foucault's later work attempted to point toward an ethic of bodies and pleasures whereby power can be resisted through the body, yet his concerns were almost largely individualized, not always linked to broader public or political dimensions to the body in culture.

Beginning in the 1980s, however, theorists sought to return a concept of agency to the center of culture. According to recent theory, culture is no mere set of conceptual rules and sociality no mere relationship between individuals and groups. Rather, society is a mode of intersubjectivity and interexperience that is highly volatile and contestable and is continually the subject of negotiation by cultural agents. This field of intersubjective life is likewise permeated by power, charged with activity and agency (struggles and vying interests) that are themselves mediated in practice.

So in order to understand culture, one must understand the world of bodies and objects as well as the field of cultural determinants. Agency, practice, and emotions are all rooted in the body. Human intersubjectivity is embodied; social reality is itself incarnate and corporeal, insofar as social activity can neither be reduced to linguistic patterns nor seen as mere supplements to other cognitive acts. The body, then, is no inert object on which the mind inscribes meaning but is itself a source of and a conduit for such meaning, as in the embodied religion of Berrigan ritual protest. Phenomenology shows that human consciousness and experience have an immediacy and a transformative power that is not private or subjective only, in narrow construals of these terms. In order to understand the experiences of the persons who profess and act on religious belief, phenomenology attempts to eschew evaluative schemes in order better to describe an experience as it appears to consciousness. By focusing on the intentionality of the practitioner (e.g., the Berrigans in their rituals), one can appreciate how religious practice generates meanings, constitutes relations, and embodies an alternate mode of social interaction.[61] This focus reveals the importance of embodied action in the constitution of social and political worlds. As Maurice Merleau-Ponty wrote, "The body is our general medium for having a world . . . and it projects thereby around itself a cultural world."[62]

Christian antiliberalism cannot be understood, then, without a richer understanding of embodiment in culture. It matters not whether the interpreter believes as the Berrigans do. One must be able to appreciate that their ritual protest does not merely attempt to substitute antiliberal ideas for liberal ones but rather is experienced by them as a real and efficacious manifestation of the divine in and through their corporal practices. Thus, ritual actions constitute a form of practical knowledge whereby the cultural domain is defined not only in terms of morals and discourses but also in terms of "habits" and bodily activities. The gestures of ritual—making the sign of the cross, bowing the head in prayer, smearing ash on the forehead—constitute the sense and knowledge of the world, a visceral mode of cultural understanding. Against the fashionable notion of the body as a "signifier," a kind of fleshy "text" on which the social is written, Berrigan ritual protest exemplifies the ways in which the body is not a passive carrier of cultural norms but a vehicle of intersubjectivity and agency that helps to construct meaning.

Ritual protests are enactments of religious and moral ideals, whereby the ritual actions of individual bodies enter into the moral world of the body politic. By performing the very religious beliefs they believe liberalism seals off, the Berrigans experiment with roles they believe mainstream politics crowds out. The authority of their protest comes not from the nation-state or from conventional political metanarrative but rather from the symbolic, rhetorical, and embodied power of religion, its "strategies of signification and grammars of opposition."[63] Against a representational approach, in which the body has and reveals social meanings inscribed on it, ritual is an experimentation with different states of mind (in the same way that Iris Marion Young insists that gender is not "out there" but is embodied and constructed by motility and materiality).[64]

The Berrigans hope that by embodying a different mode of valuation and social interaction, they can urge others to step into the world they make, one beyond the options available in a liberal regime. They hope to inspire others to mimic their actions and thus to inculcate a particular form of "virtue" other than that which liberalism demands. At the intersection of performance, audience, and exhortation, it is possible for the Berrigans to subvert fixed ideologies and to challenge taken-for-granted assumptions about politics and religion. The very gestures of ritual protest are constituted as "other" in a political order that prizes individualism over collective identity, has institutionalized a suspicion of religious devotion in political spheres, and privileges abstract jurisprudential discourse. Religious practice, when publicly enacted in opposition to political power, becomes a form of unruly conduct and expression that challenges the legitimacy of state power. The moral, social, and aesthetic possibilities that unfold in ritual cannot be constrained by normal semantic or political orders.

If, as Iris Marion Young writes, the orientation of the body toward its environment defines the relation of subjects to their world, then the out-of-place-ness of Berrigan bodies relative to the conventional arrangements of liberalism constitutes a definitive challenge to those arrangements.[65] When a group of prayerful septuagenarians fill the lobby of the "Department of Extinction," witnessing against the fallen political order, they believe they are fracturing the rational coherence of that space's operations and discourse with the alternate languages and gestures of religious devotion and critique. To the extent that state power and legitimation depend on their correlative forms of knowledge and abstract law, the Berrigans consciously use ritual protest to inject alternate meanings into, or even to overturn, those forms. Although this form of political religion falls outside what is "rational" within a liberal regime, this witness not only has meaning for those who perform it but also "ruptures the world of human meaning, like a wedge forcing an opening in discourse and creating the possibility of creative cultural change, dissolving structures in order to facilitate the emergence of new ones."[66] The ritual thus superimposes a new sense of moral order over the old.

This species of staged, dramatic protest is far less easy to codify and to name as illegal than a simpler violation of the law such as picketing or marching. The theatrical element of ritual enables the Berrigans more easily to highlight what they see as violations of God's law; the traditional resonance of ritual appeals to audiences on a more visceral level than the abstract discourse of legality. Here the very otherness of religious belief is made to serve as a critical principle whereby divine sovereignty, biblical imperatives, and sacred narratives help the Berrigans to define their grievances with liberal political order. The rituals have variously quoted from official Catholic doctrine (e.g., *Pacem in Terris*) and from Scripture (Deuteronomy, the Gospel of Matthew, Amos, and Isaiah); they have incorporated blood, fire, ash, prayer, and song in their attempt to anoint the ground of the state—razed, as they see it, by the powers of death—with new life and redemption through sacrifice and suffering.

This form of witness must also be seen as incarnational, in a way consistent with Catholic social teaching (in which charity is exercised in direct relational form between people, at the smallest level of subsidiarity) and also in its attempts to transform nature through an infusion of divine grace. It is in this sense that the trespass against human or political boundaries is not a scandal to the Berrigans or their supporters but a way of supporting a particularly Catholic set of practices, of mediating and narrating the divine forces that they believe shape their subjectivity and community. We can see, then, that resistances that are often understood as "political" frequently grow out of indigenous or local practices that we call "religious." By exerting a form of personal or communal control over the sphere of the political, literally by inscribing alternate understandings and actions into the political through protest, Berrigan ritual protest challenges the political representations of state power.

"It's Impolite Not to Tell the Judge He's Terrible": The Berrigans in Court

The Berrigans' conflict with liberal political order has time and again brought them to ground zero of the liberal landscape: the courtroom.[67] In this space—where abstract legal discourse reigns, actions are defined and codified, and the judgment of the state is handed down—the Berrigans have attempted to extend their protest by using the courtroom itself as a space for raising issues of conscience and employing discourses alien to the law. Beginning with the infamous trial of the Catonsville Nine and continuing with the contemporary trials in which Philip Berrigan warns the court to "watch," the Berrigans have used their court appearances to point out the structural coerciveness and systemic injustice of liberal political culture.[68] If the courts are the sacred spaces of American civil religion and trials its high rituals, the Berrigans' courtroom antics can be seen as attempted reclamations of the language of right and justice in the name of their understanding of divine obligation.

Daniel Berrigan stated as early as the Catonsville era his contempt for American jurisprudence. The courts, he claimed, are insensitive to the moral and religious sensibilities he sees as the appropriate response to contemporary social problems. To cut against the "fatty excrescence" of the courts, the Berrigans have sought consistently "to use the courtroom in order to achieve some public audibility about who [they] were and what [they] were about."[69] Their courtroom behavior resembles their other ritual protests, whereby they dramatize their differences from liberalism, particularly the contrast between the abstract scholasticism of legal speech and the moral concerns they express "simply and directly."[70] When their religious and moral concerns are not addressed by the legal and political system, the Berrigans subject that system to the imperatives of their religious worldview, doing so publicly, theatrically, and disruptively in court.

The prophetic justice of their religious tradition "puts the persecutors and judges in the dock for crimes against humanity[,] . . . [since] the system could never be made to function well, even according to its own debased rules."[71] By explicitly drawing the legal system itself into their moral and religious struggle, the Berrigans attempt to challenge the ubiquity of legal conclusions and legal definitions of conscientious action. For example, in the trial of the Catonsville Nine, Arthur Murphy's summation for the U.S. government exemplifies the ways in which Berrigan ritual protest is classified by the state. Claiming that no law can be violated in the defense of "higher" beliefs or principles, Murphy warns that "if you allow this kind of law to develop in the United States, each individual can then, for his own motive or for his own purpose, select the law which he chooses to violate, irrespective of how sincere he may be, and know that he will be excused."[72] Using this kind of slippery-slope argument, the courts have consistently imposed gag rules on the Berrigans' discussion of their religious concerns and even of international law. Daniel Berrigan calls this "a courtroom in which the world is excluded . . . [;] our moral passion is outside the consideration of this Court, as though the legal process is an autopsy upon us."[73]

To the Berrigans, the courts represent a concentration of state power insofar as they are the spaces wherein life and death decisions are made. To challenge this authority, the Berrigans and their followers have attempted to make the courts into human spaces, seizing or undermining the power of the state to name, define, or fix the meanings of acts that come from religious practice. Where the prosecution defines ritual protest outside the terms of religious and moral concern, the Berrigans' defense often resembles a teach-in, an improvised community and dialogue, in which they admit the facts of the case while denying the state's interpretation thereof. Instead, they take recourse to the "higher laws" that animate their actions. Daniel is fond of saying the Our Father in court, an act that inevitably irritates the judge and disrupts the trial. Philip has often cited the Sixth

Amendment against the court's use of gag rules. What is even more scandalous to the court, the Berrigans often charge the judges themselves with violation of the law.[74] During the trial of the Harrisburg Seven, for example, the Berrigans announced their disdain for the legal system, which they called a part of the "war machine of the state" and whose political trials they dismissed as "Broadway seasons."[75]

Exemplifying both this disdain and the increasingly theatrical nature of their own trial performances, the Berrigans' performance in the King of Prussia trial was uniquely antagonistic. Plowshares activists were prepared once again to admit the "facts"—that they had illegally entered the General Electric plant and damaged property—but they repeatedly redefined the terms of the case to the judge and the trial lawyers. For example, regarding the charge of destruction of private property, Daniel countered that "to apply the word 'property' to nuclear warheads is to degrade and cloud the issue of what is proper to us."[76] Repeatedly pestering Judge Samuel W. Salus with the implications of both Catholic teaching and international law for nuclear weapons, Daniel and Philip argued that in fact it was America's complicity in "war crimes" that should be tried in the courts, rather than the mere trespassing of witnessing citizens.[77]

During the course of the trial, Salus grew ever more frustrated with the Berrigans' violations of courtroom protocol. After his pleas that issues of faith be tabled for more "objective" matters of legality, the Berrigans (and even some jurors, when questioned after the ruling) claimed that these distinctions were difficult to make. Salus's exasperated response was, "But what if the judge instructed you to leave out all *extraneous* influences—religion, culture?"[78] Daniel in particular made great sport of these and other statements by the judge, mocking Salus for his by-the-numbers liberalism and contrasting the identity of the Plowshares activists as Christians with the authority of the court. In fact, Berrigan claimed, "The charges, it was clear, were a juridical effort to name, not so much our crimes as *ourselves* . . . to *nail us*."[79] Just as it was Caesar's justice that crucified Christ, so Caesar's justice today threatens the innocent; hence, the witnessing Christian cannot abide by Caesar's justice in this case, lest Christ have died in vain. So it is that faith in Christ necessitates confusing the "facts" of the courtroom, inverting the priorities of law, and distorting the court's "distortions" of the activists' actions. Amid such rhetorical gamesmanship, it is no surprise that Daniel likens being in court to "gazing on our images in the crazy mirrors of the state fun house."[80] Where the state tears up the script of their ritual actions, the Berrigans respond by staging a different kind of play within the courtroom itself. According to the Berrigans, the courts attempt to dismantle the truth of symbolic action with legal rationality, to rip the symbols of hammer and blood from their context and ultimately from their meaning.

Aside from the disruptive, theatrical elements of the Berrigans in court, their defense typically rests on a series of substantive claims made against liberalism. At the March 19, 1984, trial of the Griffiss Plowshares, Elizabeth McAlister articulated one of these claims to Judge Howard Munson. "The religion of national sovereignty or nuclearism," she said, "is . . . violating our freedom of religion. This state religion not only compels acts that are prohibited by the laws of God but the state religion also prohibits the free exercise of religion."[81] Resting on the time-honored distinction between God's laws and the laws of the state, these claims against liberalism enable the Berrigans to indict not only the military but the U.S. government itself.[82] Using trespassing or property damage trials to open up a much wider drama concerning the legitimacy of the state and the rule of divine law, the Berrigans frequently claim (as they did in Elizabeth City, North Carolina, for the December 7, 1993, action at Johnson Air Force Base) that the state is guilty of the crime of building bombs and promoting militarism; then they pray, sing, and turn their back on judges, who usually find the Plowshares defendants to be in contempt of court (a charge the Berrigans find terrifically amusing).

The Berrigans employ a strategy of rhetorical tacking, reversing position whenever it is to the disadvantage of the judge to do so. For example, though they have steadfastly refused to pay bail after any of their arrests (insisting that to do so would be to concede that their actions were somehow illegal), they also often admit quite happily to the illegality of trespass and destruction of property, but only within the context of charging the state and the courts with the "real" illegality. For example, a Plowshares activist once equivocated mightily, "Well, yes, by your laws I can see how you might construe that I am guilty, but in fact the way we see it is that we're not guilty."[83] Prosecution lawyers generally insist that the real issue is not whether the arms race is legitimate but whether the state can allow its citizens to violate laws with which they disagree. But for the Berrigans, the law itself is tainted, serving only to protect the wealthy and to safeguard the means of destruction rather than citizens.

As part of this critique of law in a liberal regime, the Berrigans often invoke a "necessity defense," a well-established Catholic position, arguing that their actions are necessary to save the lives of children. They contend that their violation of state laws is necessary to prevent greater harms and that conventional methods of disobedience and suasion are wholly ineffective in this prevention. This defense has not been looked on kindly by the judges presiding over the Berrigans' trials. Judge James Buckingham, for example, who presided over the appeal of the King of Prussia decision, refused to allow expert testimony, dismissed the necessity defense, and claimed that the Plowshares activists' commitment to the Gospels was "irrelevant."[84] Plowshares defendants have also argued their case on the premises of international law, charging that the U.S. government consistently violates international treaties (and United Nations human rights declarations) that prohibit, or limit the scope of, warfare. They cite the Hague conventions of 1899 and 1907 (as well as the Kellogg-Briand Pact of 1928) as clearly presumptive against the slaughter or endangerment of innocents, the pact having sought in particular to limit all force to self-defense and to render all settlements of conflict "pacific."[85] If these international standards are being railroaded in the name of social order, the defendants contend, citizens are therefore justified in resisting the authority of the state.

Judge Buckingham set a Berrigan precedent by placing a gag rule not only on religious speech but on argumentation rooted in international law (on the grounds that the U.S. government was not on trial). Richard Falk, Milbank Professor of International Law at Princeton, testified on the Berrigans' behalf, denouncing the court's gag rule on international law arguments as a "procedural preemption" that overstepped its legal and political authority.[86] Yet despite the power of these testimonies and arguments, the Berrigans have persistently been met with the stern indifference of the legal system. Their speech and their activism are charged with a symbolism, and a metaphorical suggestiveness, that contrast directly with the unidirectional nature of legal discourse, which attempts to fix language and meanings. McAlister's statement to Judge Munson at the Griffiss Plowshares trial exemplifies this poetic, metaphorical divergence from legal discourse. "Our . . . intention was not to damage property," she said. "Indeed, we ask ourselves, the court, our friends, what property? Nothing proper here to human life. Nothing fitting, suitable in institutions of mega-death. In truth, no property. Our purpose was that death be robbed for a change of the last word and to say that these instruments of death constitute improper work so that people might begin a new day in peace."[87]

Willfully exceeding the discursive limits set by the courts, the Berrigans raise issues and stage debates that are not "proper" to the courtroom space. The trial becomes a theater where the defendants put the law itself on trial in an attempt to remove what they believe is the moral "mask" of liberalism. When the court insists that the only relevant issue is a violation of federal statutes, the Berrigans invoke Scripture, divine law, and blood; when the court reminds the defendants to respect the gag rule on religious speech, Plowshares supporters stand with scarves and towels around their mouths to call attention to these discursive limits. Even in recent Plowshares trials—as in that concerning the action on *The Sullivans*—the courtroom pattern persists. Against repeated outbursts and protestations by Philip, Assistant U.S. Attorney Helene Kazanjian steadfastly insisted, "We looked at his conduct, and we thought it was worthy of prosecution and charged him based on what he did. He caused a substantial amount of damage to the ship and that warranted prosecution."[88] Judge Gene Carter demanded that Plowshares defendants cease reference to international law and refrain from arguing that the existence of warships violates the international nuclear nonproliferation treaty.[89]

These actions generate a number of complicated implications for thinking about Christian antiliberalism. Considering the Berrigans' courtroom tactics in conjunction with their broader repertoire of ritual protest, it is evident that these actions together constitute a disruption of the political exchanges, values, and authority on which liberal political order depends. Using the inherent polyvalence of religious symbol and narrative and exploiting the multiple meanings inherent in religious rituals and actions, the Berrigans attempt to expose the gap between what they believe constitutes the *real* and what they judge the unreality of liberalism. These endeavors are especially significant given how central naming and classification are to political order. Berrigan trials show how, in the words of Richard Fenn, "the state prefers to objectify actions into performances that it can define according to its own categories of acts."[90] In other words, the state engages the Berrigans only to pronounce that the spirit and motivations behind their actions are irrelevant. Although the state recognizes the potency of the religious challenge, its response is to depoliticize this challenge by flattening its moral contours and constraining its rhetorical authority. Yet when this classificatory system is fractured through the use of metaphor, ritual, symbol, and counternarrative, a powerful challenge to the political status quo is thus enacted. In this sense, when the Berrigans act in ways they believe consistent with the demands of the Kingdom of God, they act in a way that is intrinsically subversive of state power. The play and ambiguity of ritual protest subvert political determinations; religious narratives, symbols, and actions engage and challenge those of the larger society.

These actions mark a boundary between "the cities of God and Caesar."[91] In a political order in which most institutions (especially the courts) have strict rules for reducing and restricting the content of religious speech, the Berrigans' use of the moral languages of Catholic social justice and the embodiment of Christian sacrifice both highlight the "state's unwillingness to argue its case in the courtroom on equal terms with the individual."[92] The state's refusal to recognize the authoritative discourse of religious tradition comes from its suspicion that religious language is "merely symbolic" or even "manipulative" or perhaps from its fear that this discourse is otherwise.[93] Certainly religious language often eludes the institutionalized distinctions between literal and metaphorical truth that pervade the courtroom space, and religious rhetoric further resists efforts to fix its meaning in the argot of political order.

We are left, then, with a kind of discursive double effect: each party contends that the other's language conceals what is relevant or true. For the Berrigans, judicial definitions of their actions and constraints on their speech summon images of the trials of Jesus before Pilate and the Sanhedrin. For the liberal state, the Berrigans' language and actions seem like nothing less than the audacious and potentially undemocratic attempt to place the world itself on trial. The Berrigans have argued that they act merely out of a consistency between belief and action, one that is part of a recognizably Christian form of protest.[94] Unsurprisingly, however, the court's rules for defining credibility and justification took precedence over the rules that might justify the Berrigans speaking in their own defense (i.e., rules internal to a particular tradition). And in this fashion, the Berrigans grow ever more frustrated with what they see as the system's dogged efforts to obscure the moral clarity of the situation: "what liturgical action puts together, judicial rules of discourse tend to put asunder."[95]

In the Belly of the Whale: Jonah House and Community

It is at Jonah House that the Berrigans lick the wounds incurred from battles with liberal political order. When the religious worlds created in ritual protest are rent asunder, the results can be as disruptive to the Berrigans as their rituals are to the state: jail terms, the depletion of community, the scorn of fellow religionists, and increased isolation. The Berrigans thus see the maintenance of community over time as necessary not only for the continuance of protest but also for the ways in which community itself constitutes a sign of contradiction and resistance to political power. Dan Berrigan, censured routinely by the hierarchy but still a Jesuit, has recently moved from Fordham University in the Bronx to Manhattan's Upper West Side, where he teaches and works with AIDS patients at hospices, among other activities. It is in Jonah House, therefore, that the dynamics of resistance community are most apparent.

McAlister is quick to point out that the residents of Jonah House cherish its relationship to Christian tradition. They maintain a very marginal relationship with the hierarchy—although the Archdiocese of Baltimore owns the land of St. Peter's, it interacts with Jonah House through an organization called the St. Peter's Cemetery Restoration Foundation, effectively keeping the hierarchy from all official contact with the Berrigans.[96] The residents consider themselves still connected with the spirit that animates the church, however, including the sacraments and sometimes also extending to individual members of the hierarchy (such as Baltimore's Bishop Frank Murphy). Nonetheless, the dominant self-understanding at Jonah House is that the community exists as a space outside the world of political power, where consciences are converted and the powers of death repudiated.

In the early period of their activism, when the Berrigans saw themselves as reformers of institutions whose ties with humanity and morality were in danger of being severed, they asserted that "the quality of life" within their communities was exactly what they had to offer those who sought to reform American politics.[97] This followed a strand within the Catholic Worker movement that asserted not only that the church and democracy needed reform but also that they were *worthy* of it and *already* contained resources for the promotion of human dignity. Dorothy Day saw community building as an effort to realize the doctrine of the Mystical Body of Christ, whereby all humans are the members of one another.[98] She identified the collective poor with Jesus the carpenter Messiah, and she likened her early work on behalf of the poor—in various forms of direct action such as picketing, pamphleteering, and marching—to the ministry of Saint Paul, "when you get out on the street corners with the word."[99] Day believed that these liturgical and doctrinal connections would ensure that community was not separate from Catholic tradition but would instead reform that tradition from within by employing traditional symbols, stories, and rituals for new and more socially responsible purposes.[100]

Religious criticism was thus connected to and done for the sake *of* traditions. Until roughly the end of the 1960s, both Berrigan brothers, under the influence of Day's vision, were keenly aware of their status as representatives of the church. Philip recalls, "We were being forced to articulate how we, as representatives of the church, should conduct our lives [in light of the challenges of the Vietnam era]".[101] Daniel likewise proclaimed that he was interested simply in "the stance of the Church before mankind."[102]

Their regard for democratic politics was connected in the same fashion. Even as a fugitive in the underground, Daniel still claimed that his purpose in life was not to set up an alternative to the U.S. government: "We want to say no to everything that is antihuman, and to suggest new ways for human beings to get on with each other."[103] Philip charged that confrontations with the state should only be in the service of "bearing with community life."[104] Interpreted in this way, the actions at Catonsville were intended to summon the conscience of fellow citizens and to goad them into building new forms of community that were less self-interested.

These communal aspirations resembled the traditional Catholic social doctrine of subsidiarity, which contends that "the smallest possible unit of society, individual, family, or local community, should deal with social problems wherever possible rather than involve the state and higher political organizations."[105] In addition, community should ideally be patterned after the stories of Jesus' life and ministry and after the ritual life of the church, both of which might serve as models for new forms of community and solidarity that could challenge egoism and materialism. Jonah House was initially founded in 1973 to serve as a model for building and sustaining local communities.[106] Since then, however, the purposes for which the community was founded have changed in ways largely due to the Berrigans' own loss of faith in the traditions they once sought to reform. Although they cherish their relationship to the spirit of the church, they no longer seek to enact incremental reform of the tradition. And the marginal hopes they once held for democratic politics have been largely abandoned since 1980, when the actions of Jonah House began explicitly to serve as acts of witness *against* the political order. In the twenty years since, the language of political hope has disappeared and with it any strong sense that political institutions matter.

When Ronald Reagan was elected in November 1980, the Berrigans felt overcome by frustration and powerlessness in the face of a skyrocketing arms race, deepening national debt, and atrophying social programs. McAlister, looking back on the Reagan and Bush administrations, said, "You don't live through twelve years of that without being profoundly scarred by that, having to say 'there is no hope here.'"[107] Despite deepening despair about the hope for political change, the actions that continue are deeply informed by a sense of *religious* hope, in the ultimate triumph over the powers of death. In ways very similar to those of Sojourners activists, McAlister speaks of the community's marginality and of its apparent inability to affect national military or economic policy, insisting that to think in terms of tangible accomplishments and material changes is inimical to the needs of sustaining hope and sustaining community. She sees the logic of "numbers games" as an abandonment of Christian existence for an abstract bureaucratic way of thinking that "has nothing to do with the spirit entering and with justice."[108]

Paralleling the shift in political hope has been a shift in tone and the sources of justification. Until the late 1960s, the Berrigans justified their actions according to commonly held norms of democratic practice and Catholic teachings on social justice and human rights. But in the Jonah House era, they have relied only on a literal interpretation of the Gospels for justification and hoped to achieve as much distance—spiritual, moral, and geographical—from the outside world as possible. Berrigan and McAlister, in their account of Jonah House's first fifteen years, claim that the only valid form of community in a nuclear age is one modeled after a literal reading of the Gospels. "Community finds its authority in Christ's mandate," they write, "'where two or three are gathered in my name, there am I in the midst of them,' Matthew 18:20."[109] The only organizing principle for community is found in the New Testament's Beatitudes and in the Book of Acts.

If death is the reigning feature of contemporary political order, then those who profess the Kingship of Christ understand themselves to be professing life when they disrupt that order, go to jail, or form communities of resistance. Patterned after the "fugitive" existence of the apostles (Acts 4:1–3), these communities attempt to embody the new life of the Resurrection, serving as public calls to conversions. Most important to the residents, this resistance is understood as an act of love and service on behalf of a fallen world. When "normal" politics cannot conquer the powers of death, those who feel love will follow the "abnormal" path of resistance.[110]

The Berrigans cling to the image of Jesus as not merely a nonconformist but a criminal. Public witness thus yields for them the possibility of immobilizing the state by clogging the courts and the jails with religious criminals and holy outlaws. Christian social thought—from as early as Tertullian's writings and expressed formally by Martin Luther, among others—has always contended that the church possesses an inner dynamic against the world.[111] It is this dynamic that has historically animated the Berrigans' practice and more recently the day-to-day life of Jonah House as well. In perhaps their most powerful inversion of the values of the social order, the Berrigans attempt to make concrete through ritual what the liberal state obscures with its "empty abstractions, sterile loyalties, crippling fears and hates": the wretched of the earth, the human cost of the arms race, the inequities of the global economy, and the simple acts of charity and compassion they place at the center of Christian life.[112]

Although more frequently scorned by the hierarchy and their co-religionists than not, the Berrigans see their actions and resistance as not only consistent with but central to their religious tradition. Their ambitions for political reform remain dim, yet Daniel in particular hopes to "rewrite the tradition for the sake of our people."[113] At Jonah House, the rewriting often mixes the mundane with the more spectacular ritual protests. The spring of 1999 was frequently given over to demonstrations at the Baltimore County probation office. Susan Crane, Michelle Naar-Obed, and Greg Obed—all recently released from prison, where they had been serving sentences in relation to Plowshares activity—were being sought by the authorities, who defined their return to Jonah House ("a site of ongoing criminal activity") as a violation of parole. Although Philip Berrigan was allowed to cohabit with McAlister after his release from prison, the other three full-time residents became wanted as soon as they came home.

McAlister, Berrigan, and others promptly convened at the probation office, demonstrating outside and questioning loudly, "Who's guilty of ongoing criminal activity?" They urged both employees and passersby that bombings in Iraq and Kosovo were far more criminal in their minds than the simple gesture of three people returning to their home. Nonetheless, U.S. marshals came frequently to Jonah House that spring. McAlister was sure that, despite their efforts to alert the public to their predicament, all three would be arrested and "violated."[114] On one visit, the marshals thought that McAlister was Susan Crane; McAlister responded to this charge by wheeling her wheelbarrow through St. Peter's weeds, telling the marshals, "This is my criminal activity for the day."[115] She hoped to expose the absurdity of their pursuit of Crane and others, suggesting that mowing lawns, servicing machines, painting, and food distribution can hardly be considered criminal.[116]

Of course, McAlister's protestations to the authorities are disingenuous, coming from one who has so gleefully thumbed her nose at state power for so long. In constructing a dramatic, intentionally provocative, and deeply traditional series of protests, the Berrigans not only exult in and brandish boldly the criminality of their actions but also demand that their audiences recognize themselves as actors in the drama the Berrigans enact. By incorporating various government employees into their actions, the Berrigans firmly deny the notion of there being "innocent bystanders" to state militarism. Although they may have grown increasingly unsure of the value of this drama for the church or the government, the Berrigans have remained insistent that it is an authentic representation of a moral and spiritual crisis that affects all who live in the age of the bomb. Their own communal response is intended to serve as a model of long-term faithful resistance, embodying the "No" that "prophetic" justice shouts to the state.[117] The moral exigencies of this "No," as with other Christian antiliberals, demand action and reflection that cut across inherited lines of religious tradition or doctrine. As stated at the outset of this study, it is for these reasons, among others, that Christian antiliberalism not so much resembles a religio-political orthodoxy that follows a predictable pattern or sequence of criticism but rather is a new species of religio-political discontent.

Working from within the Catholic tradition to unmask the powers of liberal political order, the Berrigans strive at Jonah House to make personal connections on the local level and to pursue the task of exposing what they believe are the lies of imperial power. Maintaining a marginal relationship with the institutional church, Jonah House conducts home liturgies for a small group of Baltimore residents. Those who celebrate there gather in a kind of voluntary displacement from the norms and practices of liberalism, "moving from one's 'ordinary' or 'proper' place in this society . . . into a life of solidarity with the countless millions who live disrupted lives."[118] This "small universe" clings to four basic convictions: that liberal political order subsists on a long-term addiction to war; resistance is more necessary in the post-Vietnam era, since public passion is much lower; new community models are needed; and God's Word is subversive of "human dis-order."[119] The community struggles to maintain itself as a counterforce to consumerism, prizing contemplation, nonviolent resistance, and Scripture as viable alternatives.

Yet there are those who, despite the power and drama of the Berrigans' long-term ritual protest, reject this manner of political criticism and community building. Anonymous sources in Catholic peacemaking circles have claimed that "it's so much easier to jump fences than do the nitty-gritty, grassroots work required to stop nuclear power and end the arms race."[120] Indeed, one must wonder whether the Berrigans possess a vision of positive political order. There is certainly a politics to their religious compassion, and it is clear that for them liberal political order must be resisted, but one wonders whether they consider the only authentic community a resistance community and if there is any hope for constructive politics beyond this limited scope. If the abuse of power creates ruptures in earthly community, and if the regenerate then engage in risk and sacrifice to counter this abuse, what is the new creation for which they work? If hope is made new in Christ, and if humans are ultimately redeemable, how is the peace of Christ won?[121]

The Berrigans are adept at pointing out not only the shortcomings of conventional politics but also the moral compromises they believe are incurred through mainstream political participation. Philip Berrigan counsels resisters against participating in the capitalist economy, paying taxes, voting in regular elections, and so forth. Alternately, "you can vote with your feet, you can vote with your whole person, you can protest and be resistant and register an infinitely more emphatic vote."[122] When the Berrigans infuse the public sphere with religious imagery, symbolism, ritual, and protest, they register such a "vote," challenging both particular policies and conventional ways of thinking about the practice of religion and politics. The gap between Christian self-understandings and liberal politics is starkly exposed in the Berrigans' insurgent, disturbing, antiliberal politics. It is through such protest activity that a truly different understanding of what it means to be political and religious is manifested, a style of politics that visibly marks its distance from conventional understandings of these areas. When blood is spilled, ashes smeared, hammers pounded, or liturgies conducted, spaces on the map of Christian resistance emerge in relief. They may yield no vision of community or politics that admits of long-term institutional reform or even of coalition building. And yet these actions, and the devotional poetry that accompanies them, do indeed register emphatically. When seeking to understand this antiliberalism, the Berrigans suggest only that perhaps the real drama lies not in the answer to such questions but in the need to ask them at all. As Daniel Berrigan asks, "As the need of the time passes from being in public to being locked up against public and the jailbird sings sweetest of all—who will come along with us then?"[123]

Joy Cometh with the Morning

Democracy, Power, and Christian Antiliberalism

*Your Honor, I have stated in this court that I am opposed
to the form of our present government; that I am opposed
to the social system in which we live; that I believe in the
change of both. . . . Let the people take heart and hope
everywhere, for the cross is bending, the midnight is
passing, and joy cometh with the morning.*
  —EUGENE V. DEBS

*In the dynamic of corporate capitalism, the fight for
democracy thus tends to assume anti-democratic forms.*
  —HERBERT MARCUSE

*Man's capacity for goodness makes democracy possible;
man's capacity for evil makes democracy necessary.*
  —REINHOLD NIEBUHR

In the past decade, it has become more commonplace to read about religious social criticism in academic discourse. A seeming response to the
fuzzy political options of the post–Cold War era, talk of religious engagement with politics was welcomed by many as a shot of passion straight to
the heart of liberal democracy. As books about religious social criticism
proliferated on bookshelves, it seemed for a time that nearly every public
intellectual wanted to comment on the subject. Philosophers opined about
the public uses of "the sacred"; old-style social democrats wrote of the
need for an enlarged sense of moral and religious pluralism; and cultural
theorists effused over the possibilities waiting to be uncovered "between

God and gangsta rap."[1] Across the pages of such books, readers encountered passages about what religious social critics or "freedom fighters" should or must do.[2] A curious second-order tone, an almost metadiscursive veneer, evolved in these discussions of the political meanings or directions of religious energy. Yet where amid all this reflection and theorization, one might wonder, were the religious social critics themselves? Where were those who, rather than follow the imperatives of theorists, were actually doing things, creating forms of political practice from the resources of their traditions? Did the devout, fiercely concerned about politics and justice, embrace this rhetoric, or did the jargon effectively mark a distance between the worlds of theory and practice?

In previous chapters, I have described a powerful mode of religious social criticism currently flourishing in the United States, one that I believe eludes the theoretical writings, and perhaps even the political vision, of those who would interpret political religion. The three groups I have named exemplify the broader impulse of Christian antiliberalism through their active protest—manifested in the specific qualities of political illegibility, the sacred registers of politics, ritual protest, and koinonia—against the policies of federal, state, and local governments. In describing the parameters of this protest, I have attempted to sharpen some political and theoretical issues in the study of American religion through descriptions of Christian antiliberalism's practices and beliefs. Here I wish to focus on this phenomenon's implications not only for the study of American religion but also for deliberation about religion's place in the public sphere. Christian antiliberalism challenges us both academically, in terms of the way we think about political religion in general, and politically, through the contestation it brings to liberal political order.

The place of religion in the public sphere has become a popular lens through which to speculate about the future of American democracy. A wide range of interpretations have emerged, viewing the resurgence of political religion as evidence of anything from cultural authoritarianism to a long-overdue restoration of "values" to American life. Despite the glut of commentary, many such interpretations are marked by omissions: the genealogy, beliefs, aspirations, political tactics, and, most important, cultural significance of political religions have received only cursory attention of the sort that is both historically and politically truncated. Frequently, commentary on political religion is occasional, crafted in response to isolated events, and mostly fails to touch on the larger enduring and pervasive political and religious significance of the events. Alternately, academic discourse about political religion is often pulled into the orbit of establishment clause interpretation, ethical analysis of religious reasoning, the theoretical heavyweight bout between liberalism and communitarianism, or one of several standard approaches within the field of American religion.

Most contemporary studies of power and politics in American religion tend to be submerged either in the subdiscipline of "cultural studies" (which, for all its theoretical sophistication, often focuses narrowly on "micropolitical" strategies of resistance—themselves often turning on issues of identity politics such as race, class, and gender—in a way that avoids the larger contextual issues shaping American political religion), in Foucauldian analyses of "discourse" (which largely aim to monitor or uncover the construction and arrangement of social power through the control of both practical and theoretical knowledge), or in social scientific studies of particular denominations or organizations (which prove immensely helpful in the provision of raw data but are less illustrative in issues of culture and meaning making).[3] In other words, studies of American religion tend to be faced with either a political deficit or a historical deficit, and the work of social and political theory is often saddled with a cultural or anthropological deficit. Those who attend to the specificity of religion frequently lose the larger context in which religion is located, whereas those who attend to the larger questions of politics and society all too often ignore the particularity of religious creations.

My explorations of the religio-political creations of the Berrigans, the New Christian Right (NCR), and Sojourners have attempted to redress these deficiencies and to integrate approaches in a suggestive way. I have striven to achieve an interpretive distance from the ways of studying political religion just mentioned, as well as from those more conventional approaches familiar to students of American religion: studies of "reformism" or backlash, chronicles of particular denominational stories, organizational histories, or concentration on issue-specific religious activism. Instead, I have attempted to generate a new series of questions about political religion and have also proposed a new set of categories for orienting analysis and interpretation. I believe this approach to the study of American political religion—and specifically, to the study of Christian antiliberalism— is attentive not just to standard modes of American religious history but also to issues of cultural anthropology and political meaning making.

In this chapter, my goal is twofold. I explore the fourth feature of Christian antiliberal practice—koinonia—and, through this investigation of local activism, I situate my own work in ongoing theoretical conversations about American democracy. Here, too, I hope to distinguish my contribution from mainstream debates about political religion in America. Theoretically, it seems of little use to me to debate endlessly, as so many theorists have done, the question of whether a liberal democratic regime should "allow" religious activism or participation in the public sphere (or, in a somewhat related matter, to expend intellectual energy scrutinizing the political merits of that elusive species of discourse known as "religious arguments"). Even the casual observer of American history will quickly see that American religions have always been active in the public and show no signs of stopping; they are there regardless of how much hand-wringing occurs in the academy. So perhaps the presence and growing influence of Christian antiliberalism present an opportunity to pose new questions and to rethink the ways in which political religions are engaged. The relevant question concerns not whether religions are "allowed" in the public political spheres but rather how to respond in a democratic fashion—as both scholars and citizens—to this presence. It is this question I wish to address now, at the end of my study.

The Shapes of American Religion

This is not a work of political theory; it is a work *about* political religion. Instead of attempting to endorse and defend a particular institutional or governmental response to the realities of political religion, my aim has been to describe a particular phenomenon or impulse on the American religious landscape and to highlight the lingering questions about American politics this phenomenon raises. There are inferences to be drawn from Christian antiliberalism for thinking about the shifting shapes of American religion and politics in our era. In the beliefs and practices of Christian antiliberals, one sees the ways in which Christian groups are re-creating and reconstituting themselves, not solely in relation to matters of theology or liturgy but also around and between the spheres of education, national defense, and economy and, most important, around broader questions put to political order itself. Certainly Christians have always been socially and politically engaged in multiple ways.[4] Yet the very publicity of Christian antiliberalism makes manifest the renewed cultural and historical importance of these engagements.

Historically, Christian antiliberalism is evidence of the larger redirection of American politics in the postwar era and also of the increasingly politicized nature of American Christianity itself. Although linked to older traditions of American dissent—both religious and secular—Christian antiliberalism captures many of the historical developments of the late twentieth century and beyond. Politically, this phenomenon is evidence of the pressing need to rethink the position and role of religion in American society. Religiously, it manifests the extension of several recent American (and possibly global) trends.[5] The pluralization of "traditional" Christian identities—whereby Christians diversify and split off as new issues and challenges are raised and the corollary process involving the precedence of social over denominational bonds—is amply evident in Christian antiliberalism.[6] Yet there is more to this protest impulse than the generation of new public practices from "common" religious and moral commitments. Although Christian antiliberalism is indeed constituted in part by recognizable forms and features, the study of political religion must also attend to the religious creations emergent outside the "common" and at the multiple intersections between religions and politics. Indeed, even the boundary between these two contested terms—"religion" and "politics"—is ever blurrier. It is clear when we engage Sojourners, the NCR, and the Berrigans that the religion/politics distinction is not theirs but rather one external method of mapping these groups' complicated relation to liberalism.

So when one seeks to engage and understand a conservative evangelical home school, a Plowshares action involving the use of hammers on a warplane, or the rhetorical or symbolic slipperiness of a Sojourners practice, there are questions and distinctions that are more and less helpful. As I noted in the introduction, questions oriented primarily around external qualifiers such as institutional or ideological affiliation are partially helpful at best in generating understanding of political religions. Instead of asking which political party an activist supports or to which denomination she or he belongs, I find it more illustrative, more helpful, more basic to ask, "To what extent are the groups contesting conventional discourse through political illegibility?" or "How is political order being experienced in the sacred registers?" These questions may yield answers that are more disturbing or more unwieldy, but they address elements of political religion that must not be overlooked.

The terms around which I have oriented this study—political illegibility, the sacred registers of politics, ritual protest, and koinonia—have helped delineate the specific features of Christian antiliberalism. The broader criticisms of liberal political order—that it is insensitive to the demands of religious practice, that its "bigness" and bureaucratic reach are hostile to robust forms of political participation, and that it relies on juridical and deliberative abstraction that obscures the moral issues most important to public politics—are made and remade through specific experiences, discourses, actions, and patterns of living. In these remakings, Christian antiliberalism emerges in ways that are politically illegible—exposing the limits of conventional ideological markers—and that exceed conventional religious categories such as denomination, ethnicity, or social class. Hence, this form of political religion exemplifies the polyvocality and the protean nature of political religions in America.

It is for these reasons that I describe Christian antiliberalism as a religio-political style or dynamic (a "coalition of resentments") rather than as a movement, for even though antiliberal practitioners share antipathies and styles of practice (manifested through political illegibility, the sacred registers of politics, ritual protest, and koinonia), they do not display any larger theological, ideological, or institutional affinities with one another. Rather than self-identifying exclusively as leftists or Catholics or conservatives, then, Christian antiliberals work in and around liberalism to redirect the patterns of thought and the practices that they feel violate their self-understandings as Christians.

It is here, in these elisions of liberalism, that patterns and consistencies are revealed among different groups of antiliberals. One of the most notable of these features is the use of liberal rights talk and political vocabulary to undermine the legitimacy of liberalism itself. New Christian Right educational activists decry state schooling for its "underhanded" propagation of the "religion of secular humanism," a "deceit" that they claim unconstitutionally establishes a religion as part of the state and that they consequently feel jeopardizes the salvation of NCR children. The Berrigans, too, condemn the state for violating their First Amendment rights, charging that the government tries to force them into "false worship" of nuclear weapons; under such duress, the only way they could be true to their faith, and also to the constitutional terms liberalism claims to honor, is to violate the law.[7] Although Sojourners do not make claims quite this stark, they nonetheless contend that American liberalism is all too often incompatible with the imperatives of "prophetic" politics. Another way of parsing these claims is to note that Christian antiliberals believe, for various reasons, that "the state has usurped the role of the Church as the guardian of public morality."[8] These words are Philip Berrigan's, yet they could just as easily have been delivered by Michael Farris, Jim Wallis, or any number of other protesters. It is true of them all that their activism emerges from an indignation over this perceived usurpation. Sensing themselves responsible for the authority claimed by liberal political order, Christian antiliberals attempt a reclamation.

In these efforts it is clear, as noted earlier, that particular groups of antiliberals embody one element of antiliberalism practice in a highly illustrative way: Sojourners' prophetic politics exemplifies the political illegibility common to Christian antiliberals; the NCR captures the antiliberal engagement with or experience of liberalism at the sacred registers of identity politics; and the Berrigans demonstrate the centrality of ritual protest to antiliberal critique. Each group, however, possesses all of these qualities in addition to the final quality of koinonia. The Berrigans and the NCR share Sojourners' belief that the standard political terminology used to designate paths of citizenship and activism—"left" and "right," "liberal" and "conservative"—is too blunt to capture the religious roots of their practice, too reductive to merit any religious validation, and all but insensitive to the concerns of the faithful. Sojourners and the Berrigans also believe that their identity as Christians marks them as deviant in a liberal regime and that politicization of the sacred registers of politics constitutes a countersign to that regime. And both the NCR and Sojourners are regular practitioners of the arts of ritual protest, dramatizing their religious concerns within the spaces of the liberal public sphere.

These crosscutting features suggest that American religion remains anything but static or passive and that religious participation in public politics has only intensified of late. The very otherness of religion in a liberal regime is used by Christian antiliberals as a critical principle, one that serves to introduce a plurality of meanings into public spheres these practitioners judge devoid of moral orientation. These meanings transect older religious and political boundaries, revealing that shared antipathies to the standing political order are at least partially determinative of the shapes of American Christianity.

The public acts and rituals of Christian antiliberalism are central to the constitution of identity. When such acts are analyzed, it becomes clear that religious and political components are not easily divisible, as the protest itself reveals religion as the site of negotiating identity and of testing the boundaries of the political. Cultural creations such as religions are the subject of politics, and vice versa, but each is far too polyvalent to be reducible to the other, to be rendered equivalent. Christian antiliberalism emerges partly in response to political developments; indeed, antiliberal beliefs and practices serve to articulate grievances and to negotiate for access to power. This proliferation of religious identities and practices around the political raises questions about how political space is defined, who has access to it, and what degree of participation it enables. From the point of view of Christian antiliberals, these are questions about the nature of witness, Christ's triumph over death and sin, or the effort to redeem a fallen social order. They are also questions about political power, the limits and possibilities of democracy, and the ubiquity of conflict in a pluralistic society. I am interested in Christian antiliberalism not because I believe that its practitioners hold the keys to our political and moral future or that they possess the wisdom necessary to guide our culture but because I believe that thinking along with these critics can yield insight both into why liberalism has come under such great scrutiny and into the new shapes of political religion in America.

A Refuge from Liberalism

As William Greider has written, the mutual dependence between citizens and government on which democracy relies has eroded, leaving little more than mutual contempt.[9] Contemporary politics has become more deeply Weberian, centering on the specialized knowledge and money required for entry into the process and utilizing a rationalized language that Christian antiliberals feel renders their religious and moral concerns remote from the political process. This widespread sense of frustration and powerlessness has produced a kind of "righteous isolation, contemptuous of all traditional ways of connecting with government."[10]

A typical narrative of post-1960s politics conceives of protest as a marginal activity forever threatened by the state's capacity to absorb and normalize dissent. The implication in such accounts is that "pragmatic" or "realist" politics are the only available outlets for activism in advanced capitalism. Flying in the face of this apparent good sense, Christian antiliberals have engaged in a willfully antisystemic practice—opposed to the hierarchy, planning, bureaucracy, and leadership of the liberal order—that collapses the boundaries between religion, politics, and culture through its use of a political logic, ritual protest idiom, and registers of identity that are often not on "normal" political grids. As a challenge to the abstract formalism of "the system," Christian antiliberals often eschew the rules of the liberal regime in favor of staging dramatic confrontations with power. Sometimes these confrontations involve organization building (as with Michael Farris and the Home School Legal Defense Association), at other times simply the cultivation of a religious community, such as Jonah House. In each case, however, Christian antiliberalism attempts to create a space for refuge from liberal political order.

In a context of relative disillusionment and powerlessness, Christian antiliberals attempt, in ways that are both admirable and worthy of concern, to empower citizens in their everyday lives and to provide a sense of meaning through direct political action rooted in the life of a community. This practice I call koinonia, recalling the fondness of Christian antiliberals for claiming inspiration from the lives and communal witness of the apostles as described in the Book of Acts. Outside of their direct confrontations with liberal political order, Christian antiliberals seek to craft the kind of community life they feel exemplifies those virtues crowded out of a liberal regime. As noted earlier, Sojourners claim that conventional political logic and discourse obscure or prevent meaningful forms of religious engagement with social problems such as poverty, and one of their most consistent strategies of response has been the cultivation of local community institutions in Washington, D.C., in addition to their locally oriented brand of public practice. The NCR's concerns about public education have frequently eventuated in the generation of small-scale initiatives that, though often tied to larger national organizations, strive to focus on precisely those felt experiences of emotion and character they believe are so crucial to the development of young people. The Berrigans' response to the perceived failures of both church and state has been the founding and maintenance of the resistance community Jonah House.

These responses embody different concerns and assume different shapes, both programmatic and institutional, but they all seek to constitute authentically Christian communities that embody the residents'/participants' sense of religious ethics and criticism. They all serve as refuges from a political order perceived as hostile. In response to their engagement with the very liberalism they experience as difference in the sacred registers, Christian antiliberals at times may disengage in koinonia. Certainly the desire to retreat from a political order perceived as hostile is an understandable one; if one believes that acquiescence to liberalism risks compromise or possible endangerment of one's tradition, then seeking refuge is a quite rational response, for it is in these spaces, too—in the schools and homes of the NCR, in the resistance ethos cultivated at Jonah House, in and around the Sojourners' neighborhood—that Christian antiliberal identity is worked on and protected. Yet the establishment of such spaces of refuge raises questions, as have the other elements of antiliberalism, about the relationship between American political religions and the ongoing project of American democracy.

Conceptual and practical confusions haunt these endeavors, concerning both their motivations and ultimate aspirations. For example, it is often unclear if Christian antiliberals possess a positive, rather than a critical, vision of community and democracy that might succeed liberalism. Without attention to the constructive details of community building, with all the attendant risks of such projects, Christian antiliberals may be fated to march in time to "the tragic rhythm of American radicalism."[11]

Certainly some elements in the critique of liberal political order are worthy of affirmation. Its proceduralism and its abstract rationality do not possess the kind of legitimacy required in a democratic regime. The administrative maze of American politics is rightly being assailed in the name of wider and more robust political participation. The antiliberal koinonia also embodies an admirable concern for deliberation and local activism.

And yet Christian antiliberalism's responses to these realities can be deeply troubling, filled as they are with the rhetoric of judgment and devoid as they are of moral or political compromise. Although these responses are linked to a critique of extant democracy, they frequently have a questionable relation to the very democratic norms they find lacking in liberalism. It may be, then, that Christian antiliberals are not always opposed to political authority as a matter of biblical principle or in the name of a more decentralized model of participatory democracy; one might reasonably conclude that some antiliberals would like to see their authority (re-)inscribed on the social order, to see koinonia become a model for social existence more broadly. Christian antiliberal use of religious power against the political—the invocation of an authoritative tradition that passes judgment on political order and that attempts to broaden the range of public discourse and practice—does not necessarily free practitioners or citizens from the pull of a different kind of authority; nor does it necessarily embody the multiple meanings or promote the irredeemable contestation on which democracies depend.

There is a curious ambiguity in Christian antiliberal practice, which serves simultaneously to contest and to reinforce extant politics. This practice raises important questions about, and highlights disturbing shortcomings in, contemporary American liberalism. Yet three potentially antidemocratic tendencies are shot through this ambiguous practice: the danger of excluding or "other-ing" those with different understandings of religion; the tendency of antiliberal protest toward aversion to any kind of political organization; and encouraging majoritarianism at the local level.

For example, the Berrigans' abandonment of mainstream reform initiatives and dismissal of attempts to transform political order have frequently been marked by a kind of religious righteousness that on occasion condemns not only the nonreligious but also those among the faithful who choose to work within extant political systems. This kind of separatism—whether devotional or spatial—can undermine the positive role that different kinds of political institutions and different scales of activity can play in reform and activism. Further, it quite possibly constitutes a retreat from rather than an engagement with politics, in all its messiness and fractiousness. Although the Berrigans are wisely suspicious of the deficiencies of liberal democracy and have continued to challenge state policies, their lack of hope for reform has transformed the language of Christian social criticism into a forbidding and extreme idiom.[12] The Berrigans may, in fact, have robbed themselves of an important resource for challenging the tactics of such groups and for presenting their own form of witness, for without the willingness to criticize traditions, institutions, and practices from within, religious social critics such as the Berrigans will find their voice only in a wilderness that, for all the moral legitimacy it may seem to confer, is increasingly remote from the world they hope to change.

Jonah House's separatism and its stark social criticism resemble other forms of Catholic separatism, such as Peter Maurin's agrarianism in the Catholic Worker movement of the 1950s, but also the kind of antiworldly orientation frequently found in NCR communities. Since the 1970s, the Berrigans have not so much altered their social criticism as shifted its location. Their abandonment of the reformist hope central to their 1960s activism has allowed conservative religious activists to gain a monopoly on the moral languages of Christian social criticism. In its disgust with the public's dwindling capacity for moral outrage, Jonah House paradoxically ends up using some of the rhetoric and tropes favored by extreme religionists such as the Christian militias or Operation Rescue, whose condemnatory tones brook no degree of compromise. It is clear that the Berrigans and these other extremists are different in their orientation and practice. But these odd overlaps between them call attention not only to liberalism's failure to secure its own political legitimacy but also to the very real possibilities and pitfalls of religious politics. The all-important questions of generating a positive communal vision or a cogent institutional alternative to a political system denounced as irredeemable are dismissed as extrinsic to the demands of Christian devotion.

A similar animosity toward institutional life is evident also in NCR practice. Activists such as Michael Farris and the parents and educators who share his educational priorities see themselves as promoting a type of human dignity that only "Bible-based" education can free from the shackles of liberal society. The theological worlds of conservative American evangelicals and Catholic pacifists are extremely different; but it is important to note that they have rhetorical, critical, and practical commonalities. The growing sense in Jonah House that the Scriptures are sufficient, for example, mirrors the literalism found in a Christian educational manual or textbook. Each is confident that the New Testament is the paradigmatic guide for political activity and can address the range of political or moral alternatives that are necessary. The NCR's suspicion of academia, the liberal media, and secular humanism—a mistrust that now constitutes something of a lingua franca in American political life—is heartily endorsed by the Berrigans.[13]

The NCR is unique, however, in its focus on public education. In its vociferous critique of nearly every facet of American liberalism, it inevitably decries those features of liberal political order it disagrees with as antidemocratic. Like the Berrigans in the courtroom, the NCR discloses liberalism's aversion to strong moral or religious commitment, its constraint of public discourse, and the ways in which this aversion can disempower citizens at the local level. Yet the goals of the NCR are often equally undemocratic: it risks unchecked majoritarianism in its desire to replace the particularist world of political liberalism with its particularist understanding of Christianity. Although it is not quite accurate to say that the NCR seeks the establishment of a theocracy, it is correct to suggest that it is opposed to the political order only insofar as this order does not represent or legislate on the basis of *its* concerns. To claim that public education is not "neutral" or "rational" and that it may contain biases against the kind of religious values found in the NCR is one thing; but it is quite another to suggest that the public education curriculum must be jettisoned in favor of topics such as creation science, the teaching of abstinence instead of sex education, and the study of Scripture. Such a move would substitute one form of public exclusivity for another and jeopardize the educational rights of students without the religious views of the NCR. The same cautions would obviously hold true for other features of the NCR's domestic and foreign policy commitments.

Sojourners, though seemingly the most palatable and centrist of the activists discussed in this book, also face questions concerning the democratic aspirations they claim are central to their work. On the one hand, Wallis, Sojourners, and Call to Renewal (CTR) claim to be more ecumenical and inclusive than other religious activists; yet they also insist that "prophetic politics" is the only authentic avenue toward spiritual-political integrity. Sojourners' demand that every social and political issue be seen as a moral and religious issue is not altogether different from the claims of other Christian antiliberals. Yet there are two ancillary features of "prophetic politics" that complicate this claim in potentially disturbing ways. First is the notion that Christians must be outsiders, willing to "speak truth to power." If the prophetic Christian insists on refraining from institutional or conventional political involvement, one might justifiably call CTR's public criticism moralizing or hypocritical. More substantively, if the Christian's obligations do not extend beyond the local geography in more than a rhetorical sense, one might well wonder if "prophetic politics" is more beneficial to the moral self-worth of its practitioners than to the poor and disenfranchised.

The second feature is the rhetorical indeterminacy of "prophetic politics" itself. Wallis's reliance on the language of "civility," "compassion," and "compromise" may sound inviting, and yet this same language is employed by the figureheads of NCR organizations in ways that are used to label their opponents and construct them as "other." Sojourners do little to distinguish their use of these notions from those of more conservative figures. So great is their need to distance themselves from conventional political affiliation, indeed, that they stop short of important conceptual and practical distinctions from those whose social vision opposes theirs. If Sojourners can provide citizens with no cogent way of understanding their programs as alternatives to those of Gary Bauer or William Bennett, what is to prevent loose notions such as "civility" from becoming available for endless manipulation? Sojourners' use of Scripture is similarly loose. It is self-evident that the writings of the prophets of the Hebrew Bible, to say nothing of Scripture more broadly, contain mixed messages about the social and political responsibilities of the devout. Yet Sojourners insist that theirs is the authentic reading of Scripture no less than the NCR does of its (opposing) readings. Is there not, in this insistence, a religious arrogance, a sense that those whose answers to social problems differ from Sojourners' are politically fallen?

Underlying all three antiliberal worldviews is the notion that "every action of the government is seen as sinister, duplicitous, and illegitimate."[14] Politics is seen as inherently confrontational, with little middle ground between detachment and embattlement. This does not mean that the conspiratorial tone in Philip Berrigan's writings is comparable to a Christian "patriot" militia's fears of a Zionist-Occupied Government. But the antiliberal antipathy toward political order in any form cuts against the more reformist tendencies of antiliberalism and in so doing raises unsettling questions about power and religion in American democracy. If koinonia is freighted with disdain for the democratic process, it can risk not only insularity or detachment but potentially social violence as well.

Power, Religion, and Democracy

How, then, should such increasing political uncertainty, social discontent, and attendant issues of social power be understood? What themes, frameworks, and categories can generate the cultural dialogues needed to address these questions and issues? I have insisted throughout that this work cannot proceed without engaging the specific forms of pluralism and discontent that it aims to address. In order fully to understand the nature and scope of specific challenges such as Christian antiliberalism—and in order to make any effort at addressing or responding concretely to such challenges—it is imperative to combine a rigorous empirical approach to such phenomena with an appreciation for the thorny issues of power and democracy they broach.

The political system challenged by Christian antiliberals is an heir to classical European liberalism, which generally seeks to ward off social disorder while still protecting political rights by avoiding potentially discordant questions of meaning and morality in the public sphere. According to this model of liberal order, the individual rights enjoyed by citizens are premised on the good of social cooperation. As we have seen, Christian antiliberals believe that this model of social cooperation demands of them that they either ignore or falsify commitments and practices that are central to their lives. At the center of this conflict with liberalism is the unwillingness of practitioners to sacrifice their particular beliefs in order to gain access to public politics. It is difficult to imagine, for example, a situation in which a Christian schools advocate on a local school board would sacrifice his or her religious beliefs in a conversation about science curricula. (It would be politically difficult to stomach the notion that democracy can flourish only if such individuals are kept off school boards.)[15]

These are the very real issues and concerns that occupy citizens in a liberal democratic regime. Although it is practically implausible to suggest that no decision or collective undertaking is legitimate without addressing the specific concerns of each citizen involved, it is equally implausible to ignore the sources of conflict about which liberalism may rightly be fearful. Some political theorists, such as Stephen Holmes, fear that such engagement with religious concerns and practices could unwittingly generate support for antidemocratic legislation. Holmes and others may rightly fear religiously supported legislation such as Colorado's 1992 Amendment 2, which sought to overturn a bill granting equal recognition and rights to same-sex domestic partnerships, yet these concerns cannot be applied categorically to political religions.[16] A deeper engagement with history and culture would not necessarily transform liberal political order, but without such an engagement there is little hope of understanding better and navigating a culture as complex and fractious as ours, much less that liberal principles could secure legitimacy.

To insist on the continued "privatization" of religion, or to insist that religions are inconsequential to the work of democracies, is to misconstrue the very "problem" with which democracies are rightly preoccupied. A strategy of radically circumscribing the public sphere and confining religion to the private sphere only invites the hostility of activists and protesters such as Christian antiliberals. Liberalism may not engage in the active institutional constraint of religious speech and practice, as some religious social critics believe; yet in liberal political order there are nonetheless tacit assumptions about what constitutes socially acceptable religion, assumptions that function to exclude certain forms of religion from the conversation.[17] I contend that the understandable animosity resulting from these tendencies could be addressed, if not quelled, by a fuller public engagement with the sources and motivations of such specifically religious discontent. Such engagement would not only put democratic decision making and participation on firmer philosophical grounds but would also address a key criticism motivating antiliberals.

In making these suggestions, however, I do not ally myself with those challenges to the liberal model of politics made in the name of "values" or "community" loosely defined. Such challenges—often affiliated with communitarian theory, frequent antagonist of Rawlsian liberal theory—criticize liberal procedures for their lack of attention to moral discourse, community, and narrative context, all of which are celebrated as necessary for a healthy political life. The primary concern in this charge is that liberalism weakens communities and alienates citizens from one another in a way that threatens to fray the connective tissues on which democratic life depends.[18] In these critics' view, liberal philosophy is plausible only with a conception of the self divested of the central aspects of identity (such as communal ties, moral worldview, or religious commitment) that make people who they are. If liberalism's conception of the self is faulty, it is reasoned, so too is the type of politics to which it is linked.

There is merit to the communitarian critique of procedural liberalism, particularly in its rejoinder to what Stephen L. Carter calls the trivialization of religion. Certainly religions ought not to be dismissed as illegitimate contenders in political and legal discourses, and any potential judicial or political constraints on religious practice might rightly be regarded as antidemocratic. Yet there is something about this communitarian argument that is too enamored of the notion that religion or "values," however vaguely these might be defined, might prove a necessary antidote to the ills of liberalism. These observations, in other words, are undermined by a certain vagueness and breeziness about religion as it exists on the ground in America. Communitarianism's laudable desire to have religion taken seriously on the collective political agenda leads to an intellectual overcompensation. Certainly not all political religion is illiberal, but it is folly to suggest that "values"—religious or otherwise—are prima facie sources for remedies to liberalism's legitimation crisis. It is far too simplistic to suggest that public life cannot get along without religion, to insist that if we could only "get religion," then we would have a political panacea. These assumptions, like those of the liberalism under such scrutiny, are plausible only at a significant remove from what religions actually are. Religions do not always play by the rules. Religions do not always conform to the demands of conversational restraint or the bracketing of deeply contentious religious beliefs. The "moral voices" of religions are frequently inflected with antidemocratic potential. Zeal to criticize liberalism should not lead critics to valorize uncritically the claims of religious and local communities, as if their very localism or religiousness granted them a sort of epistemic or even political privilege.

It is no service to democracy, in any of its multiple forms, simply to evoke a culturally grounded form of politics without thinking through its relation to the world into which it must fit. My point is that it is altogether too superficial to sacralize values-based or values-neutral politics; each of these "solutions" is, in some important ways, an attempt to sidestep the difficulties of reckoning politically with the multiple, fractious, and potentially irresoluble debates of a democratic society. Ignoring the issues of meaning that are central to people's lives can clearly generate acrimony, yet so too can a simplistic embrace of these same issues of meaning. In a pluralistic society such as ours, it is far from clear which forms of community or which sorts of values—if any—might be relevant in any given political context or situation. Problems of pluralism and identity are not necessarily captured well by categories such as "values" or "community" or by "neutrality" and "rationality"; rather, these are inevitably issues saturated with social power. It is this issue of religious power, both exclusionary and dissenting, that is so clearly foregrounded in Christian antiliberal practice.

Political and social theories should be applauded for their attempts to reckon with growing social discontent. Yet such theories often reveal more about each other than they do about the world they seek to engage. These theoretical conversations explicitly link themselves with political events and practices that go beyond the esoteric world of philosophy; and indeed, they have helped shape and reshape the political order that Christian antiliberalism challenges. Yet there remains a "strange silence" to both these theories: they are ironically detached from the political world they seek to engage.[19] This does not mean that theory is bankrupt; rather, theory's vast resources are not used often enough and are unnecessarily shielded from history and culture.

The presence of antiliberalism raises questions about the meaning, scope, and shape of American democracy at the beginning of a new century. It is a valuable effort to grapple with this phenomenon theoretically, to seek a comparative language and a categorical framework that may enable closer analysis and substantive response. Hence, it is vital on both a normative and a practical level not to disallow or depoliticize Christian antiliberalism. The only theoretical response that will work is one that is historically and culturally informed. The ground of politics has shifted beneath our feet. Ignorance of these shifts will yield very real cultural, political, and legal consequences—not just for religious activists but for American politics in general, as its legitimacy and very functioning are undermined by increasingly antagonistic critics. Without rethinking the presuppositions that frame interpretations of political religion, the problems of this encounter will only be exacerbated.

I call attention to these issues of power and social authority in Christian antiliberalism not because I hope to reconstruct a theory of the political that can address all these issues. Rather, I more modestly suggest that the shapes of this particular type of American political religion are themselves saturated with social power and that these complexities determine the direction of Christian antiliberalism's religious expression. The thorny issues of power and coercion, freedom and constraint, are *part of* the religious practice itself. It is not the telos of my project to argue for a particular institutional response to the realities exemplified in Christian antiliberalism. Others have more cogently addressed the need for, and the desirability of, intermediary institutions that can accommodate a more robust form of political participation.[20] Still, the presence of this Christianity, with its attendant issues of power, practically demands that its observers draw some inferences for thinking about democratic politics. I simply highlight, rather than attempt to resolve, issues raised by Christian antiliberalism that must be addressed more fully in a democratic society: the centrality of deliberation, the value of institutional pluralization, respect for identity, and challenges of local community building. These are also religious issues and concerns, ones that need to be foregrounded in the study of political religion in America.

Antiliberalism is everywhere, and its challenges must be acknowledged and met in a democratic fashion. American liberalism is, of course, not in immediate danger of replacement; Christian antiliberals do not wait in the shadows to mount a revolution. But liberalism nonetheless lacks energy and consent, and if its problems are not cataclysmic ones, they remain significant.[21] It is in this context that many theorists have displayed a resurgence of interest in democracy and civil society. The organizational emphasis of Christian antiliberals clearly parallels the spaces of civil society; koinonia is consistent not only with the philosophical turn to identity but also with the challenge to centralized authority. When Christian antiliberals believe that liberal political order undermines communal self-determination, they respond by working from local institutions and traditions to empower citizens in much the same way as do proponents of a revitalized civil society.

The terrain of localism and koinonia is thus not only the arena in which the impact of the state is most acutely felt but also the space for challenging illegitimate authority and empowering citizens. Here, new identities are enacted, new political issues contested, and the scope of the liberal state challenged. What is so crucial to this observation, and so confounding to observers of political religion, is that Christian antiliberalism's valuable emphasis on participation and local activism is precisely the point at which the antidemocratic risks of its activities are sharpest.

Amid the plurality of meanings that converge on the term "democracy" —meanings that range from "rulers" who are ratified by the people to a government that serves as citizens' caretaker—a crucial common theme is the notion that democracy is a political form constituted and governed by the people themselves. Yet when the people themselves determine the shape of the political sphere, the issues of power, conflict, and majoritarianism are unavoidable. Particularly when citizens are informed by antagonistic political religion such as Christian antiliberalism, democracy opens up into danger. Religious power is maintained and deployed both on the organizational level and at the deepest registers of subjectivity, emotion, and moral sensibility. It is in these registers, with their potential for passion and zeal, that the dangers of Christian antiliberalism are strongest and least likely to submit to the requirements of a democratic polity.

The central question with which Christian antiliberalism confronts us, then, is how to reconcile the need for a more democratic politics with the potential for antidemocratic practice this may invite. Does Christian antiliberal resistance strive for a larger political transformation? Does this religious criticism aim to restore legitimacy to the shared features of a democratic order? Or is it instead a rejection of these goals in favor of righteous separatism or worse? Most interpretations of political religion ignore these sorts of questions in their insistence that religion is, for one reason or another, either not fit for politics or absolutely necessary to democracy. I believe it is wrong to focus solely on the potential dangers or benefits of Christian politics; we should begin also to focus on liberalism's limits.

First, theorists must take more seriously phenomena such as the Christian challenge to liberal political order, rather than dismissing it as a novelty or a passing phenomenon. This challenge is part of a recognizable political tradition in the United States, one whose reemergence needs to be addressed in a substantive and democratic fashion. Additionally, theoretical engagement with these issues must avoid underwriting a form of politics that sidesteps the challenge to conventional politics and its call for more democratic participation.

Second, serious engagement with political religion and its challenges demands rigorous inquiry into and descriptions of the religionists themselves. By placing the study of American religions in conversation with these larger political and theoretical concerns, I hope to have made clearer some of these complexities by using comparative categories (e.g., political illegibility) that can assist richer interpretations of political religions. A deeper, historically informed grasp of political religions can enable clearer thinking about their implications for American democracy. Only with such understanding can a more democratic solution to the problems of religion in the public sphere be assayed. To facilitate this understanding, the study of American political religion should link together disparate strands of knowledge (from the sociological study of new social movements, the religious study of ritual protest, and the political theory of liberal democracy) to tell the story of presences such as Christian antiliberalism. This grounded work puts theory on more solid footing, keeping it from straying too far from the terrain of political practice, from the daily messiness of political life.

Finally, a more democratic response to political religions is needed. This is not intended to echo facile calls for "religious values" in the public sphere, for religion is now, and always has been, in the public sphere. The salient question is how we can more democratically reckon with the implications of this presence. Since both religion and politics are assuming new forms, albeit with resemblances to older traditions, it is important to rethink what democracy requires in this new context. Although the liberal goals of individual liberty and public civility are not themselves anachronistic, different methods are now needed to secure those goals.

I contend that a radical democratic politics is better able to grapple with these shifts. Radical democracy does not identify the democratic ideal (whereby the people are responsible for their own political self-determination) with the mechanisms of governance (i.e., the state or the federal bureaucracy) or with the market. In order that the people might become more involved in the processes of their own governance, radical democracy seeks to restore political power to citizens by encouraging participation at the local level, creating spaces where citizens may form issues and debate them, and ensuring that the political sphere is open to issues that are relevant to both particular identities and the nation at large. This response to political religions seeks a way out of the liberal-communitarianism impasse in three ways: it is rooted in the mediating space of civil society; it is open to the claims of "value" and "identity" that underlie antiliberalism; and it is committed to a robust form of participation that also recognizes the partiality of such participation and the danger of allowing any single vision of the good to achieve hegemony. So these efforts are chastened by a sense of political tragedy and a sensitivity to the dangers courted in widening the scope of political participation. Although these theoretical aims are not unique to my project, they are made sharper when conjoined with the challenges of Christian antiliberalism.

Widening the political sphere to recognize the political claims of groups such as Christian antiliberals does not commit anyone to agreement with them. Rather, such recognition acknowledges that to seal off religious participation actually fuels the acrimony underlying antiliberalism. There is a greater chance of contending with antiliberal challenges by creating a more democratic public sphere that recognizes the existence of spaces between the private sphere and the state and strives to create local outlets for deliberation and contestation. Illiberalism is already a part of our public life, and it can be negotiated only through open debate and political practice.

Christian antiliberals may not always invoke the language of democracy, but it is precisely the ideal of more vigorous political participation that animates their critique of the liberal state. It is in the political spaces that belong neither to the "private sphere" nor to the state that Christian antiliberals have attempted to reinvigorate the political process itself, in the struggle for identity through organizing publics, coalescing political identities, and moral suasion. And it is in these political spaces that religious and social powers come to the surface. So although Christian antiliberalism and its multiple tactics call attention to the need for a more democratic and participatory politics, they also confront us with the need to establish limits to such a politics. Democracy must include widespread political contestation, a demand that challenges the domesticated and boundaried politics of the modern liberal state, and must acknowledge the impossibility of final adjudication on any political matters. Only in the presence of such a deliberative contest can a democratic society achieve legitimation.[22] Yet if democracy thereby trespasses the boundaries that enforce sameness, rigidity, and even stability, we must reckon once again with the dangers that its contestation invites, particularly with regard to political religion.

Certainly from one point of view, "civil society" and democracy are not threatened by religious activism or discourse. Religious commitment may depend on the kind of robust worldview of the sort with which some procedural liberals are uncomfortable, yet there is a sense in which the comprehensive worldviews of the devout are no less robust as moral commitments than those of other identity-based activists or intermediate institutions. The dangers posed by political religion in general, and by Christian antiliberalism in particular, are not exclusively those of religion but issue instead from the attempt to impose moral or political commitments (whether these are religious or not) on others. It is here that the study of American religion can help more fully to delineate the shapes of these commitments, their historical and devotional roots, the motivations behind publicizing them, and the goals they pursue. From the perspective of such study, democratic citizens might leave behind the abstract conundrum of whether religion and politics should mix to focus instead on determining precisely which aspects of these realities are detrimental to the causes of democracy and which are not.

I am not suggesting, therefore, that the residents of Jonah House should replace the Joint Chiefs of Staff, that NCR school activists should be proportionally represented on local school boards, or that Sojourners might know how best to manage the Federal Reserve. To call for a democratization of American liberalism is not a tacit endorsement of religious majoritarianism; it is an acknowledgment of political religion's historical importance in addressing a new constellation of political problems and religious realities in American society. In other words, although political order is not obligated to legislate on the basis of these deliberations, it is obligated to guarantee the expression and acknowledgment of citizens' multiple viewpoints.

Happily, some religious activists are able to work within this kind of robust democratic framework. There are occasions on which Sojourners or CTR embodies what might be called the "virtues" of democratic participation, those qualities named earlier. For example, CTR has moved further toward acknowledging the local commitments and priorities of the chapters it establishes, encouraging local citizens to become involved in the political process. In addition, religious affiliates of the Industrial Areas

Foundation—such as the East Brooklyn Congregations or Texas Valley Interfaith—acknowledge that the demands of religious activism are not incompatible with those of a democratic polity. Certainly, not all Christian antiliberals will be satisfied by the arrangements I modestly note here. It is difficult to imagine either the Berrigans or the NCR assenting to the all the procedures of democracy if this entailed a sacrifice of their goals. And yet these very ways and processes, I believe, constitute a way to deal with their potential dissatisfaction.

This normative argument for a more democratic politics also possesses an eye to political consequences. Democratic politics only guarantees that religious activists have the right to participate, not that their programs will succeed. Deliberation involves subjecting the programs and practices of such groups to scrutiny on the basis of shared democratic norms. This more democratic way of meeting the challenges of Christian antiliberalism is able to create more spaces for participation in a culture that finds such spaces increasingly threatened by bureaucracy and the market. The antidemocratic tendencies of Christian antiliberalism are more likely to be checked through an open and deliberative politics of this sort. For example, if the trials of the Berrigans ceased reliance on the undemocratic use of gag rules, the splenetic quality of the Berrigans' protest might be diminished. If the educational concerns of the NCR were not dismissed as insular or backward and allowed expression as a legitimate public interest in a recognizable forum, then the charges of "religious bigotry" that so animate the NCR might abate.

Liberalism's goals are worth protecting, but the effort to achieve them has too often employed antidemocratic mechanisms that constrain participation. Now the political landscape has shifted, and liberalism can better survive amid these changes by welcoming multiple forms of action and accepting the politicization of new areas of public life. Doing so does not abandon liberal values but represents the critical engagement with them in dialogue with cultural change. Such an approach may actually better serve to protect individual liberty and public civility than does extant liberalism. Outlets for discussion and debate about value questions could help satisfy the "need" Christian antiliberalism exemplifies by engaging citizens in problem solving and political empowerment, which help to reduce alienation and anxiety. Religious activists may participate and argue with fellow citizens, but their policies and practices will be measured against the norms of legality, publicity, pluralism, and association. If the practices and policies do not overlap with democratic norms, they cannot be legislated or enforced. This constitutes a set of boundaries and limits not to be overstepped.

Democracy sanctions neither license nor majority tyranny but is, instead, a less coercive way of dealing with the problems such as those raised by Christian antiliberals. This argument clearly begs questions of institutional arrangement. What does civil society look like and what practices are conducive to it? How can deliberation be institutionalized when citizens are often so apathetic? No one yet has the answers to these questions. Political norms are always in transition, and the political space for civil society exists only tenuously. My claim that these challenges can be managed only in the democratic process itself does not yield any certainties.

I make these suggestions skeptically, in the spirit more of Reinhold Niebuhr than of Stephen Carter. I hold no illusions about the ease with which such spaces for deliberation might be created or by which citizens might be politically energized. As both H. Richard and Reinhold Niebuhr argued, Christ is central for Christians, but not for everyone. Religious practices, narratives, and symbols are categories within particular communities of identity but, especially in a democracy, cannot be made binding for the political community at large, for if one thing is central to the vitality of a democracy, it is that the contest over the issues and decisions of import to its citizens be continuous, that the changing viewpoints and conditions of its communities be reflected in the deliberative practice that sits at the heart of democracy. This emphasis on unending conversation and contestation is born of no romantic or optimistic view of human capacities and tendencies but from the recognition of human tendencies toward selfishness and power struggles. Because we humans are often unrealistic about power, self-interest, and the fragmentary character of historical achievements, we require the openness of democratic participation to subject our decisions and achievements to revision and legitimation.

The Stubborn Quality of Truth and Experience

The study of religion is fraught with epistemological challenges that are perhaps unique in the interpretation of cultures. The discipline of religious studies has long been identifiable by its methodological self-consciousness, by its tendency to agonize over the possibility or desirability of studying religions "objectively" (a consideration that raises further questions about what is entailed by objectivity, social scientific standards, or merely some form of interpretative disinterest). Yet for well over thirty years it has been axiomatic in the humanities that "objectivity" and "disinterest" are, along with other robust species of truth claims, at best misrepresentations of the kind of knowledge that limited human subjects can have about one another and at worst illusions that are saturated with power. In light of the disrepute into which aspirations to objectivity have fallen, some scholars of religion have pondered whether one ought simply to "confess" one's interests in the study of religion, to acknowledge one's material and intellectual situatedness in a way that supposedly is forthright about the biases that inevitably creep into scholarship. After the postmodern turn, it is reasoned, there are no longer any substantive reasons to support pretensions to objectivity.[23] Still more recently, such debates have been expanded to question the very utility of the term "religion." Is it even reasonable to think that a single analytic category can capture the wide variety of human practices and traditions? Furthermore, is it possible that the very use of the term "religion" is part of a hierarchical system that ranks acceptable and unacceptable forms of "religion," that distinguishes "our" religion from "theirs," "good" religion from "bad"?[24]

Raising these kinds of issues in the study of American political religion not only helps to achieve distance from breezy accounts about religion in public life but can also serve as a way to gain some clarity about the presuppositions behind such study, my own and others'. In attending to the specifically religious character of Christian antiliberalism, I am in no way suggesting that there is a fixed essence of "religion"; indeed, religions are as protean as any other form of human identity or organization. Rather, when religious activists are judged by the political standards of liberal order, their religiousness (in all its fractiousness and diversity) is generally what marks them as politically other (which, of course, is a status embraced by many protesters). The construction of the term "religion" is a vivid reminder of how political and legal power can shape an orientation toward American religions.

In reckoning with a specific form of political religion, I have striven to avoid projecting my own presuppositions about religion and politics— whether these are scholarly presuppositions or other kinds—onto the practitioners before documenting their beliefs and aspirations as fully and, as it were, faithfully as possible. Although it is impossible fully to avoid such dangers—my very attention to these kinds of issues in American religion, these specific practitioners, and the questions of legitimacy they raise are marks of my own interest and my own position as both citizen and scholar—I have tried nonetheless to keep my focus on the fragile relationship between these religious social critics and political order. This relationship is particularly vexed in the United States, since American liberalism's historical commitments to safeguard the rights of conscience and religious belief have been pursued through the construction of "religion" as a general category of experience that is off limits to the state and other citizens. Yet the social critics I describe have resisted the specifically liberal conceptions embodied in this understanding of "religion": a definition of citizens as disinterested and rational individuals and a conception of political order as minimalist and morally neutral. These critics have also contested the institutional or practical pursuits consistent with these conceptions, specifically the formulation of "religion" as an individual phenomenon, one that centers around belief over action and that is practiced in "nonpolitical" spaces, those clearly demarcated from the public realm of the state.[25] Liberals have generally sought to continue protecting "religion," generically speaking, out of a concern that unchecked social power could threaten pluralism; critics of liberalism, on the other hand, see the liberal strategy as antithetical to religions as they are actually lived and instead seek greater recognition for the multiple forms "religion" may take in a pluralistic society. Writing in the shadow of this dilemma, students of political religion must reflect on the meanings of provocative and often unsettling encounters between religions and the political.

Attending to the details of Christian antiliberalism, as well as to the broader political directions therein, can only benefit those who would think scrupulously about political religions in America. Particularly with such a trenchant form of critique, a fine-grained intellectual response should calibrate itself to the concreteness of lived religion, to what Jean Bethke Elshtain calls the "stubborn quality of truth and experience."[26] We are witness not only to broader trends in political religion—whereby North American Christians challenge "the basic principle of state sovereignty as well as the proposal to replace the state system with transnational materialism"—but to the ways in which these critiques and ritual protests often emerge outside established church structures and flourish instead at the level of popular religiosity as well as through the four analytic features I have used to describe Christian antiliberalism.[27] This kind of political religion helps reconstitute devotional identity around shared political antipathies in a way that merges "seemingly incompatible beliefs into one worldview, serving different constituencies and different purposes at the same time."[28]

In the contemporary context of American liberal democracy, the study of American religion itself acquires a political immediacy, for Christian antiliberalism is indicative of a wider confluence of religious and political meaning making that is transforming the shape of American religious practice. Amid all the religious creativity and innovation that have flourished in the United States, the specters of coercion, manipulation, and social conflict have hovered close by. A democratic society may depend on pluralism and contact, yet these very elements raise the risk of conflict and antidemocratic activity. The stuff of public religion *is* the stuff of power, self-interest, compromise, ego, and conflict. Christian antiliberalism may testify to the importance of community organizing and the need for citizens to defy power and create political projects of their own. But this political energy is all too susceptible to a politics of difference, of manipulation, or of scorn for public order. Christian antiliberals may hit the mark in some of their criticisms of liberal political order, yet their responses remain troubling, even to the most sanguine interpreter.

The need to address these tensions is pressing, insofar as Christian antiliberalism raises troubling questions about political legitimacy. It is essential, therefore, that chroniclers of American religion reject the all too prominent notion that religious social criticism is a mere morality play, that it lacks the substance to merit hard-nosed religious or political scrutiny, or that it is unambiguously a good thing. I describe the Christian rebuke to political order because I am convinced of its significance in the study of American religion more broadly. I am further convinced that a sufficient understanding of such phenomena must incorporate newer and more supple modes of analysis that can track the overlapping meanings, powers, and cultures in political religion. The categories I have used in this book are my contribution to this work. And it is my hope that they may achieve a broader utility in the study of political religions.

In these endeavors, it is crucial that interpreters of American religion not adopt a separatist stance that mirrors the political separatism of some antiliberals. Some elements of antiliberal critiques (e.g., the scorn for all political authority) and certainly a number of their programmatic suggestions (e.g., the rejection of public education) may rub scholars the wrong way, but the study of American religion depends on avoiding the construction of "a normative hierarchy of religious idioms" that acts to exclude those religious creations that are beyond the pale of disciplinary tolerance.[29] Although it may revolt some people to think that Christian antiliberals are poised to annex local school boards or city councils or that antiliberal rhetoric may contain the urge to dominate the civic order by imposing a narrowly fundamentalist conception of the good, "it is the challenge of Religious Studies to hold our horror, desires, needs, hopes, and fears in creative tension as we work towards understanding the other."[30]

By refusing to constitute Christian antiliberals as either religiously or politically other, we can begin to appreciate the complexities of their creations and the challenges they pose both to those who seek to understand American religion and also to fellow citizens concerned about the fate(s) of American democracy. Certainly these creations exist in tension with the demands of democracy; but they also raise important questions about the meanings of democracy itself. Indeed, one need not insist that Christian antiliberalism is itself a democratic practice, or that its presence is beneficial for democratic politics, in order to recognize that the questions it raises are important ones that evince new religious sensibilities expanding the boundaries of the political.

These questions call for a kind of political engagement on the part of chroniclers of American religion. The best contribution to be made is as full a documentation of political religion as possible in order to facilitate the hard-nosed political analysis clearly necessitated in our context. It is in this complicated space where the dangers and the promises of religious social criticism commingle that I believe the study of American religion proves useful in the work of political reflection and theorization. Mapping the contours of phenomena such as Christian antiliberalism provides a way to speak, out of the silences of contemporary theory, about the challenges that currently beset American democracy and about new religious and cultural movements that challenge us to rethink older approaches to the study of religion in public life.

The stakes of such considerations are high. We live in a chastened moment, one that has seen a heightening of concern with and awareness of the intersecting problems of power, religion, and democracy. Most of this awareness centers around the presence of religiously oriented terrorist groups such as the Al Qaeda network responsible for the events of September 11, 2001. The irruption of such violence into American public life raises questions about the conventional parameters of recent political discourse. The liberal triumphalism of the post–Cold War years now seems like a distant relic, its optimism weak in contrast not only with September 11 but also with Rwanda, East Timor, and Kosovo. Similarly, protestations that liberal political order is nothing but the thinly disguised will to power of elites now seems too self-important, too dismissive of the real value to be found in searching for common political projects and procedures. It is thus time for renewed reflection on power, religion, and democracy, not only as global concerns but as issues fundamental to American political culture and history.

Religious antiliberalism is, as I mentioned in the introduction, a global phenomenon. Yet although it is important to situate my own project in this broader context, my aim here has not been to generate a global theory of political religion. Any such theory, however, would need to be conducted in ways similar to my study of Christian antiliberalism. What I mean by this is not that my approach to political religions is the only worthwhile one but simply that the measure of a theory of political religion is not its breadth of scope or its potential value to international diplomats and State Department officials. Even those acts with the most wide-ranging of intentions and consequences need to be studied in their immediate local context, since this is the ground of such actions. It may be true that, as Mark Juergensmeyer and others contend, notions of cosmic warfare shape and structure these actions to a degree; yet equally, and probably more, important are the local structures of kinship ties, customs, relational networks, public space, and the tangled web of experiences of political frustration or hope that are felt in the home and at the most intimate levels of human experience. Certainly this focus on the local level—at which Christian antiliberals experience their world in its immediacy—has been central to my study: Sojourners are angered at the arrangement of and access to public space in their neighborhood; the NCR experiences its moral crisis over books in the local library or curricula in the local classroom; and the Berrigans see the public housing projects behind Jonah House as symptoms of a larger political order gone awry. This is not to say that these claims and experiences are not directed outward and related to larger concerns, for they surely are (and this, too, has been central to my study). But if one is to understand this redirection, one must seek first to comprehend the initial experience and perception of disorder that lead Christian antiliberals to attempt a reordering of their worlds. Their specific religiosity is working with and against a specific political world; neither "religion" nor "politics" can be essentialized in these considerations.

I care deeply about pluralism (religious and otherwise) and about the ability of political order to safeguard it. Conflict is ubiquitous in a pluralistic society, and so dialogue and compromise are necessary. Not every distinct or competing worldview generates policies or patterns of life that are consistent with the norms of a democracy or with its legal structures. Yet in order to avoid the twin pitfalls of privileging a single normative vision (of "religion" or of politics) or of allowing the legitimacy of the law to erode, there is an urgent need to generate public forums for the airing of differences and, it is hoped, for the construction of political consensus through reflective, critical discourse. Only through such robust deliberation and participation can the challenges of religions and political power be met.

Christian antiliberalism constitutes a challenge to think differently about what democracy requires. Indeed, it problematizes many of the keywords that guide the study of political religion. Terms such as "reactionary," "fundamentalist," "liberal," "democratic," and "postmodern" are frequently used as explanatory categories for this sort of protest activity, but in the body of this study it has become apparent that these terms now lack a certain precision and that a different vocabulary is required to make sense of the contemporary context.

A sufficient understanding of what politics is, and of what is at stake in Christian antiliberalism, must recognize that old modes of analysis are insufficient partly because they fail to recognize the extent to which politics is constituted by overlapping meanings, powers, and cultures. History, religion, space, work, biology, and environment are all at work in Christian antiliberalism. It has been my goal to raise and to answer the new questions that confront us: What kinds of creations are Christian antiliberal practices? How specifically do they create a different understanding of politics? What is made in these practices, specifically and comparatively? To what extent could one say that political and religious creativity exists on the margins or in the in-between places (the cracks in our political culture)? Which discourses are converging on Christian antiliberalism, or, perhaps, on which discourses does Christian antiliberalism converge?

Grappling with antiliberalism's challenges to democracy invites the risks and dangers of widening the political sphere. Christian antiliberalism can often be bound up with antidemocratic or intolerant tendencies or a propensity toward excessive quiescence or capitulation. The eruption of Christian antiliberalism suggests that spaces for political participation are increasingly closed off and that political demands are crowded out in a way that promotes backlash. The tasks of creating more democratic ways of dealing with the complexities of religion in public life, and of preserving a wider space for democratic participation, will yield considerable conflict and will leave us without the old political certainties. But such a politics may be the only kind now available to us.

Notes

Introduction

1 David Meyer also refers to this Plowshares action. He rightly recognizes the importance of the Berrigans, but he commits several perplexing errors. His attention to their religious beliefs is almost cursory; he claims that the May 1968 Catonsville action was their first, whereas the October 1967 Baltimore Four action preceded it; he asserts that their rhetoric and moral commitment are unchanged since the 1960s, a claim whose inaccuracy is documented in chapter 4; and he labels their actions as civil disobedience, a term the Berrigans themselves reject. See Meyer, "Civil Disobedience and Protest Cycles."

2 Detailed accounts of this and other Berrigan actions appear in chapter 5. On the Maine action, see Charles Radin, "Former Priest Sent to Prison for Damaging Ship in Protest," *Boston Globe*, October 28, 1997; Paula Span, "One Man's War," *Washington Post*, July 28, 1997; and "Berrigan Sentenced to Two Years for Damage to Destroyer in Bath," *Brunswick (Maine) Times-Record*, October 28, 1997.

3 I explain this term in further detail later.

4 This is only a general interpretation of the Founding era. The Founders debated fiercely about religious freedom and other matters, and the extent to which citizens sought self-government during this period is debatable. See Williams's *Contours of American History* and Wood's *Radicalism of the American Revolution*.

5 Ribuffo, "Response to Nicolas Laarman."

6 Kramnick and Moore, *Godless Constitution*.

7 See Kazin, "Politics of Devotion."

8 See Edsall and Edsall, *Chain Reaction*, and Greider, *Who Will Tell the People?*

9 The events of September 11, 2001, are also of obvious relevance here, though religious terrorism is quite different from political religion, however antagonistic the latter may be.

10 The past decade has seen an important growth of work on global "fundamentalist" movements that challenge certain features of political orders. Particularly notable is Marty and Appleby's Fundamentalism Project.

11 Participation in Catholic, Latter-Day Saints, and Pentecostal communities

is increasing. In time, the so-called megachurches may redirect this trend in mainline Protestant denominations, as well.

12 One might plausibly see in the later Catholic Worker movement's pessimism (from roughly the late 1950s through the Vietnam era) about the state a form of criticism similar to that of Christian antiliberalism. However, Day rarely criticized the political philosophy or the conception of citizenship employed by the state, simply focusing on its encroachment into the "sphere" of religion (a very liberal way of conceptualizing this relationship, it bears mentioning).

13 Kintz, *Between Jesus and the Market*.

14 For a full account of legibility and illegibility, consult Scott, *Seeing Like a State*.

15 According to Walzer, a "connected critic" aims to change an institution or tradition by using commonly recognizable language and symbols, whereas a "critic in exile" explicitly detaches from these shared meanings in order to dramatize his or her difference.

16 For example, both postmodernists such as Connolly and theorists involved in the liberal-communitarian debate—both of whom purport to be engaged with concrete issues such as these—are preoccupied either with metaquestions about the philosophical grounds for evaluating religious discourse or with the perplexing and paternalistic question of whether religions should be "allowed" into the public sphere. I address these literatures in more detail in my concluding chapter.

Chapter One

1 Clifford Geertz, "The Pinch of Destiny: Religion as Experience, Identity, Meaning, Power," lecture delivered April 7, 1998, at Indiana University.

2 Wuthnow, *Restructuring of American Religion*.

3 See Tyler, *Freedom's Ferment*.

4 Brinkley, *Liberalism and Its Discontents*, ix.

5 Morone, *Democratic Wish*, 141.

6 Ibid., 1.

7 Goodwyn, *Democratic Promise*, xii.

8 Lind, *Next American Nation*, 39.

9 Goodwyn, *Democratic Promise*, xii.

10 On the emergence of this brand of politics, see Weinstein's *Corporate Ideal in the Liberal State* and Williams' *Contours of American History*.

11 See Craig's *Religion and Radical Politics*.

12 See Brinkley's *Voices of Protest* and Kazin's *Populist Persuasion*.

13 See Bennett, *Party of Fear*; Coates, *Armed and Dangerous*; Crawford, *Thunder on the Right*; Kazin, *Populist Persuasion*; Ribuffo, *Old Christian Right*; and Stock, *Rural Radicals*.

14 On the former group, see Crunden, *Ministers of Reform*.

15 Stock, *Rural Radicals*, 109.

16 Weinstein, *Corporate Ideal in the Liberal State*, 31.

17 Brinkley, *End of Reform*, 269.
18 See Lyons, *New Left, New Right, and the Legacy of the Sixties*.
19 See Lind, *Next American Nation*; Lyons, *New Left, New Right, and the Legacy of the Sixties*; and Allitt, *Catholic Intellectuals and Conservative Politics*.
20 Rossinow's *Politics of Authenticity* explicitly links the existential quest for meaning with the political innovations of the era.
21 Miller, *Democracy Is in the Streets*, 52. See also Mendel-Reyes's *Reclaiming Democracy* and Rossinow's *Politics of Authenticity*.
22 It should be noted, however, that many observers of American progressive politics have expressed hope, in the wake of the 1999 Seattle protests at the World Trade Organization/World Bank summit, that such a movement might be reappearing.
23 Some political historians insist that the welfare state has not only weakened but died. Although the European welfare state's fortunes have experienced a decline, many of its basic social programs and legal commitments remain intact despite the growth of so-called Third Wave liberal democracy. See Gornick, "Cancel the Funeral."
24 Clecak, *Crooked Paths*, 9.
25 Weidenbaum, "New Social Contract for the American Workplace."
26 Rifkin, *End of Work*.
27 See Greider, *One World, Ready or Not*.
28 See Bruce Bartlett, "Tax Spending, Not Savings," *New York Times*, July 6, 1997; Kapacyr, "Middle Class Blues"; and Vogelstein, "Giving Credit Where Credit Is Due."
29 See Greider's *One World, Ready or Not* and Barber's *Jihad vs. McWorld*.
30 The literature on identity politics is vast. Excellent theoretical sources include Cohen and Arato's *Civil Society and Political Theory* and Taylor and Gutmann's *Multiculturalism*. Fine historical sources include Jasper's *Art of Moral Protest*.
31 See Dionne's *Why Americans Hate Politics*; Gitlin's *Twilight of Common Dreams*; Greider's *Who Will Tell the People?*; and Lasch's *True and Only Heaven*.
32 Wallis, "Interview with Daniel and Philip Berrigan, and Elizabeth McAlister."
33 A fine account of second- and third-wave feminism is Stimpson's "Women's Studies and Its Discontents." The best introduction to subaltern studies is Guha's *Subaltern Studies*. Jackson's *Paths toward a Clearing* is a good introduction to cultural anthropology open to phenomenological methods.
34 Fukuyama, "The End of History?"
35 Bell, *Cultural Contradictions of Capitalism*. Among Habermas's works, see especially *Legitimation Crisis* and *Communication and the Evolution of Society*.
36 Brinkley, *End of Reform*.
37 Lyotard, *Postmodern Condition*, and Rorty, *Contingency, Irony, and Solidarity*.
38 Carter. *Culture of Disbelief*, 16.
39 Political liberalism's primary texts are, of course, Rawls's *Theory of Jus-*

tice and *Political Liberalism*. See also Holmes, *Anatomy of Antiliberalism*, and Shklar, "Liberalism of Fear."

40 On "comprehensive doctrines," see Rawls's revised preface to *Political Liberalism*.

41 I refer here to liberal political theory, but this theory emerged from the sociohistorical conditions described earlier and has helped legitimate the practices of the liberal regime.

Chapter Two

1 Wallis, introduction to *Cloud of Witnesses*, 3.

2 See Wallis, *Soul of Politics*.

3 I borrow the term "illegible" from Scott's *Seeing Like a State*.

4 Ibid., 2–3.

5 Ibid., 83.

6 Bobbio, *Left and Right*, 1.

7 Gitlin, *Twilight of Common Dreams*.

8 Shibley, *Resurgent Evangelicalism in the United States*, ix.

9 Hatch, *Democratization of American Christianity*.

10 For an exceptional account of this trial, see Larson's *Summer for the Gods*.

11 Fowler, *New Engagement*.

12 Ibid., 115.

13 Wallis, "Recovering the Evangel," 3.

14 Michaelson, "Crucible of Community," 20.

15 It is worth noting that, in their emphasis on collective decision making, Sojourners may be drawing not only from the New Left but also from the historical example of Anabaptist communities, particularly the Mennonites. Indeed, the group often favorably cites the theology of John Howard Yoder.

16 Rossinow, *Politics of Authenticity*, and Gish, *New Left and Christian Radicalism*.

17 In Wallis, "Keeping Faith, Doing Justice, Building Community," 12.

18 Wallis, "Rebuilding the Church," 11.

19 Verhulst quotation from personal conversation, April 12, 1999.

20 See Jaffe and Sherwood, *Dream City*.

21 Hollyday, "Awakening on Belmont Street," 20.

22 Wallis, "Mammon's Iron Thumb," 4.

23 Hollyday, "Out of the Mouths of Babes," 30–31.

24 Stentzel, "Night Hospitality," 30.

25 Tamialis, "Ten Years of Keeping the Faith," 17.

26 One wonders whether local poor parents could easily afford the enrollment fee of six hundred dollars per child. Tracy's *Direct Action* provides a vivid account of Moses' activities.

27 Duin, "Where Have All the Christian Communities Gone?," 29.

28 Personal conversation, April 12, 1999. There is evidence of discontent with Wallis's leadership, as many have gotten involved in bookkeeping or

editing, activities removed from the passions that originally drew them to Sojourners.

29 Wallis, "Confessing Community," 4.

30 Sabath, "The State," 30.

31 Davids, "God and Caesar," 28.

32 Myers, "In Word and Deed," 18.

33 Perkins, "Concrete Theology," 13.

34 "Offensiveness" recalls neo-orthodox thinkers such as the Niebuhrs and Barth, who insisted that the Word subjected all earthly norms and practices to radical critique.

35 Ginsburg, "From Little Things, Big Things Grow," 122.

36 McSorley, "Siege at Seabrook," 16–18.

37 Wallis, "Higher Loyalty," 4.

38 Myers, "By What Authority," 11.

39 See Kellerman's "Subversive Calendar of the Heart," 32.

40 Kari Verhulst related that Sojourners protests against NATO bombings in Kosovo had been linked to conversations "about the role of world governing bodies . . . challenging [them] to be more [democratic]." Personal conversation, April 12, 1999.

41 Wallis, "Let the Goodwill Prevail," *Washington Post*, December 25, 1996, A23.

42 Significantly, Sojourners have recently devoted less print space to women's issues (though their practice has not dwindled). Some discontented activists feel that Wallis has "tabled" feminism out of fear that its controversies might hamper CTR's success.

43 Wallis, "Worth Fighting For," 13, reprints Boston's "10-Point Plan to Mobilize the Churches," an oft-used model for religious groups hoping to address this issue.

44 Jim Wallis, introduction to Wallis, *Rise of Christian Conscience*.

45 Perhaps significantly, it was during this time period—in early 1998, to be specific—that what Verhulst calls "the community with a capital 'C'," the actual houses in which Sojourners once lived together full-time, dissolved into several separate communities.

46 Jones, "Evangelicals in Several Stripes," 3.

47 Romney, "Group Promotes Image of Christians as Political Moderates," *Los Angeles Times*, November 18, 1996, A3.

48 Both quoted in Wallis, "No Ways Tired," 8.

49 Wallis, "What to Do about the Poor," 10.

50 Wallis, *Who Speaks for God?*, 3.

51 Cohen, "Why I'm Still 'Left'."

52 Isaac, "Toward a Politics of Democratic Ambivalence," 84.

53 Quotation from Elshtain, *Real Politics*, viii.

54 Wallis, *Who Speaks for God?*, 159.

55 Wallis, "Confessing Community," 3.

56 Wallis, *Soul of Politics*, 133.

57 Ibid., 178, 157.

58 All this information is readily available at www.calltorenewal.com.

59 See reader Michael McGinnis's letter in *Sojourners*, May 1993, 9.

60 Personal conversation, November 23, 1996.

61 Francis X. Clines, "A Religious Tilt toward the Left," *New York Times*, September 16, 1996, A1.

62 Wallis, "Court Prophets," 3.

63 Quotation from McCarthy, "Wallis Offers Credible Christian Vision," 3.

64 Wippsa, "Christian Left Organizes to Oppose Religious Right," 3.

65 Quoted in "Briefs" section of *National Catholic Reporter*, December 29, 1995, 7.

66 Laurie Goodstein, "Christian Leaders Challenge the Right," *Washington Post*, May 24, 1995, A14.

67 See Bob Herbert, "Saving the Cities," *New York Times*, July 2, 1998.

68 Wallis, "Giving Religion a Bad Name," 50.

69 Bonnie Honig's term "remainder" nicely captures not only the exclusionary qualities of conventional political thought in a liberal regime but also its quantitative features.

70 Wallis, *Soul of Politics*, 21.

71 Ibid., 159.

72 Wallis, "Come to the Table," 1.

73 www.calltorenewal.com.

74 Personal conversation, April 12, 1999.

75 Collum, "Big Picture," 14.

76 Personal conversation, April 12, 1999. Verhulst elaborated on this point: "The whole approach to faithfulness as spreadsheet . . . that you can come up with a chart for what you've done and achieved and contributed and all that, that to me is dangerous. . . . And the whole theology of needing to justify your place in the universe is degrading. I just don't think it's true to the way that God sees us, and I don't think it's much of a sustainable foundation for being in the world."

77 Quotation from ibid.

78 Wallis, "Living in Hope," 285.

Chapter Three

1 The use of the term "New Christian Right" may be perplexing, since I argue that Christian antiliberalism rejects the terms "left" and "right." I use the term, however, because it is the one most widely used in theoretical and historical literatures to describe the activists and causes that concern the work of this chapter.

2 There are numerous sources on the NCR's post-1960s political resurgence. A good overview is Wilcox's *Onward Christian Soldiers?*. Recent scholarship, such as Carpenter's *Revive Us Again*, demonstrates that, though out of the public eye, Christian conservatives were quite active in the decades between the Scopes trial and the 1960s.

3 Marsden, "Preachers of Paradox," 156.

4 Quoted in Martin's *With God on Our Side*, 118.

5 For a liberal defense of such programs, see Macedo, "Liberal Civic Education and Religious Fundamentalism."

6 Martin, *With God on Our Side*, 120–24. I put the term "Christian" in quotes as a reminder that, though the NCR often uses the term as if its meanings were self-evident, the NCR's voice is one among the myriad of Christian voices in North America.

7 Quoted in ibid., 118.

8 Lemann, "Reed in the Wind," 32; Kramnick and Moore, *Godless Constitution*, 11.

9 Ribuffo, "Response to Peter Laarman," 391.

10 See Hatch, *Democratization of American Christianity*. Hatch ignores how this supposedly democratic religious idiom constituted a set of social differences that excluded women, African Americans, Catholics, and others from the public sphere.

11 Marsden, *Fundamentalism in American Culture*, 6–7.

12 Kazin, *Populist Persuasion*, 150.

13 See Dionne's *Why Americans Hate Politics*.

14 Marty and Appleby, *The Glory and the Power*, 33.

15 Quoted in ibid., 72.

16 Moen, *Transformation of the Christian Right*. For example, in the Ninety-seventh Congress the NCR barred the Legal Services Corporation from accepting cases on homosexual rights and also opposed a District of Columbia plan to lessen jail sentences for rapists.

17 Quoted in Lienesch, *Redeeming America*.

18 Francis, "Message from Mars," 68.

19 Quotation from Marsden, "Preachers of Paradox," 157. Although anti-Catholicism and anti-Semitism remained part of the heritage of Christian conservatives, the NCR sought to include conservatives of all backgrounds to "enlist" in the struggle against liberalism.

20 Lienesch, *Redeeming America*, 13.

21 A great plurality of organizations remains. For every political action committee and Christian lobby, there are separatist groups such as Randall Terry's Operation Rescue. At the extremes, the most establishmentarian NCR practitioners may affiliate themselves with the Republican Party, whereas others may avow total independence from political order.

22 This last term is from Shibley's *Resurgent Evangelicalism in the United States*, 53.

23 Members of the NCR often write and speak of liberalism in these terms. In conversation with a member of Promise Keepers, for example, I was told that American social problems were attributable to the lack of "godly men" in politics. The sense is that liberalism's aversion to values has paradoxically led to the disorder it sought to avoid. See Whitaker, *New Right Papers*, and Reed, *After the Revolution*.

24 See Reed, "What Do Religious Conservatives Really Want?"

25 Ed Dobson claims that the NCR is not politicized by single issues such as abortion rights but by a "perceived threat" from liberalism. See Cromartie, *No Longer Exiles*, 52.

26 Viguerie, "Ends and Means," 32.

27 Quoted in *Dallas Morning News*, February 20, 1996.

28 Francis, "Message from Mars," 68.

29 This phrase is from Kintz's *Between Jesus and the Market*, 20.

30 Sara Diamond notes that a key factor in nurturing these self-understandings is the NCR's vast informational network, including broadcasters, book publishers, newspapers, state-based think tanks, and law firms. See Diamond, *Facing the Wrath*, 43.

31 Quoted in Moen and Gustafson, *Religious Challenge to the State*, 75.

32 This concern is everywhere in the NCR. In my research I was frequently given copies of pamphlets and outraged open letters. Bradley's "From Prodigal to Preacher" thunders that "with the onslaught of evil-lution, higher criticism of the Bible, atheism, Marxism, liberalism, easy believ-ism, and the hippie-drug-radical-free-sex revolution of the sixties, the Bible and all its doctrines have been heartily flushed down the toilet" (3).

33 In 1974, Weyrich's Heritage Foundation was one of Moore's key benefactors. In 1969, civil rights lawyers sued the IRS for recognizing the tax-exempt status of private schools that remained segregated. The courts de-segregated these schools, many of which were operated by NCR churches. As Rabkin reports in "Supreme Court in the Culture Wars," this enraged the NCR, which believed that the courts used a double standard allowing taxpayers to challenge expenditures on religion but not on any other public expenditure.

34 Martin, *With God on Our Side*, 175.

35 Ibid., 182.

36 On the link between NCR activism and anxieties about family and sexuality, see Kintz, *Between Jesus and the Market*, 72–76.

37 Central to these efforts is the NCR's vast funding empire, without which the defense of homeschooling or the establishment of Christian schools would be more difficult. This empire includes funding organs such as the Capital Resource Institute in Sacramento, NCR law firms such as the Ruth-erford Institute, and "anonymous" funding sources such as Third Century Publishers, whose profits are funneled into major NCR organizations such as the Religious Roundtable. In a fascinating coincidence, the pecuniary activities of Third Century Publishers were first exposed by Sojourners in 1974.

38 Peters's *Judging Jehovah's Witnesses* places *Cantwell* and similar cases in a broader narrative about the post–World War II expansion of civil rights under an activist judiciary.

39 See Rabkin, "Supreme Court in the Culture Wars."

40 Smith, *American Evangelicalism*, 140.

41 Quoted in ibid., 141.

42 Randall, "Culture, Religion, and Education," 71.

43 Most states provide some aid to nonpublic schools (e.g., transportation, health care, or school lunches) or participate in "shared time" classes as long as these schools meet state standards. Christian schools often see these standards as onerous. According to Doerr and Menendez (*Church Schools and Public Money*), evidence suggests that voters would rather decline state aid. Since 1966, eighty-eight referenda on funding for religious schools have been held in thirteen states. Voters have consistently supported church-state separation in education with overwhelming numbers.

44 See Nord's *Religion and American Education*.

45 LaHaye, *Battle for the Public Schools*, 10.

46 Quotations from ibid., 13, 14. LaHaye's claims about standardized testing are almost entirely undocumented, though he does cite an article from the *National Enquirer* on page 15.

47 LaHaye (ibid.) notes ominously that Soviet literacy rates rise as U.S. rates fall.

48 Ibid., 55.

49 Ibid., 127. LaHaye's research relied on textbook reviewers Mel and Norma Gabler, who report that mandatory sex education is linked to wife swapping and bestiality.

50 Ibid., 269.

51 This figure is based on 1992 reports from the Department of Education, quoted in Manatt, *When Right Is Wrong*, 130.

52 Quoted in Peshkin, *God's Choice*, 259.

53 Menendez reviews sixteen of these textbooks in *Visions of Reality*.

54 Ibid., 62.

55 Dewink and Herbster, *Effective Christian School Management*, 10.

56 See ibid., 25. The majority of my research for this chapter was conducted in Raleigh, North Carolina, and Bloomington, Indiana. In both communities many churches sponsor schools. In Bloomington, the largest are First Church of the Nazarene's Journey Christian School and the independent Lighthouse Christian Academy. North Carolina has a large number of such schools (and the number of home schools is now more than seventeen thousand). Raleigh-area schools include Paideia Academy (where social studies classes discuss Noah and the Ark), Fayetteville Christian School (linked, like many institutions, to the Association of Christian Schools International), and Cresset Christian Academy. These schools have elaborate applications that include a confessional pledge and many questions concerning one's religious background and beliefs.

57 Ibid., 76–77.

58 Wagner, *God's Schools*, 11.

59 Ibid., 100.

60 Rose, *Keeping Them out of the Hands of Satan*, 11.

61 Dewink and Herbster, *Effective Christian School Management*, 190.

62 This educational culture extends to universities such as Bob Jones Univer-

sity, Jerry Falwell's Liberty University, Pat Robertson's Regent University, and now Farris's Patrick Henry College, which caters specifically to home-schooled students.

63 Farris filed suit against the U.S. Congress for deliberating too long about the Equal Rights Amendment. More commonly, he sued school districts and libraries for stocking materials he and his constituents considered immoral. See Carol Ostrom, "Conservative Christians Fear 'Humanist Takeover,'" *Seattle Times*, April 9, 1983, 3.

64 Note the similarities to the ways the Berrigans use their trials to challenge liberalism.

65 Rozell and Wilcox, *Second Coming*, 96.

66 Farris quoted in ibid., 98.

67 For an excellent documentary account of this case, see Bates, *Battleground*.

68 Ibid., 20.

69 Ibid., 55. See Farris, "Fundamentalists Often Targets of Bigotry," *USA Today*, August 11, 1986, A8.

70 Bates, *Battleground*, 116.

71 Stevens, *Kingdom of Children*, 4.

72 Ibid., 26.

73 Ibid., 72. Stevens also notes that, though "traditional" models of male headship are promoted, practically homeschooling arrangements extend conventional women's roles. Many conservative women continue to demonize feminism even as they seek to exercise forms of leadership and self-determination that appear ironically indebted to feminism.

74 Ibid., 172. Other homeschoolers—mostly libertarians linked to the 1960s "free school" movement—object to the NCR's efforts to "Christianize" the culture.

75 Ibid., 99.

76 See Diamond's *Spiritual Warfare*, 83–110, and her *Facing the Wrath*, 57–64.

77 See Doerr and Menendez, *Church Schools and Public Money*.

78 Farris, *Where Do I Draw the Line?*, 13, and Farris, *Home Schooling and the Law*.

79 Farris, *Where Do I Draw the Line?*, 110, 11. Farris notes with horror that, in his estimation, public schools forbid children from singing Christmas carols but force them to read "anti-Christianity" books by the likes of Gordon Parks. He also warns against the use of self-esteem and image-enhancing texts such as *Bright Beginnings*, whose Pumsy the Dragon character is singled out as an advocate of "New Age channeling" on page 51.

80 Ibid., 17.

81 Ibid., 24. An account of Farris's skirmishes with American Civil Liberties Union officials is in Jason Vest's "Mike Farris, for God's Sake," *Washington Post*, August 6, 1993, C6.

82 Farris, *Where Do I Draw the Line?*, 77.

83 Quotations from ibid., 211, 209. The AACS describes its legislative goals as: "1) To protect our schools and ministries from government entanglement, 2) To promote the causes of religious freedom, Christian education, and

family values, 3) To influence legislation that would help or hurt our cases, 4) To inform our legislators of our concerns and compliments, and 5) To challenge our nation to consider biblical answers for man's problems." Ibid., 207.

84 Rozell and Wilcox, *Second Coming*, 98.

85 Ibid., 100.

86 Both quotes from ibid., 101.

87 Ibid., 103.

88 See Kennedy, "House Learns Civics Lesson," 76. As of 2002, the HSLDA continues to use its vast organization and funding to influence local, state, and national legislation that pertains to homeschooling. The HSLDA is currently pursuing cases in every state (recently its attorneys have argued several times before the North Carolina State Supreme Court, among others, to contest allegations of abuse in home schools), and the organization has even begun to expand its operations abroad.

89 This refers to sociological understandings of religions as means by which practitioners use their traditions to reclaim social goods of which modernity "deprives" them. In terms of identity of social movement theory, this would be carried out when religions form a lobby or an interest group, seeking representation in the state as a form of compensation.

90 Aronowitz, *Politics of Identity*, 4.

91 Quotation from Taylor, "Politics of Recognition," 68.

92 In the past decade, seemingly dozens of "left" commentators have rushed into print claiming that identity politics saps energy that might otherwise be used on good old-fashioned materialist issues. David Hollinger, Todd Gitlin, Michael Tomasky, and Michael Lind, among others, express these kinds of reservations.

93 Gitlin makes this claim in *The Twilight of Common Dreams*, 3.

94 See Stolzenberg, "'He Drew a Circle That Shut Me Out.'"

95 See Habermas, *New Conservatism*.

96 Habermas, "Struggles for Recognition in the Democratic Constitutional State," 109.

97 Ibid., 116.

98 Ibid., 137.

99 See Connolly, *Ethos of Pluralization*, xix.

100 Ibid., xx. Indeed, this is very similar to the points I make in chapters 1 and 5.

Chapter Four

1 Personal conversation with McAlister at Jonah House, April 13, 1999.

2 See Piehl, *Breaking Bread*, and Baxter, "Notes on Americanism and Catholic Radicalism."

3 This ambivalence about state power appears often in American Catholicism.

4 McNeal, *Harder Than War*.

5 Burns, *Frontiers of Catholicism*, 72.

6 Wills, *Bare Ruined Choirs*, 232.

7 Berrigan, *Fighting the Lamb's War*, 36.

8 Ibid., 81.

9 See Tracy, *Direct Action*.

10 Quoted in Diggins, *Rise and Fall of the American Left*, 17.

11 Tracy, *Direct Action*, 13.

12 Berrigan, *Widen the Prison Gates*, 31.

13 Fenn, *Liturgies and Trials*, 11.

14 Personal conversation at Jonah House, April 13, 1999.

15 Fisher explores this theme in *The Catholic Counterculture in America*.

16 Laffin and Montgomery, *Swords into Plowshares*, 30.

17 Berrigan and McAlister, *Time's Discipline*, 110.

18 Subheading quotation from Berrigan, "Two Secretaries of State Require Heart Surgery," 22.

19 Fisher, *Catholic Counterculture in America*, 72.

20 Carey Goldberg, "Times Have Changed; the Berrigans Haven't," *Chicago Tribune*, November 30, 1997.

21 Personal conversation at Jonah House, April 13, 1999.

22 Stringfellow and Towne, *Suspect Tenderness*, 67.

23 Gray, *Divine Disobedience*, 171.

24 Berrigan and Coles, *Geography of Faith*, 124.

25 Quoted in Gray, *Divine Disobedience*, 100.

26 Nelson and Ostrow, *FBI and the Berrigans*.

27 Berrigan and Coles, *Geography of Faith*, 85.

28 Berrigan, *Widen the Prison Gates*, 157.

29 Berrigan, *Fighting the Lamb's War*, 7.

30 Ibid., 99.

31 Quotation from ibid., 202.

32 Ibid., 184.

33 Wallis, "Interview with Philip and Daniel Berrigan, and Elizabeth McAlister," 23.

34 Berrigan, "Reflections on Isaiah," 16.

35 Laffin and Montgomery, *Swords into Plowshares*, 12.

36 Ibid., 25.

37 Quotation from Berrigan and McAlister, *Time's Discipline*, 131.

38 Subheading quotation is from ibid., xii.

39 Chronologies of Plowshares actions are in McNeal, *Harder Than War*, and Laffin and Montgomery, *Swords into Plowshares*.

40 See Gallagher, *Laws of Heaven*.

41 Ibid., 80.

42 Berrigan and McAlister, *Time's Discipline*, 75.

43 Ibid., 82.

44 Philip Berrigan, prologue to Halpert and Murray, *Witness of the Berrigans*, xiii.

45 Berrigan and McAlister, *Time's Discipline*, 110.

46 Personal conversation at Jonah House, April 13, 1999.

47 Note the parallel between these charges and those made by NCR activists such as Farris.

48 Berrigan and McAlister, *Time's Discipline*, 84.

49 Ibid., 108.

50 This account, and all quotations in this paragraph, are from Philip Berrigan's letter to Plowshares, reprinted at www.nonviolence.org/plowshares/berrigan.html.

51 Personal conversation at Jonah House, April 13, 1999.

52 Ibid.

53 Ibid. McAlister told me that at her arrest a policeman asked her about the blood. She told him that it was her own, to which he responded, "Well that really makes a point, doesn't it?" McAlister explained to me that the authorities "get it right away" and, what is horrible to her, choose nonetheless not to change their policies.

54 Berrigan. *America Is Hard to Find*, 18.

55 In Halpert and Murray, *Witness of the Berrigans*, 76.

56 Ibid., 141.

57 Contemporary theory of space has explored the politics of architecture, geography, landscape, and access. Among others, Michel Foucault, Edward Soja, Mike Davis, and Alex Wilson have contributed to this work.

58 Scott, *Domination and the Arts of Resistance*, xiii.

59 Ibid., 8.

60 Critics of phenomenology worry that it is too narrowly focused or subjective to grapple with broader social issues. In contrast, I understand phenomenology to posit that all consciousness is relational and intersubjective and hence that religious ritual is not "private" but a powerfully public form of social being.

61 The literature on phenomenology is vast, in both its philosophical and anthropological variations. See Best, *Philosophy and Human Movement*; Bourdieu, *Outline of a Theory of Practice*; Merleau-Ponty, *Phenomenology of Perception*; and Young, *Throwing like a Girl*.

62 Merleau-Ponty, *Phenomenology of Perception*, 146.

63 Ibid., 30.

64 See Young, *Throwing like a Girl*.

65 Ibid., 143.

66 Csordas, "Embodiment as a Paradigm for Anthropology," 24.

67 Subheading quotation from Mary Scoblick, member of the Harrisburg Seven, quoted in O'Rourke, *Harrisburg Seven and the New Catholic Left*, 10.

68 See Papke's *Heretics in the Temple*.

69 Berrigan, *No Bars to Manhood*, 37.

70 Ibid., 38.

71 Berrigan, "Reflections on Isaiah," 32.

72 In Bannan and Bannan, *Law, Morality, and Vietnam*, 136.

73 Ibid., 146. Interestingly, Berrigan's critique here echoes criticisms made

against political theorist John Rawls's "original position," which stated that justice can most fairly and accurately be generated by disinterested agents who are shorn of their "accidental" characteristics such as race, class, or religion.

74 Paul Mayer recalls that the defendants in the trial of the Milwaukee Fourteen, resisters inspired by the Berrigans, violated a gag rule by reciting parts of *Pacem in Terris*. See Halpert and Murray, *Witness of the Berrigans*, 40.

75 O'Rourke, *Harrisburg Seven and the New Catholic Left*, 106.

76 Norman, *Hammer of Justice*, 139.

77 Ibid., 146.

78 Ibid., 150; italics mine.

79 Ibid., 6. Aside from these blunt references to the Crucifixion, the Berrigans have likened the American legal system to that of Stalinist Russia, whose show trials the Berrigans darkly allude to in their own theatricality.

80 Berrigan, "Swords into Plowshares," 62.

81 Berrigan and McAlister, *Time's Discipline*, 133.

82 These claims ironically mirror the NCR's charges against liberal education. For a vivid description of such an indictment, see Gallagher's *Laws of Heaven*, 120.

83 Quoted in Wilcox, *Uncommon Martyrs*, 94.

84 Ibid., 97.

85 Ibid., 99.

86 Ibid., 100.

87 Quoted in ibid., 104.

88 Quoted in Goldberg, "Times Have Changed."

89 Report from UPI, reprinted in the *Chicago Defender*, May 8, 1997, 10. Longtime resident Ardeth Platte's journal from the *Sullivans* trial can be read at www.plowshares.org.

90 Fenn, *Dream of the Perfect Act*, 127.

91 Fenn, *Liturgies and Trials*, xxxiv.

92 Ibid., 21.

93 Ibid., 53.

94 When Fenn discusses the rhetorical implications of the Catonsville trial, he relies on Habermas's term "speech-act immanence" (which conveys the internal logic, consistency, and tradition supporting a statement or truth claim). Ibid., 66–67.

95 Ibid., 187.

96 In McAlister's words, "We say to them 'listen, we think that it would be very good . . . that there not be a direct relationship between the diocese and Jonah House. . . . That way you aren't responsible for us and we aren't responsible for you.'" Personal conversation at Jonah House, April 13, 1999.

97 Berrigan, *America Is Hard to Find*, 94.

98 Day, *Long Loneliness*, 147.

99 Ibid., 204.

100 See Day, *On Pilgrimage*, 8.

101 Berrigan, *Fighting the Lamb's War*, 53.

102 Berrigan and Coles, *Geography of Faith*, 128.

103 Ibid., 77.

104 Berrigan, *Fighting the Lamb's War*, 169.

105 Allitt, *Catholic Intellectuals and Conservative Politics in America*, 95.

106 Berrigan and McAlister had recently been excommunicated, for their clandestine marriage, prior to Jonah House's founding.

107 Personal conversation at Jonah House, April 13, 1999.

108 Ibid.

109 Berrigan and McAlister, *Time's Discipline*, 112.

110 See Stringfellow and Towne, *Suspect Tenderness*, 100.

111 See Berrigan, *Prison Journals of a Priest Revolutionary*.

112 Berrigan, *Widen the Prison Gates*, 171.

113 In Bannan and Bannan, *Law, Morality, and Vietnam*, 149.

114 Personal conversation at Jonah House, April 13, 1999.

115 Ibid.

116 As it happens, McAlister's fears were realized, albeit under slightly different circumstances. On December 19, 1999, Philip Berrigan and Susan Crane, along with two other Plowshares activists, "disarmed" two A-10 Warthog aircraft at the Warfield Air National Guard Base in Middle River, Maryland. For damages incurred by hammering on the aircraft, the defendants were ordered to pay restitution of $88,622.11. Bail was set at $90,000 cash, and on March 23, 2000, at the Baltimore County Circuit Court, sentences were handed down: Crane was sentenced to twenty-seven months in prison, Berrigan to thirty months.

117 See Berrigan, *Dark Night of Resistance*, 26.

118 McAlister, "Lenten Meditations from Prison," 38–39.

119 Berrigan and McAlister, *Time's Discipline*, xiv, xx.

120 Quoted in Wilcox, *Uncommon Martyrs*, xiv.

121 Significantly, when I asked McAlister some of these questions, she responded either that these concerns were antithetical to Jonah House residents' religious self-understandings or that Jonah House itself was response enough.

122 In Wallis, "Interview with Philip and Daniel Berrigan, and Elizabeth McAlister," 24.

123 Halpert and Murray, *Witness of the Berrigans*, 104.

Chapter Five

1 See Dean, *Religious Critic in American Culture*; Walzer, *What It Means to Be an American*; and Dyson, *Between God and Gangsta Rap*.

2 The best example of this rhetoric is found in West's *Keeping Faith*.

3 On the first, see Garber and Walkowitz, *One Nation under God?*; on Foucault, see the recent collection *Foucault and Religion*, edited by Jeremy R. Carrette; and on the last, see Stone, *On the Boundaries of American Evangelicalism*.

4 Two fine collections chart the social complexity of American religions: Tweed, *Retelling U.S. Religious History*, and Hackett, *Religion and American Culture*.

5 On the global dimension of these developments, see Casanova's *Public Religions and the Modern World* and Juergensmeyer's *Next Cold War*.

6 See Wuthnow, *Restructuring of American Religion*.

7 Wilcox, *Uncommon Martyrs*, 165.

8 Berrigan and McAlister, *Time's Discipline*, 41.

9 Greider, *Who Will Tell the People?*, 12.

10 Ibid., 162.

11 This phrase is Richard Hofstadter's, quoted in Clecak's *Radical Paradoxes*.

12 Perhaps more significant, it is quite possible that the abandonment of "connected criticism" by the Berrigans (and "progressive" Christians more broadly) has left the language of reform and incrementalism to Christian conservatives.

13 Daniel Berrigan has even recently become involved in antiabortion politics, the political shibboleth for NCR members, though of course his motivations come from what some Catholic thinkers call a "consistent ethic of life." Wills, *Under God*, 325.

14 Barkun, *Religion and the Racist Right*, 240.

15 See Isaac, Filner, and Bivins, "American Democracy and the New Christian Right."

16 Holmes, *Passions and Constraint*.

17 For an understanding of these constraints on religious practice, see Connolly, *Ethos of Pluralization*; Isaac, Filner, and Bivins, "American Democracy and the New Christian Right"; and Stolzenberg, "'He Drew a Circle That Shut Me Out.'"

18 The most prominent of these communitarian critical works are Sandel's *Liberalism and the Limits of Justice* and *Democracy's Discontent*.

19 The term "strange silence" is from Isaac's *Democracy in Dark Times*.

20 For example, see Habermas's *Between Facts and Norms*; Kari and Boyte's *Building America*; and Mark Warren's *Democracy and Association*.

21 See Isaac, *Democracy in Dark Times*, 35.

22 Benhabib, "Toward a Deliberative Model of Democratic Legitimacy," 77.

23 Here I am thinking primarily of theologically inclined scholars such as Stanley Hauerwas, Michael Baxter, and George Marsden.

24 Notable here is Jonathan Z. Smith's recent work, especially "Religion, Religions, Religious."

25 In these passages, I am partially incorporating writing from my piece "'Religion' and Religions in Legal Studies," forthcoming in *Religious Studies Review*.

26 This phrase is from Elshtain's *Real Politics*, viii.

27 Quotation from Gustafson and Moen, *Religious Challenge to the State*, 7.

28 Ibid., 63.

29 Orsi, "Snakes Alive," 5, in manuscript copy. Published as "Snakes Alive: Resituating the Moral in the Study of Religion," in Fox and Westbrook, *In Face of the Facts*.

30 Ibid., 16.

Bibliography

Newspapers

Brunswick (Maine) Times-Record
Chicago Tribune
Los Angeles Times
New York Times
Seattle Times
USA Today
Washington Post

Books, Articles, and Essays

Allitt, Patrick. *Catholic Intellectuals and Conservative Politics in America, 1950–1985*. Ithaca, N.Y.: Cornell University Press, 1993.

Aronowitz, Stanley. *The Politics of Identity*. New York: Routledge Press, 1992.

Bannan, John F., and Rosemary S. Bannan. *Law, Morality, and Vietnam: The Peace Militants and the Courts*. Bloomington: Indiana University Press, 1974.

Barber, Benjamin. *Jihad vs. McWorld: How Globalism and Tribalism Are Reshaping the World*. New York: Ballantine Books, 1995.

Barkun, Michael. *Religion and the Racist Right: The Origins of the Christian Identity Movement*. Chapel Hill: University of North Carolina Press, 1994.

Bates, Stephen. *Battleground: One Mother's Crusade, the Religious Right, and the Struggle for Control of Our Classrooms*. New York: Poseidon Press, 1993.

Baxter, Michael. "Notes on Americanism and Catholic Radicalism: Towards a Counter-Tradition in Catholic Social Ethics." In *American Catholic Traditions: Resources for Renewal*, edited by Sandra Yocum Mize and William Portier, 53–71. Maryknoll, N.Y.: College Theology Society/Orbis, 1997.

Bell, Daniel. *The Cultural Contradictions of Capitalism*. New York: Basic Books, 1976.

Benhabib, Seyla. "Toward a Deliberative Model of Democratic Legitimacy." In *Democracy and Difference: Contesting the Boundaries of the Political*, edited by Seyla Benhabib, 67–94. Princeton: Princeton University Press, 1996.

Bennett, David. *The Party of Fear*. New York: Vintage Books, 1995.

Berrigan, Daniel. *America Is Hard to Find*. Garden City, N.Y.: Doubleday, 1972.

———. *The Dark Night of Resistance*. Garden City, N.Y.: Doubleday Books, 1971.

———. *No Bars to Manhood*. Garden City, N.Y.: Doubleday, 1970.

———. "Reflections on Isaiah." *Sojourners*, January 1989, 15–16.

———. "Swords into Plowshares." In *Swords into Plowshares: Nonviolent Direct Action for Disarmament*, edited by Arthur J. Laffin and Anne Montgomery, 54–63. San Francisco: Harper and Row, 1987.

———. "Two Secretaries of State Require Heart Surgery." *Sojourners*, June 1982, 22–23.

Berrigan, Daniel, and Robert Coles. *The Geography of Faith*. Boston: Beacon Press, 1971.

Berrigan, Philip. *Prison Journals of a Priest Revolutionary*. New York: Ballantine Books, 1971.

———. *Widen the Prison Gates: Writings from Jails*. New York: Touchstone Books, 1972.

Berrigan, Philip, and Elizabeth McAlister. *The Time's Discipline: The Beatitudes and Nuclear Resistance*. Baltimore: Fortkamp Publishing, 1989.

Berrigan, Philip, with Fred A. Wilcox. *Fighting the Lamb's War: Skirmishes with the American Empire*. Monroe, Maine: Common Courage Press, 1996.

Best, David. *Philosophy and Human Movement*. London: Allen and Unwin, 1978.

Bobbio, Norberto. *Left and Right: The Significance of a Political Distinction*. Chicago: University of Chicago Press, 1997.

Bourdieu, Pierre. *Outline of a Theory of Practice*. Cambridge: Cambridge University Press, 1977.

Bradley, Rick. "From Prodigal to Preacher: The Rick Bradley Story." Lancaster, Tex.: Revival Promotion Press, n.d.

Brinkley, Alan. *The End of Reform: New Deal Liberalism in Recession and War*. New York: Vintage Books, 1995.

———. *Liberalism and Its Discontents*. Cambridge: Harvard University Press, 1998.

———. *Voices of Protest: Huey Long, Father Coughlin, and the Great Depression*. New York: Vintage Books, 1982.

Burns, Gene. *Frontiers of Catholicism*. Berkeley: University of California Press, 1992.

Carpenter, Joel A. *Revive Us Again: The Reawakening of American Fundamentalism*. New York: Oxford University Press, 1997.

Carrette, Jeremy R., ed. *Foucault and Religion: Spiritual Corporality and Political Spirituality*. New York: Routledge, 1999.

Carter, Stephen L. *The Culture of Disbelief: How American Law and Politics Trivialize Religious Devotion*. New York: Anchor Books, 1993.

———. *The Dissent of the Governed: A Meditation on Law, Religion, and Loyalty*. Cambridge: Harvard University Press, 1998.

Casanova, Jose. *Public Religions and the Modern World*. Chicago: University of Chicago Press, 1997.

Clecak, Peter. *Crooked Paths: Reflections on Socialism, Conservatism, and the Welfare State*. New York: Harper Torchbooks, 1977.

———. *Radical Paradoxes: Dilemmas of the American Left: 1945–1970*. New York: Harper Torchbooks, 1973.

Coates, James. *Armed and Dangerous: The Rise of the Survivalist Right*. New York: Hill and Wang, 1987.

Cohen, Jean, and Andrew Arato. *Civil Society and Political Theory*. Cambridge: MIT Press, 1992.

Cohen, Mitchell. "Why I'm Still 'Left.'" *Dissent*, Spring 1997, 43–50.

Collum, Danny. "The Big Picture: Where We Are and How We Got Here." *Sojourners*, May 1986, 14–19.

Connolly, William E. *The Ethos of Pluralization*. Minneapolis: University of Minnesota Press, 1995.

———. *Why I Am Not a Secularist*. Minneapolis: University of Minnesota Press, 1999.

Craig, Robert H. *Religion and Radical Politics: An Alternative Christian Tradition in the United States*. Philadelphia: Temple University Press, 1992.

Crawford, Alan. *Thunder on the Right: The New Right and the Politics of Resentment*. New York: Pantheon, 1980.

Cromartie, Michael, ed. *No Longer Exiles: The Religious New Right in American Politics*. Washington, D.C.: Ethics and Public Policy Center Press, 1993.

Crunden, Robert M. *Ministers of Reform: The Progressives' Achievement in American Civilization, 1889–1920*. Urbana: University of Illinois Press, 1982.

Csordas, Thomas J. "Embodiment as a Paradigm for Anthropology." *Ethos* 18 (1990): 5–47.

Davids, Peter. "God and Caesar." *Sojourners*, May 1981, 24–28.

Day, Dorothy. *The Long Loneliness*. San Francisco: Harper Collins, 1981.

———. *On Pilgrimage: The Sixties*. New York: Curtis Books, 1972.

Dean, William. *The Religious Critic in American Culture*. Albany: State University of New York Press, 1995.

Detweiler, Fritz. *Standing on the Premises of God: The Christian Right's Challenge to American Public Schools*. New York: New York University Press, 1999.

Dewink, James W., and Carl D. Herbster. *Effective Christian School Management: How to Start and Operate a Christian School*. Greenville, S.C.: Bob Jones University Press, 1982.

Diamond, Sara. *Facing the Wrath: Confronting the Right in Dangerous Times*. Monroe, Maine: Common Courage Press, 1996.

———. *Spiritual Warfare: The Politics of the Christian Right*. Boston: South End Press, 1989.

Diggins, John Patrick. *The Rise and Fall of the American Left*. New York: Norton Books, 1992.

Dionne, E. J. *Why Americans Hate Politics*. New York: Touchstone Books, 1991.

Doerr, Edd, and Albert J. Menendez. *Church Schools and Public Money: The Politics of Parochiad*. Buffalo, N.Y.: Prometheus Books, 1991.

Duin, Julia. "Where Have All the Christian Communities Gone?" *Christianity Today*, September 14, 1992, 24–25.

Dyson, Michael Eric. *Between God and Gangsta Rap*. New York: Oxford University Press, 1995.

Edsall, Mary, and Thomas Edsall. *Chain Reaction*. New York: Norton Books, 1991.

Elshtain, Jean Bethke. *Real Politics*. Baltimore: Johns Hopkins University Press, 1997.

Farris, Michael P. *Home Schooling and the Law*. Paeonian Springs, Va.: Home School Legal Defense Association, 1990.

———. *Where Do I Draw the Line?* Minneapolis: Bethany House Publishers, 1992.

Fenn, Richard K. *The Dream of the Perfect Act: An Inquiry into the Fate of Religion in a Secular World*. New York: Tavistock Publishers, 1987.

———. *Liturgies and Trials: The Secularization of Religious Language*. New York: Pilgrim Press, 1982.

Fisher, James Terence. *The Catholic Counterculture in America, 1933–1962*. Chapel Hill: University of North Carolina Press, 1989.

Fowler, Robert Booth. *A New Engagement: Evangelical Political Thought, 1966–1976*. Grand Rapids, Mich.: Eerdmans Publishing, 1982.

———. *Unconventional Partners: Religion and Liberalism in the United States*. Grand Rapids, Mich.: Eerdmans Publishing, 1989.

Francis, Samuel T. "Message from Mars." In *The New Right Papers*, edited by Robert W. Whitaker, 64–83. New York: St. Martin's Press, 1982.

Fukuyama, Francis. "The End of History?" *National Interest* 16 (Summer 1989): 3–18.

Gallagher, Michael. *Laws of Heaven*. New York: Ticknor and Fields, 1992.

Garber, Marjorie, and Rebecca Walkowitz, eds. *One Nation under God?* New York: Routledge Press, 1999.

Geertz, Clifford. "The Pinch of Destiny: Religion as Experience, Identity, Meaning, Power." Lecture delivered April 7, 1998, at Indiana University.

Ginsburg, Faye. "From Little Things, Big Things Grow: Indigenous Media and Cultural Activism." In *Between Resistance and Revolution: Cultural Politics and Social Protest*, edited by Richard G. Fox and Orin Starn, 118–44. New Brunswick, N.J.: Rutgers University Press, 1997.

Gish, Arthur. *The New Left and Christian Radicalism*. Grand Rapids, Mich.: Eerdmans Publishing, 1970.

Gitlin, Todd. *The Twilight of Common Dreams*. New York: Metropolitan Books, 1995.

Goodwyn, Lawrence. *Democratic Promise: The Populist Moment in America*. New York: Oxford University Press, 1976.

Gornick, Janet C. "Cancel the Funeral." *Dissent*, Summer 2001, 13–18.

Gray, Francine du Plessix. *Divine Disobedience: Profiles in Catholic Radicalism*. New York: Knopf, 1970.

Greider, William. *One World, Ready or Not*. New York: Touchstone Books, 1997.

———. *Who Will Tell the People?* New York: Touchstone Books, 1992.

Guha, Ranajit, ed. *Subaltern Studies: Writings on South Asian History and Society*. Vol. 1. Oxford: Oxford University Press, 1982.

Habermas, Jürgen. *Between Facts and Norms*. Cambridge: MIT Press, 1996.

———. *Communication and the Evolution of Society*. Boston: Beacon Press, 1979.

———. *Legitimation Crisis*. Boston: Beacon Press, 1975.

———. *The New Conservatism*. Cambridge: MIT Press, 1992.

———. "Struggles for Recognition in the Democratic Constitutional State." In *Multiculturalism*, edited by Charles Taylor and Amy Gutmann, 107–48. Princeton: Princeton University Press, 1994.

Hackett, David, ed. *Religion and American Culture*. New York: Routledge Press, 1997.

Halpert, Stephen, and Tom Murray, eds. *Witness of the Berrigans*. Garden City, N.Y.: Doubleday, 1972.

Hatch, Nathan O. *The Democratization of American Christianity*. New Haven: Yale University Press, 1989.

Hollyday, Joyce. "Awakening on Belmont Street." *Sojourners*, August 1979, 20–22.

———. "Out of the Mouths of Babes." *Sojourners*, September 1978, 30–31.

Holmes, Stephen. *The Anatomy of Antiliberalism*. Cambridge: Harvard University Press, 1993.

———. *Passions and Constraint: On the Theory of Liberal Democracy*. Chicago: University of Chicago Press, 1995.

Isaac, Jeffrey C. *Democracy in Dark Times*. Ithaca, N.Y.: Cornell University Press, 1998.

———. "Toward a Politics of Democratic Ambivalence." *Dissent*, Spring 1997, 83–86.

Isaac, Jeffrey C., Matthew F. Filner, and Jason C. Bivins. "American Democracy and the New Christian Right: A Critique of Apolitical Liberalism." In *Democracy's Edges*, edited by Ian Shapiro and Casiano Hacker-Cardon, 222–63. Cambridge: Cambridge University Press, 1999.

Jackson, Michael. *Paths toward a Clearing: Radical Empiricism and Ethnographic Inquiry*. Bloomington: Indiana University Press, 1989.

Jaffe, Harry S., and Tom Sherwood. *Dream City: Race, Power, and the Decline of Washington, D.C.* New York: Simon and Schuster, 1994.

Jasper, James. *The Art of Moral Protest*. Chicago: University of Chicago Press, 1997.

Jones, Arthur. "Evangelicals in Several Stripes." *National Catholic Reporter*, September 9, 1994, 3.

Juergensmeyer, Mark. *The Next Cold War: Religious Nationalism Confronts the Secular State*. Berkeley: University of California Press, 1993.

———. *Terror in the Mind of God: The Global Rise of Religious Violence*. Berkeley: University of California Press, 2000.

Kapacyr, Elia. "Middle Class Blues." *National Review*, November 7, 1994, 14–15.

Kari, Nancy, and Harry Boyte. *Building America: The Democratic Promise of Public Work*. Philadelphia: Temple University Press, 1997.

Kazin, Michael. "The Politics of Devotion." *The Nation*, April 6, 1998, 16–18.

——. *The Populist Persuasion*. New York: Basic Books, 1995.

Kellerman, Bill. "A Subversive Calendar of the Heart." *Sojourners*, January 1985, 32–33.

Kennedy, John. "House Learns Civics Lesson." *Christianity Today*, September 14, 1994, 76.

Kintz, Linda. *Between Jesus and the Market: The Emotions That Matter in Right-Wing America*. Durham, N.C.: Duke University Press, 1997.

Kramnick, Isaac, and R. Laurence Moore. *The Godless Constitution: The Case against Religious Correctness*. New York: Norton Books, 1996.

Laffin, Arthur, and Anne Montgomery, eds. *Swords into Plowshares: Nonviolent Direct Action for Disarmament*, San Francisco: Harper and Row, 1987.

LaHaye, Tim. *The Battle for the Public Schools: Humanism's Threat to Our Children*. Old Tappan, N.J.: Fleming H. Revell Co., 1983.

Larson, Edward J. *Summer for the Gods: The Scopes Trial and America's Continuing Debate over Science and Religion*. Cambridge: Harvard University Press, 1997.

Lasch, Christopher. *The True and Only Heaven: Progress and Its Critics*. New York: Norton Books, 1991.

Lemann, Nicholas. "Reed in the Wind." *New Republic*, July 8, 1996, 32–36.

Lienesch, Michael. *Redeeming America: Piety and Politics in the New Christian Right*. Chapel Hill: University of North Carolina Press, 1993.

Lind, Michael. *The Next American Nation: The New Nationalism and the Fourth American Revolution*. New York: Free Press, 1995.

Lyons, Paul. *New Left, New Right, and the Legacy of the Sixties*. Philadelphia: Temple University Press, 1996.

Lyotard, Jean-François. *The Postmodern Condition: A Report on Knowledge*. Minneapolis: University of Minnesota Press, 1979.

Macedo, Stephen. "Liberal Civic Education and Religious Fundamentalism: The Case of God v. John Rawls." *Ethics* 105 (April 1995): 468–96.

Manatt, Richard P. *When Right Is Wrong: Fundamentalists and the Public Schools*. Lancaster, Pa.: Techomic Publishing Co., 1995.

Marsden, George. *Fundamentalism in American Culture: The Shaping of Twentieth-Century Evangelicalism, 1870–1925*. New York: Oxford University Press, 1980.

——. "Preachers of Paradox: The Religious New Right in Historical Perspective." In *Religion in America*, edited by Mary Douglas and Steven Tipton, 150–68. Boston: Beacon Press, 1983.

Martin, William. *With God on Our Side: The Rise of the Religious Right in America*. New York: Broadway Books, 1996.

Marty, Martin, and R. Scott Appleby. *The Glory and the Power: Fundamentalists in the Modern World*. Boston: Beacon Press, 1992.

——, eds. *Fundamentalism and the State*. Chicago: University of Chicago Press, 1995.

McAlister, Elizabeth. "Lenten Meditations from Prison." *Sojourners*, February 1986, 38–39.

McCarthy, Colman. "Wallis Offers Credible Christian Vision." *National Catholic Reporter*, March 1, 1996, 3.

McNeal, Patricia. *Harder Than War: Catholic Peacemaking in the Twentieth Century*. New Brunswick, N.J.: Rutgers University Press, 1992.

McSorley, Richard. "Siege at Seabrook." *Sojourners*, June 1977, 16–18.

Mendel-Reyes, Mehta. *Reclaiming Democracy: The Sixties in Politics and Memory*. New York: Routledge Press, 1995.

Menendez, Albert J. *Visions of Reality: What Fundamentalist Schools Teach*. Buffalo, N.Y.: Prometheus Books, 1993.

Merleau-Ponty, Maurice. *Phenomenology of Perception*. London: Routledge Press, 1962.

Meyer, David. "Civil Disobedience and Protest Cycles." In *Waves of Protest: Social Movements since the Sixties*, edited by Jo Freeman and Victoria Johnson, 267–76. New York: Rowman and Littlefield, 1999.

Michaelson, Wes. "Crucible of Community." *Sojourners*, January 1977, 16–21.

Miller, James. *Democracy Is in the Streets: From Port Huron to the Siege of Chicago*. Cambridge: Harvard University Press, 1987.

Moen, Matthew C. *The Transformation of the Christian Right*. Tuscaloosa: University of Alabama Press, 1992.

Moen, Matthew C., and Lowell S. Gustafson, eds. *The Religious Challenge to the State*. Philadelphia: Temple University Press, 1992.

Morone, James A. *The Democratic Wish: Popular Participation and the Limits of American Government*. New Haven: Yale University Press, 1990.

Myers, Ched. "By What Authority: The Bible and Civil Disobedience." *Sojourners*, May 1983, 11–14.

———. "In Word and Deed: Jesus' Challenge to Power in Mark." *Sojourners*, January 1987, 16–18.

Nelson, Jack, and Ronald Ostrow. *The FBI and the Berrigans*. New York: Coward, McCann and Geoghegan, 1972.

Nord, Warren A. *Religion and American Education: A National Dilemma*. Chapel Hill: University of North Carolina Press, 1995.

Norman, Liane E. *Hammer of Justice: Molly Rush and the Plowshares Eight*. Pittsburgh: Pittsburgh Peace Institute Books, 1989.

O'Rourke, William. *The Harrisburg Seven and the New Catholic Left*. New York: Thomas Y. Crowell Co., 1972.

Orsi, Robert A. "Snakes Alive: Resituating the Moral in the Study of Religion." In *In Face of the Facts: Moral Inquiry in American Scholarship*, edited by Richard Fox and Robert Westbrook, 201–26. Cambridge: Cambridge University Press, 1998.

Papke, David Ray. *Heretics in the Temple: Americans Who Reject the Nation's Legal Faith*. New York: New York University Press, 1998.

Perkins, Perk. "Concrete Theology: A Response to the Urban Crisis." *Sojourners*, September 1980, 11–14.

Peshkin, Alan. *God's Choice: The Total World of a Fundamentalist Christian School.* Chicago: University of Chicago Press, 1986.

Peters, Shawn Francis. *Judging Jehovah's Witnesses: Religious Persecution and the Dawn of the Rights Revolution.* Lawrence: University of Kansas Press, 2000.

Piehl, Mel. *Breaking Bread: The Catholic Worker and American Catholic Radicalism.* Philadelphia: Temple University Press, 1982.

Polner, Murray, and Jim O'Grady. *Disarmed and Dangerous: The Radical Lives and Time of Daniel and Philip Berrigan.* New York: Basic Books, 1997.

Rabkin, Jeremy. "The Supreme Court in the Culture Wars." *Public Interest* 125 (Fall 1996): 3–26.

Randall, E. Vance. "Culture, Religion, and Education." In *Religion and Schooling in Contemporary America: Confronting Our Cultural Pluralism*, edited by Thomas C. Hunt and James C. Carper, 59–81. New York: Garland, 1997.

———. "Religious Schools in America: Worldviews and Education." In *Religion and Schooling in Contemporary America: Confronting Our Cultural Pluralism*, edited by Thomas C. Hunt and James C. Carper, 83–105. New York: Garland, 1997.

Rawls, John. *Political Liberalism.* New York: Columbia University Press, 1993.

———. *A Theory of Justice.* Cambridge: Harvard University Press, 1971.

Reed, Ralph. *After the Revolution.* Dallas: Word Publishing, 1994.

———. "What Do Religious Conservatives Really Want?" In *Disciples and Democracy: Religious Conservatives and the Future of American Politics*, edited by Michael Cromartie, 1–15. Washington, D.C.: Ethics and Public Policy Center, 1994.

Ribuffo, Leo P. *The Old Christian Right: The Protestant Far Right from the Great Depression to the Cold War.* Philadelphia: Temple University Press, 1983.

———. "Response to Nicolas Laarman." *Dissent*, Summer 1995, 391–92.

Rifkin, Jeremy. *The End of Work: The Decline of the Global Labor Force and the Dawn of the Post-Market Era.* New York: Putnam and Sons, 1995.

Rorty, Richard. *Contingency, Irony, and Solidarity.* Cambridge: Cambridge University Press, 1989.

Rose, Susan D. *Keeping Them Out of the Hands of Satan: Evangelical Schooling in America.* New York: Routledge Press, 1988.

Rossinow, Douglas. *The Politics of Authenticity: Christianity, Liberalism, and the New Left.* New York: Columbia University Press, 1998.

Rozell, Mark, and Clyde Wilcox. *Second Coming: The New Christian Right in Virginia Politics.* Baltimore: Johns Hopkins University Press, 1996.

Sabath, Bob. "The State: An Apostolic View." In *Seeds of the Kingdom*, 30–34. Washington, D.C.: Sojourners Publishing, 1977.

Sandel, Michael J. *Democracy's Discontent: America in Search of a Public Philosophy.* Cambridge: Harvard University Press, 1996.

———. *Liberalism and the Limits of Justice.* New York: Cambridge University Press.

Scott, James. *Domination and the Arts of Resistance: Hidden Transcripts.* New Haven: Yale University Press, 1990.

————. *Seeing Like a State*. New Haven: Yale University Press, 1997.

Shibley, Mark A. *Resurgent Evangelicalism in the United States: Mapping Cultural Change since 1970*. Columbia: University of South Carolina Press, 1996.

Shklar, Judith. "The Liberalism of Fear." In *Liberalism and the Moral Life*, edited by Nancy Rosenblum, 21–38. Cambridge: Harvard University Press, 1989.

Smith, Christian. *American Evangelicalism: Embattled and Thriving*. Chicago: University of Chicago Press, 1998.

Smith, Jonathan Z. "Religion, Religions, Religious." In *Cultural Terms for Religious Studies*, edited by Mark C. Taylor, 269–84. Chicago: University of Chicago Press, 1998.

Stentzel, Cathy. "Night Hospitality." *Sojourners*, February 1978, 30.

Stevens, Mitchell L. *Kingdom of Children: Culture and Controversy in the Homeschooling Movement*. Princeton: Princeton University Press, 2001.

Stimpson, Catharine. "Women's Studies and Its Discontents." *Dissent*, Winter 1996, 67–75.

Stock, Catherine McNicol. *Rural Radicals: From Bacon's Rebellion to the Oklahoma City Bombing*. New York: Penguin Books, 1997.

Stolzenberg, Nomi Maya. "'He Drew a Circle That Shut Me Out': Assimilation, Indoctrination, and the Paradox of Liberal Civic Education." *Harvard Law Review* 106 (1993): 581.

Stone, Jon. *On the Boundaries of American Evangelicalism*. New York: St. Martin's Press, 1998.

Stringfellow, William, and Anthony Towne. *Suspect Tenderness: The Witness of the Berrigans*. New York: Holt, Rinehart and Winston, 1971.

Tamialis, Barb. "Ten Years of Keeping the Faith." *Sojourners*, September–October 1993, 17.

Taylor, Charles. "The Politics of Recognition." In *Multiculturalism*, edited by Charles Taylor and Amy Gutmann, 25–73. Princeton: Princeton University Press, 1994.

Taylor, Charles, and Amy Gutmann, eds. *Multiculturalism: Examining the Politics of Recognition*. Princeton: Princeton University Press, 1994.

Tracy, James. *Direct Action: From the Union Eight to the Chicago Seven*. Chicago: University of Chicago Press, 1996.

Tweed, Thomas, ed. *Retelling U.S. Religious History*. Berkeley: University of California Press, 1997.

Tyler, Alice Felt. *Freedom's Ferment*. New York: Harper Torchbooks, 1944.

Viguerie, Richard. "Ends and Means." In *The New Right Papers*, edited by Robert W. Whitaker, 26–35. New York: St. Martin's Press, 1982.

Vogelstein, Fred. "Giving Credit Where Credit Is Due: Wall Street Fuels Consumer Debt Binge." *U.S. News and World Report*, March 31, 1997, 52.

Wagner, Melinda Bollar. *God's Schools: Choice and Compromise in American Society*. New Brunswick, N.J.: Rutgers University Press, 1992.

Wallis, Jim. "Come to the Table." *Call to Renewal Newsletter* 3, no. 1 (1998): 1.

————. "The Confessing Community." *Sojourners*, September 1977, 3–4.

————. "The Court Prophets." *Sojourners*, September 1984, 3–4.

———. "Giving Religion a Bad Name." *Sojourners*, May 1993, 50.

———. "A Higher Loyalty." *Sojourners*, May 1983, 3–6.

———. "Interview with Philip and Daniel Berrigan, and Elizabeth McAlister." *Sojourners*, February 1977, 22–26.

———. Introduction to *A Cloud of Witnesses*, edited by Jim Wallis and Joyce Hollyday, xiii–xvii. Maryknoll, N.Y.: Orbis Books, 1991.

———. "Keeping Faith, Doing Justice, Building Community." *Sojourners*, February 1992, 12–16.

———. "Living in Hope: Remembering the Resurrection." In *The Rise of Christian Conscience*, edited by Jim Wallis, 285–87. San Francisco: Harper Perennial, 1987.

———. "Mammon's Iron Thumb." *Sojourners*, February 1978, 3–4.

———. "Not in Polite Company." *Sojourners*, April 1994, 4–5.

———. "No Ways Tired." *Sojourners*, November–December 1996, 7–8.

———. "Rebuilding the Church." *Sojourners*, January 1980, 10–15.

———. "Recovering the Evangel." *Sojourners*, February 1981, 3–5.

———. *The Soul of Politics*. New York: Orbis Books/Free Press, 1994.

———. "What to Do about the Poor." *Sojourners*, March–April 1995, 10–11.

———. *Who Speaks for God?* New York: Delta Books, 1997.

———. "Worth Fighting For." *Sojourners*, February–March 1994, 10–11, 14.

———, ed. *The Rise of Christian Conscience*. San Francisco: Harper Perennial, 1987.

Walzer, Michael. *Interpretation and Social Criticism*. Cambridge: Harvard University Press, 1987.

———. *What It Means to Be an American*. New York: Marsilio Publishers, 1992.

Warren, Mark. *Democracy and Association*. Princeton: Princeton University Press, 2001.

Weidenbaum, Murray. "A New Social Contract for the American Workplace." *Challenge*, January 1995, 51–55.

Weinstein, James. *The Corporate Ideal in the Liberal State, 1900–1918*. Boston: Beacon Press, 1969.

West, Cornel. *Keeping Faith*. New York: Routledge Press, 1993.

Whitaker, Robert W., ed. *The New Right Papers*. New York: St. Martin's Press, 1982.

Wilcox, Clyde. *Onward Christian Soldiers? The Religious Right in American Politics*. New York: Westview Press, 1996.

Wilcox, Fred A. *Uncommon Martyrs: How the Berrigans and Others Are Turning Swords into Plowshares*. New York: Addison-Wesley Books, 1991.

Williams, William A. *The Contours of American History*. New York: Norton Books, 1966.

Wills, Garry. *Bare Ruined Choirs: Doubt, Prophecy, and Radical Religion*. New York: Doubleday, 1972.

———. *A Necessary Evil: A History of American Distrust of Government*. New York: Simon and Schuster, 1999.

———. *Under God: Religion and American Politics*. New York: Simon and Schuster, 1990.

Wippsa, Leslie. "Christian Left Organizes to Oppose Religious Right." *National Catholic Reporter*, March 1, 1996, 3.

Wood, Gordon. *The Radicalism of the American Revolution*. New York: Vintage Books, 1995.

Wuthnow, Robert. *The Restructuring of American Religion*. Princeton: Princeton University Press, 1988.

Young, Iris Marion. *Throwing like a Girl and Other Essays*. Bloomington: Indiana University Press, 1990.

Index